American & British Aircraft Carrier Development

1919–1941

American & British Aircraft Carrier Development 1919–1941

THOMAS C. HONE
NORMAN FRIEDMAN
& MARK D. MANDELES

Naval Institute Press *Annapolis, Maryland*

Naval Institute Press
291 Wood Road
Annapolis, MD 21402

Library of Congress Cataloging-in-Publication Data
Hone, Thomas.
American and British aircraft carrier development, 1919–1941 / Thomas C. Hone, Norman Friedman, and Mark D. Mandeles.
p. cm.
Includes bibliographical references and index.
ISBN 1-55750-382-6 (alk. paper)
1. Aircraft carriers—United States—History. 2. Aircraft carriers—Great Britain—History. 3. United States. Navy—Aviation—History. 4. Great Britain. Royal Navy. Fleet Air Arm—History. I. Friedman, Norman, 1946– . II. Mandeles, Mark David, 1950– . III. Title.
V874.3H56 1999
359.9'435'0973—dc21 99-27347

Printed in the United States of America on acid-free paper ♾
06 05 04 03 02 01 00 9 8 7 6 5 4 3 2

To Henry and Clarice Starbuck. He rolled plate at Bethlehem. She assembled aircraft at Curtiss. Cherished aunt and uncle.

Thomas C. Hone

In memory of Capt. Hugh Nott, USN, of the Naval War College.

Norman Friedman

To my parents, Stanley and Francine Mandeles.

Mark D. Mandeles

Contents

Acknowledgments

Many people assisted us with this work. We shall try to do justice to them all. In one group were the people who encouraged and financed the study. First among these is Andrew W. Marshall, Director of Net Assessment, Office of the Secretary of Defense. Mr. Marshall set us our task and helped finance our work. Vice Adm. William C. Bowes, USN (Ret.), Commander of the Naval Air Systems Command when we conducted the original study, also saw to it that the Navy helped financially and, in addition, had the confidence to believe that an appreciation of history might throw some much needed light on current issues.

Special thanks go to Dr. William J. Armstrong, now retired as the Historian of the Naval Air Systems Command. Dr. Armstrong had, at his fingertips and in his mind, a wealth of information about the early years of U.S. Navy aviation that he shared with us. Dr. Armstrong spent a great deal of his career with the Navy trying to preserve its aviation heritage, and we drew again and again on his thoughts and on the records in his care. We hope that this study repays his efforts to serve naval aviation so faithfully for so many years.

Others came forward to volunteer the fruits of their own study. Capt. A. L. Raithel Jr., USN (Ret.), gave us Parts V, VI, and VII of Rear Adm. George van Deurs's rare manuscript, "Navy Wings Between Wars: A Narrative of Growth," as well as a compilation of papers entitled "Development of Aircraft Tactics," from the Office of the Chief of Naval Operations. These documents were invaluable. Captain Raithel is amazingly knowledgeable about the early years of aviation in the U.S. Navy, and his enthusiasm for the subject is matched only by his memory for sources. Mr. Mark A. Campbell gave us a copy of his master's thesis, "The Influence of Air Power Upon the Evolution of Battle Doctrine in the U.S. Navy, 1922–1941" (History Department, University of Massachusetts, Boston, 1992). It was an illuminating source, and we recommend it to readers. Thomas Wildenberg, author of *Gray Steel and Black Oil,* shared data on aircraft performance with us from his research in the records of the U.S. Navy's Bureau of Aeronautics.

We have many archivists to thank: Dr. Richard von Doenhoff and Richard W. Peuser of the National Archives; Dr. Evelyn Cherpak of the Naval War College; and Mr. Bernard F. Cavalcante of the U.S. Navy's Operational Archives. Thanks are due also to the staffs of the Public Record Office in London and the National Maritime Museum in Greenwich. The John Marshall branch of the Fairfax County (Virginia) public library also assisted us.

A number of people read portions of our manuscript and offered useful comments. We want to thank Prof. William R. Braisted, Emeritus Professor at the University of Texas–Austin, Barry D. Watts of Northrop Grumman, Thomas Wildenberg, Frank Uhlig Jr. of the Naval War College, Capt. Wayne P. Hughes Jr., USN (Ret.), of the Naval Postgraduate School, and then Cdrs. Jan M. van Tol and James R. FitzSimonds, USN, who were serving in the Office of Net Assessment of the Office of the Secretary of Defense when we did the study originally. Ms. Laura L. Mandeles also looked over our shoulders to make sure we wrote in a style that intelligent people could understand. Trent Hone imposed order on our manuscript's chaos.

Professors Donald Chisholm of the University of Illinois at Chicago and Jon T. Sumida of the University of Maryland provided us with inspiration and thoughtful ideas as we worked.

Finally, we want to thank Thomas S. Cushing III and Sarah Carlston Ulis for editorial assistance. Thomas Cushing compiled our original study for the Office of Net Assessment into a readable illustrated document. (Perhaps that experience is what prompted him to become a successful member of the bar.) Thanks to Jeanne Pinault, our copy editor, as well.

American & British Aircraft Carrier Development

1919–1941

Introduction

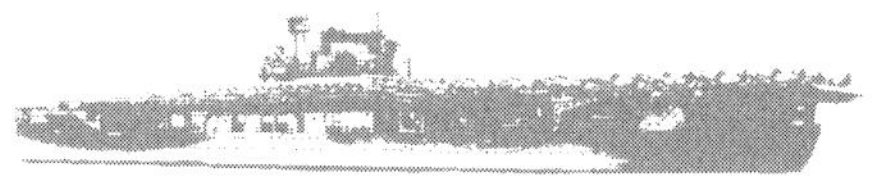

> Historically, the force which thinks best fights best. The required exchange of ideas is invariably painful and difficult, but the internal intellectual battle which it entails must be won if we are to survive.
>
> *John F. Guilmartin Jr., "Changing the Guard," Air University Review 34 (1983)*

THE PROCESS of innovation that characterizes a military revolution is multiphased, often messy organizationally and conceptually, and unpredictable. Given that such processes cannot be easily directed or controlled, historian Guilmartin is still correct: neither are successful military innovations accidental or haphazard. In this book we show that one landmark innovation, the aircraft carrier, was the product of much thought, varying degrees of experimentation, and intense professional dedication. Yet the carrier concept did not spring, full-blown, from the head of any one (or two, or three) creative military geniuses. It was developed, over time, in ways that no one person designed or even foresaw clearly. As a result, the story of the carrier concept's development is often uneven, with some surprising twists and turns.

We wrote this book to explain how two of the three leading navies of their time confronted a revolution in military affairs, specifically the emergence of the aircraft carrier. Confronted as we may well be by another such revolution, due to the proliferation of small, high-speed computers, high-capacity data links, and miniature sensors, we may gain insight by looking back to the years between World Wars I and II and examining how navies confronted the carrier concept. To do that properly, we must avoid undue reliance on what has become a popular view—that the Royal Navy failed disastrously whereas the U.S. Navy succeeded brilliantly, and that both navies narrowly avoided becoming the victims of hidebound "battleship admirals." We must understand the two navies' decisions in terms of the technology, tactics, and organizations of the 1920s and 1930s.

Any comparison of World War II with World War I must reveal the radical difference between those two terrible conflicts. On land, World War I seemed to show that the defense was dominant, because major offensives often foundered or, when successful, did not lead to further victories that knocked an opponent out of the war. At sea, the war seemed to demonstrate that more than half a century of battleship development had ended in deadlock, leaving the submarine as the most effective naval weapon in terms of damage done, given its relative cost. Yet even the submarine was defeated. The enduring image of World War I is the deadly and frustrating impasse on the Western Front. By way of contrast, World War II was a war of rapid movement, with the offensive generally dominant. Both on land and at sea, most battles ended with clear winners and losers. Something revolutionary had happened, and the measurable transformations that distinguished the two wars seemed to involve aircraft. Indeed, tactical victory on land or on the sea in World War II usually went to the side that better integrated aircraft with existing forces.

World War II appeared to end with another revolution in military affairs —one based on jet aircraft, missiles, electronics, and nuclear weapons. Soviet military thinkers, who were particularly interested in the way in which such revolutions occurred, identified another such revolution in the late 1950s and early 1960s in the form of cybernetics, the adaptation of computers to military command and control. It is not clear, as of this writing, whether we are in the midst of a new revolution at all, or in the latter stages of this "information" revolution, or whether changes in targeting and the accuracy of weapons are just gaining sufficient strength to alter dramatically the way wars are fought.

The same confusion existed after World War I. The advent of aircraft had not immediately ushered in a new era. The machine gun and fast-firing artillery had more to do with the way in which World War I was fought on the ground than all of those brightly painted airplanes. It took another generation to turn airborne fighting machines into critical military systems. Then, as now, the questions arose: Has new technology ignited a revolution in warfare? Has that revolution already commenced? And, whether it has or it has not, how can the new, innovative technology be recognized and exploited effectively?

Certainly then and later, advocates of military aviation made much of the apparent conservatism of established military leaders. For example, many Americans saw in the disaster at Pearl Harbor terrifying evidence that the Japanese had understood and exploited the striking power of aircraft, whereas our own armed forces had not. The fleet the Japanese struck consisted of battleships, and "battleship admiral" became an epithet for backward-looking senior officers. Similarly, British subjects came to see the sinking of the capital ships *Repulse* and *Prince of Wales* by Japanese naval aircraft (land-based, but trained to attack ships) as evidence of the failure of the Royal Navy to integrate aircraft into its thinking.

These judgments persisted for a long time. In 1973, for example, the eminent American historian Waldo Heinrichs said this about a peacetime navy: "It is moored to civilian life. Doctrine, precedent, routine, and habit take hold. Money is scarce and cruising is costly . . . its most pressing engagement is the battle of the budget. . . . The impulse at the top is to play safe and rely exclusively neither on the weapons of the last war nor on new, untried ones." In his view, peacetime naval establishments were "conservative, complex, and political," and they always placed "new realities within an existing framework of compromise and consensus." They did not engage in "unitary, decisive, and adaptable" planning and force development.[1] Since Heinrichs wrote these words, naval historians have found evidence that the three major navies of the world between World Wars I and II—the Royal Navy, the United States Navy, and the Imperial Navy of Japan—were not so conservative as they were made out to be by their critics. Indeed, the change began in 1974, with the appearance of Charles Melhorn's *Two-Block Fox: The Rise of the Aircraft Carrier, 1911–1929.* Melhorn's work stimulated our own and is part of a general revision of more traditional notions about peacetime navies.

Heinrichs took the view that "[n]aval aviation was an exceedingly costly initial investment. . . . To place it in the central position before the war would have required a radical restructuring of the navy that the leading admirals were not disposed to attempt." This view is common but wrong. Heinrichs and others who see peacetime military institutions as inherently conservative usually do so because they cannot conceive of the problems facing the leaders of those institutions as the leaders themselves conceived of them. For example, the senior admirals of the United States Navy did not have the option of choosing between the bomb and the battleship in the 1930s. The Washington naval agreements of 1922, reaffirmed and strengthened at London in 1930, denied that option to them. The agreements had been designed to inhibit both quantitative and qualitative arms competition, and they did just that. The leaders of the three major navies, denied "easy" options by both treaty and financial constraints, were like players with limited betting resources in a casino. Faced with great uncertainty, they "spread their bets" and hedged against a catastrophic loss, just as any reasonable person would do in a similar setting.

Moreover, the search for scapegoats—the "gun club," or the "battleship admirals"—distorts what actually happened. These navies were complex institutions, composed of thousands of trained and professional sailors and officers. Routinely, the members of these institutions took heavy ships to sea, maintained modern steam and electrical plants, ordered and stocked provisions for whole fleets, and adapted new technology—from radios to ice cream makers—to the rigors of life at sea. The leading admirals did not sit aloof from their own services. On a day-to-day basis, they faced the problem of spreading limited resources among a host of legitimate demands—for supplies, for fleet maintenance, for the support and training of sailors, for research and development, and for the construction of new weapons of war. In doing this, they acted not only as members of legally constrained and complex bureaucratic organizations, but also as individuals confronting multiple unknowns. Their critics often grasped neither the complex world in which naval leaders made decisions nor the uncertainties that they faced.

We would be unfair to Heinrichs and the other critics, however, if we didn't acknowledge one very important point that he made: military organizations may fail to develop tactics or technologies that they need to attain success in war. Outwardly impressive and efficient on a day-to-day basis, a military organization may nevertheless be flawed inwardly, and flaws may exist at one or more levels of the organization simultaneously.

HISTORIANS and social scientists typically differ about the origin and impact of military innovations in tactics and weapons. Arguments between these two groups of scholars often come down to a debate about the appropriateness of different explanatory models. What is really going on here, we believe, is a debate over what we call "levels of analysis."[2] In particular, historians tend to focus on individuals as the prime movers of innovation. Yet individuals act and think within a constellation of constraints and opportunities expressed through existing formal and informal institutions. These constraints and opportunities strongly influence the decisions individuals make. It is the social analyst's job to discover the effects of these constraints and opportunities. That is why our study examines the separate roles of *institutions* (such as a navy), *organizations* (such as the U.S. Navy's Bureau of Aeronautics), and *individuals* (such as John Towers, one of the most important U.S. Navy pioneer aviators).

But institutions other than navies also matter in our story. As Nobel laureate Douglass C. North once observed, institutions can be defined as society's "rules of the game."[3] As such, institutions reduce uncertainty for the people who accept them, just as the rules of any game we play tell us what amounts to winning and what "fair" play really is. Institutions establish a stable, predictable pattern to human interaction. The term *institution*, therefore, includes formal contracts between individuals, informal codes of conduct, conventions (such as the salutes military officers give one another), regulations, laws, and charters and constitutions. Institutions encourage some kinds of behavior and discourage others, thereby creating opportunities and constraining actions for both single persons and groups of individuals acting together. The classic example, of course, is the institution of marriage, which dramatically changes the behavior and expectations of the people who choose to accept it.

People work within the written and unwritten rules of institutions. People both accept institutions and modify them. Military institutions change as successive generations grapple with new expectations and new technology. For example, the U.S. Army had to integrate its units racially (to respond to changed expectations) *and* deal with the possibility of a "nuclear battlefield" (to respond to new technology) in less than a generation. While doing this and other difficult tasks, the Army had to maintain its ability to fight a major conventional war. That is, it had to change while still preserving the kinds of formal and informal rules that allowed it to mold effective fighting units. The history of military institutions tracks how those institutions change (or do not change) and the role individuals play in the process of change (or resistance to change).

If indeed there have been revolutions in military affairs, then we should be able to identify them by looking at whether and how military institutions have changed. We should be able to go even a step further and compare the ways in which different military institutions have reacted to the same military revolution. The comparison can illuminate the importance of individual action, of organizations, and then of the institutional framework within which individuals and organizations act.

The historian starts off the investigation by identifying the innovators themselves. The historian also "fills in the background"—identifying the "rules of the game" and describing the organizations in which and through which innovators led change. Then the social analyst identifies, where possible, the connections among individuals, organizations, and institutions. Why did one innovator succeed and another fail? Why did the members of one organization embrace change while the members of a different organization—in the same or a different nation—resisted change?

We do not want to neglect organizations. If institutions represent the rules of the game, then organizations are often the players in that game. Organizations are groups of individuals bound together for some purpose—political parties, government agencies, manufacturing enterprises, schools, churches, social clubs, laboratories, and so forth. But there are, obviously, different kinds of organizations. There is a wide gulf, for example, between what might be called a "group" and an "encounter." A group is a collection of people with a purpose who follow particular, often formal, rules in their dealings with one another and with outsiders. An encounter consists of people who come together *without* the sense that they are a group set apart by the rules of behavior they share. In a baseball stadium, for example, the spectators are having an encounter with one another. They are thrown together like the passengers on a bus. The teams on the field are groups. The players are members of very select organizations. They are rightly called "professionals." Yet it is the spectators and the teams *together* (along with owners, agents, coaches, and others) who make up the institution of baseball.

Put another way, the rules of the game (institutions) influence which organizations come into existence, how those organizations act, and whether or not the organizations have the resources—human, financial, and physical—to deal with the problems and opportunities they face. Why, for example, do children accept Little League baseball? Little League constrains the way children play baseball; it doesn't allow them the freedom that unorganized sandlot baseball offers. Yet Little League does provide resources—playing fields, equipment, uniforms, and regular schedules—that children cannot provide for themselves. Little League games also provide an audience for the children who want that attention. So Little League baseball survives as an institution, teams survive as organizations within that institution, and the whole business is sustained by the generations of individuals who pass through the teams as kids and then participate in adulthood as coaches, officials, sponsors, and parents.

Just as the institution of baseball cannot be understood without examining it from the institutional, organizational, and individual points of view, then neither can a navy be understood without doing the same. For example, the United States possessed a strong and rapidly growing manufacturing economy in the second half of the nineteenth century, but the U.S. Navy had to turn to foreign firms for special items such as armor plate. Why? The answer is that the Navy's need for armor plate was not great enough to justify any private firm's investing in the technology for making it; that is, the domestic market for armor plate was just too limited to entice commercial manufacturers to enter it. In short, naval expansion was constrained by the institution of the market. That institution rewarded organizations that took advantage of the opportunities it offered, and the Navy, to get its armor, had to acknowledge the influence of the commercial market and create incentives of its own.

As it happened, the Navy was able to foster a domestic market for armor plate (though not for guns) by playing by the rules of the game of political life. Those rules divide political authority and constrain the exercise of that authority, thereby promoting interaction (as negotiation and persuasion) among the leaders of different organizations. In plain terms, the Navy's leaders could legally and openly make their case for subsidies for armor manufacturers—to Congress, within the executive branch, and to the steel manufacturers themselves. The Navy could (and did) "play the game," using the rules to advance its cause. Simply looking inside the Navy for the factors that led to the creation of a domestic armor plate industry would miss this valuable larger institutional perspective.

At the same time, it is clear that members of military organizations have failed to accept or embrace important technological innovations—despite the opportunities offered by institutional arrangements. Historians have identified any number of lost opportunities. For example, in the 1870s and 1880s, U.S. Army Major Edward B. Williston conducted a number of systematic experiments with machine guns in an effort to determine just what influence the use of such weapons by the infantry would have on future tactics. He made a number of recommendations to his superiors. All were rejected. The U.S. Army made no effort to conduct the same sort of analysis until the early 1900s.[4] What this case and others suggest is that having institutions conducive to invention, technological change, negotiation, and discussion is a necessary but not sufficient factor in military innovation. Hence our use of multiple levels of analysis.

One reason our study concentrates on the U.S. Navy and the Royal Navy is that we have a great deal of evidence for all these levels of thought and action in these organizations. Another reason is that the United States and the United Kingdom went in very different directions with military aviation after World War I. The British government created a separate air service and air ministry. The United States government did not. This difference provides a kind of very rough test of two different organizational approaches to the problem of harnessing a new military technology to a nation's defense.

The development of carrier aviation by the Imperial Japanese Navy is also a fascinating story. Like the Americans, for example, the Japanese reacted strongly to the British World War I experience with aircraft at sea. Also like the Americans, the Japanese developed concepts for using naval aviation (including carriers) in the years before World War II that differed from those used by their British teachers. Regrettably, the evidence on the Japanese side is just not so rich, particularly at the individual level, or so reliable, especially at the organizational level, as the evidence from British and American sources, so our study touches on the Japanese only here and there.

The reliability of evidence must concern us, lest we look back and accuse individuals and organizations of failures clearly visible only in hindsight. What appears crystal clear to us now was usually very murky to those trying to make decisions at the time. The only way to understand their motives and decisions is to reconstruct the situation from their point of view, and for that, evidence is required. Also required is a healthy sense of caution, because documentary evidence may not stress or even reveal points that the participants considered obvious at the time. Voluminous evidence also will not disclose what was deliberately left out—not necessarily because the topic was clear to all concerned but because some of those involved in making a decision or developing policy were reluctant to put their ideas on paper. These problems of research will surface as we move through the chapters that follow.

There is also the problem of change. Modern navies tend to change slowly, because it takes time to build modern ships, aircraft, and weapons. Yet the political world may change at a faster rate, making a hash of earlier, thoughtful planning. After World War I, for example, the British economy was no longer superior industrially or financially to that of the United States. Yet Britain's empire, and her communication with the elements of that empire, seemed secure. Within fifteen years, Britain's security had considerably weakened. Her empire, her trade routes, and even Britain herself seemed vulnerable. Volume I of the official *History of the Second World War* (N. H. Gibbs, *Grand Strategy,* 1976) makes clear both the magnitude and the relative swiftness of the change. This might not have been such a strategic dilemma had successive British governments been able to tap an economy as strong as that of the United States, but they could not.

Even the United States, which could rely on its industrial potential, found itself by 1940 facing a situation not foreseen by its professional military planners ten years earlier: the likelihood of a two-front war. The U.S. Navy understood the advantage American industrial might gave it; appropriately alarmed, it still could muster an appropriate response. Its piece of whatever war was fought—whether across the broad Pacific against Japan or in the face of German submarines in the Atlantic, or against both simultaneously—was going to be won by the sensible, sustained application of modern industrial technology. In July 1940, the Congress gave the Navy what it had wanted for a generation: a navy superior to all the other navies of the world *combined,* the "two-ocean navy." Waldo Heinrichs, who argued that the U.S. Navy's commitment to a trans-Pacific campaign against Japan was both "unrealistic" and maintained to provide "a satisfactory bureaucratic strategy for resolving internal differences and securing external support," did not understand that the U.S. Navy's "hole card" at the grand strategy poker table was the immense industrial potential of the United States. This placed the U.S. Navy in a very different situation from that of the navies of Great Britain and Japan.

In the chapters that follow, we will try to avoid falling victim to the misperceptions which we have ascribed to others. We will dig as deep as the evidence allows to uncover why the Royal Navy and the U.S. Navy went in different directions with carrier aviation. We will move back and forth from the level of the individual officer to the level of the organization, and then from these "lower" levels to the "higher" level of the institutional context within which both individuals and organizations worked. We will also consider, particularly in the American case, those organizations and factors outside the navies that influenced their structures and tactics. Our goal is to find, as best we can, both the truth of these cases and their lessons for the future.

1 The Early Years

THE ORIGINS of the carrier concept in the U.S. Navy are complex. To sort them all out, we must first consider the beginnings of American naval aviation, which predates the development of the aircraft carrier concept. And to do that task well, we must, in starting, review the environment of technological innovation that characterized the U.S. Navy in the early years of the twentieth century.

Innovation in naval aviation was linked to innovation in other areas of naval warfare in the years before World War I. Between 1900 and 1914, the U.S. Navy became one of the world's great navies, and, like its rivals (the English, German, and Japanese navies), it pursued technology eagerly in an effort to wring the most military power out of a limited pool of dollars. The five major naval innovations that proved themselves in World War I—radio communications, the submarine, the airplane, steam turbines, and the dreadnought battleship—were all under development before the war, and their introduction in the years before the war coincided with and fueled a growing technical sophistication within the officer corps of the major navies.

LT. (JG) JOHN H. TOWERS, the Navy's third aviator, was convinced of the need to get into the air because of his service as a gunfire spotter in 1910 in *Michigan,* the Navy's first dreadnought battleship. The ship's eight twelve-inch guns could shoot just over the visual horizon, and Towers thought airplanes might solve the problem of sighting and then hitting enemy warships at such great range. He was attracted to aircraft because they promised to solve an immediate tactical problem: using long-range gunfire to best effect.

Michigan herself, however, was the product of an intense debate within the Navy over the proper interpretation of the major naval engagements of the Russo-Japanese War. The debate was over the value of battleships carrying only long-range guns. It made sense to build larger ships with an all-big-gun (twelve-inch guns and greater) battery only so long as such ships could hit opponents armed with mixed (a few twelve-inch and many ten-inch or eight-inch guns) batteries at maximum range and overwhelm them before they could bring their more numerous lighter guns to bear.

In 1900, practical battle ranges were quite short by the standards of World War I (fifteen hundred versus fifteen thousand yards), and so the mixed battery of heavy and lighter guns was appropriate. The slower-firing, heavy weapons broke through heavy armor, while the lighter weapons riddled bridges and superstructures. The heavy weapons were ship-smashers; the lighter guns killed the crew and made enemy ships unmanageable. The short battle range was due to a lack of effective fire control instruments for the large guns. At long range, gunners needed to shoot *where the target would be,* not where the target was. The reason was that shells fired at long range took a minute or more to reach the target, so shooting where the target was meant shooting, in effect, at where it had been. But to know where the target would be, given estimates of where it had been and how fast and in what direction it was traveling, required sophisticated and reliable calculators. As those calculators were developed and installed, the accuracy, reliability, and rate of fire of big naval guns increased so quickly in the years after 1900 that their potential as battle-winning weapons became obvious. The key to using them to revolutionize surface battles was the development of reliable and accurate fire control instruments.[1]

But the issue of how to do this, or, indeed, whether to do it at all, was compounded by the experience of the Russo-Japanese War, where battleships with mixed batteries fought several major engagements. In the U.S. Navy, the debate over how best to exploit the new technology of the heavy gun coupled with mechanical fire control calculators was complicated by differing interpretations of what had happened in the engagements between the Japanese and Russians. One view, presented forcefully by the world-renowned strategist Rear Adm. A. T. Mahan, was that the mixed battery was optimal. Mahan was opposed publicly by Cdr. W. S. Sims (specially appointed to improve the fleet's gunnery) in 1906. The issue of who in the Navy would control battleship design came to a head in 1908, when President Theodore Roosevelt presided over a conference to decide whether the all-big-gun design philosophy was superior. The conference endorsed the all-big-gun ship (i.e., a change in technology and tactics). It also eliminated the existing Board on Construction, a group of staff officers who had advised the secretary of the Navy on new ship designs, and replaced it with the General Board, composed of senior line officers. The new board was created to offer the civilian leadership of the Navy the best military advice on matters of strategy and policy, as well as on issues of ship design and construction. Indeed, the General Board blended, at the highest level, matters of strategy and weapons development.[2]

That same year, the chief of the Navy's Bureau of Equipment recommended to the secretary of the Navy that the latter authorize the purchase of aircraft for experimental purposes.[3] The events are related. Over-the-horizon shooting required, for maximum effectiveness, air spotting (from an airplane or a balloon). It made no sense to give battleships and fast battle cruisers the largest guns practicable if they could not use those guns effectively at maximum range. Once in the air, however, naval aviators would find other, quite revolutionary, uses for the airplane, such as bombing and antisubmarine patrolling.

The changes in naval technology that came quickly after 1900 were embraced by two communities in the U.S. Navy. The first was composed of regular line officers; the second was made up of technical officers from the Navy's bureaus of Ordnance, Steam Engineering, and Construction and Repair. Both communities were small, making it easy for the members of each to keep in touch. Both were also driven by the need to project U.S. naval power across great distances (especially the Pacific) against formidable enemies (Japan in the Pacific, Germany in the Caribbean and Atlantic). Both also looked to European navies—especially the Royal Navy—for innovative ideas and tactics. Finally, both groups had champions who were either senior in rank or close to the president or the secretary of the Navy.

Not surprisingly, the two groups sometimes differed. For example, regular line officers supported steam turbine propulsion for battleships because turbines were more compact than reciprocating engines and therefore easier to shield behind and under armor. The Navy's propulsion engineers, on the other hand, favored reciprocating steam engines for battleships because, in the early years of the competition between turbines and reciprocating engines, the latter were more fuel efficient. Yet both groups agreed that the U.S. Navy needed the most advanced technology.

The result of their agreement is clear: in the years between the war with

Spain and World War I, these two groups pressed for and managed the transformation of the Navy's technology. Even a partial list of the technological innovations is striking: steam turbines, long-range guns, fire control calculators, submarines, aircraft, radio and signals intelligence, the shift from coal to oil as a fuel for ships, and turboelectric drive (as an alternative to direct-drive turbines, useful in improving damage control). Given this rush of innovation, the Navy's interest in the airplane was a natural and indeed inevitable development.

In 1910, the Navy moved to turn interest in aviation into a program. In September, Secretary of the Navy George von Lengerke Meyer designated Capt. Washington I. Chambers as his advisor (through the secretary's Aide for Material) for aviation matters. In October, the General Board advised the secretary of the Navy that space for airplanes or dirigibles should be provided, where possible and practicable, in the designs of future ships intended to scout for the fleet. In retrospect, this looks like a simple enough decision, but it was not. There was little evidentiary support for such a proposal. As the distinguished leader of the small team of American warship designers, Rear Adm. David Taylor, stated in a paper prepared that year for the Society of Naval Architects and Marine Engineers, "If we could have a war lasting several years with a battle every month, the experience gained would of course be conclusive. . . . But when there is but a single battle, or two at most, the elements of chance may very well entirely obscure the result as regards technical matters." The members of the General Board tried to overcome this uncertainty by, as Capt. W. L. Rodgers put it in 1913, keeping "in communication with the constructive bureaus so that its recommendations shall not outrun practical possibilities." The board's willingness to draw on line *and* staff (especially technical staff) officers for expertise and opinions, and its ability to evaluate those views, not only gave the board great influence with the secretary, who was the Navy's chief procurement official, but also gave the board's members a means of anticipating technological developments.

Also in October 1910, Capt. Hutchinson I. Cone, Chief of the Bureau of Steam Engineering, informed the secretary of the Navy that aircraft would likely play an important role in naval operations and requested the authority to buy an airplane and pay an instructor to teach naval officers to fly. Cone's action is significant because he was a supporter of innovations such as the all-big-gun battleship and the steam turbine. His letter to the secretary of the Navy was consistent with his earlier and ongoing interest in technical change, and it prompted the secretary to order officers from Steam Engineering and the Bureau of Construction and Repair to investigate the status of aircraft technology. Their inquiry was favorable. The secretary was reportedly not a supporter of aviation, but the arguments of his material bureau chiefs were difficult to ignore.

So, too, were demonstrations, staged in 1910 and 1911, of the ability of aircraft to work with ships and on the water. In November 1910, for example, civilian pilot Eugene Ely flew from a wooden platform rigged to the bow of anchored cruiser *Birmingham,* in Hampton Roads, Virginia. That same month, aviation pioneer Glenn Curtiss wrote to the Navy Department offering to train the Navy's first flier. In January 1911, Ely landed on a different temporary platform fitted to armored cruiser *Pennsylvania,* at anchor in San Francisco Bay. That same month, Curtiss successfully flew his first seaplane, assisted by the Navy's first pilot, Lt. T. G. Ellyson, whom Curtiss had trained.

Aircraft, however, were still very fragile devices. The first funds appropriated specifically for "experimental work in the development of aviation for naval purposes" were given in 1911 to the Bureau of Navigation, *not* to one of the material bureaus. Given the nature of aircraft and of aeronautics at the time, that decision seems quite justified. Aviator (and ultimately rear admiral) George van Deurs's carefully illustrated memoir of the early years of naval aviation, *Wings for the Fleet,* is full of photographs of kite-like aircraft, many of them damaged or wrecked in routine flying operations. As he noted, 110 days of flying from North Island, California, in the winter of 1911–12 had not produced spectacular results: one aircraft had flown "on only one day," a second had "logged a total of 13 hours and 15 minutes on 22 days," two planes were in the air at the same time on "only three days," and "none could fly" on sixty-six days.[4]

Early airplanes were often plagued with engine and structural failures, and the training of pilots was haphazard. In 1912, as van Deurs noted, no aircraft engine in the Navy's inventory could "log regular performances of sustained flight for four hours." In the winter of 1913, pioneer aviators operating from the naval base at Guantánamo were able to fly all of their small contingent of airplanes "without accident or failure" for only one week. According to van Deurs, pilot instruction was hampered by the "uneven and chaotic development of the theory and practice of flight training." And why not? Pilots learned to fly by trial and error, from plane to plane, and from situation to situation, hoping that accidents would not kill them or wreck their fragile aircraft. As van Deurs recalled, Lt. Patrick Bellinger (later a rear admiral), in trying to land a primitive seaplane in a crosswind in 1912, unwittingly chose an approach that simply capsized his machine. It was "flying by the seat of your pants," a very primitive form of learning—forced on the pilots because of the novelty of their technology and because there was little "theory" (or codified experience) that could be used to generate manuals of instruction. Indeed, the wonder is that any of the early aviators survived at all.

On 23 June 1913, Navy Department General Order Number 41 transferred the responsibility for buying aircraft from the Bureau of Navigation to the Bureau of Construction and Repair. This move was engineered by Rear Adm. David W. Taylor, the new chief of the Bureau of Construction and Repair, because he foresaw potential in the primitive aircraft then flying. The Bureau of Engineering was given the authority to procure aircraft engines, radios, and generators. Navigation kept the responsibility for training, operations, and aviation personnel assignments.

Rear Admiral Taylor had already (February 1913) approved construction of a wind tunnel in the Washington Navy Yard so that his staff could begin systematic experiments in aerodynamics that would resemble work already being done in hydrodynamics at the Yard's towing tank. Because the Navy already had an agreement with MIT to support the latter's research in return for the training of uniformed naval architects in the Bureau of Construction and Repair, Taylor applied this precedent to aviation as well. On 12 June 1913, the secretary of the Navy agreed to send naval constructor Lt. Jerome C. Hunsaker to MIT to set up a course in aeronautical engineering in the Department of Naval Architecture there. For guidance, Hunsaker journeyed to Europe. On his return in 1914, he established the first master's degree program in aeronautical engineering in the United States.[5]

In May 1913, the Navy had nominated two representatives to the Advisory Committee for the Langley Aerodynamical Laboratory of the Smithsonian Institution. One of them was Lt. Holden C. Richardson, a pioneer aviator and naval constructor who later (after 1921) served in the Navy's Bureau of Aeronautics. His appointment was one sign that naval aviation had evolved from a promising novelty to a discipline in which senior officers such as Taylor recognized military potential, including gunfire spotting and reconnaissance at sea, and the potential for much future technical progress. Even the chairman of the House Naval Affairs Committee agreed.

That recognition came none too soon. The lack of standardization in aircraft design and in pilot training was endangering the whole enterprise of military (Army *and* Navy) aviation. On 20 June 1913, for example, the Navy suffered its first pilot fatality in a crash that also nearly killed Lt. John Towers, a key innovator and crack pilot. Towers was even then a key figure in naval aviation. In the first two years of Navy flying, Towers had made over a fourth of all flights, logging nearly twice as many hours in the air as any of the other twelve Navy fliers. The crash, coupled with similar fatal accidents on the Army side, triggered a reaction to the unregulated way in which military aviation had (unavoidably) developed. In August 1913, the General Board reported to the secretary of the Navy that "the organization of an efficient naval air service should be immediately taken in hand and pushed to fulfillment." The board argued "that a 'complete and *trained* [*sic*] air fleet' had become 'a necessary adjunct' to the navy."[6]

Less than six weeks later, the acting secretary of the Navy (Franklin D. Roosevelt) appointed a special board, headed by Capt. Washington Chambers (chief aviation advisor to the secretary of the Navy), to study naval aviation's requirements and its future. The group drew up the first "comprehensive plan for the organization of a Naval Aeronautic Service." Their primary concern was to coordinate the actions of the technical bureaus that controlled aviation: Construction and Repair, Engineering, and Navigation. The members recommended that every major warship should carry aircraft. Yet the aviation they had in mind did not include aircraft carriers. Instead, it emphasized aircraft flying from land bases on extended scouting missions over water and seaplane scouts and spotters that could accompany ships to sheltered anchorages.[7]

On 10 April 1914, cruiser *Birmingham,* flagship of the destroyer squadrons, U.S. Fleet, arrived in Pensacola, Florida, on her way to Mexican waters, where a crisis was brewing that would draw U.S. forces into Mexico's civil war. Capt. William S. Sims, on board *Birmingham* as commander of destroyer squadrons, met with Lt. Cdr. Henry C. Mustin and Lt. John Towers, commander and executive officer, respectively, of the new aviation training center. Mustin and Towers persuaded Sims to take some of their seaplanes to Mexico, "and the Navy Department authorized placing three on board the *Birmingham.*" These three were soon augmented by an additional two aircraft brought from Pensacola by the small battleship *Mississippi.*

The meeting at Pensacola foreshadowed the conflict within the ranks of naval aviation over how best to take aviation to sea: on aircraft-carrying ships or separately, as ship-supported seaplanes.[8] It also brought together three of the most influential officers in the early history of naval aviation. Sims was a reformer; he was articulate, intelligent, an excellent writer, and possessed of a strong personality. Towers was the expert pilot—the adventurer, dashing and debonair, yet intensely professional. Mustin, who had already worked with Sims, was an expert gunner and tactician. Like Towers, he was convinced that airplanes were the key to the most effective use of the artillery carried by battleships and battle cruisers. Their interests and skills complemented one another and gave aviation the level of passion and professional skill it would need to grow from an auxiliary arm to the prime striking power of the Navy.

Their common problem was figuring out how best to guide this new technology. Pressure to do so quickly mounted after war began in Europe. Mustin, Towers, and others were dispatched to Europe to track the development of military aviation there. All were galvanized by the rapid strides in the design and production of military aircraft funded by the French, British, and German governments. As Mustin, fresh from a whirlwind tour of France in August 1914, wrote to Capt. Mark Bristol, the new Director of Naval Aviation, "The standard Curtiss or Wright is nothing but a lot of junk in comparison to a Morane-Saulnier, Bleriot or Nieuport."[9]

Mustin's thoughts on the importance of aircraft as instruments of naval fire control paralleled earlier thinking within the Royal Navy on the benefits to be gained from coupling effective long-range gunfire with very high sustained ship speed. Royal Navy officers such as Adm. Sir John Fisher had grasped at this combination as a means of preserving British naval supremacy over Germany without at the same time driving the British treasury to bankruptcy. Mustin became the first serious advocate of the aircraft-carrying ship, because he understood just how devastating long-range heavy gunfire was and also how such gunfire, effectively controlled by aircraft, could win an engagement in minutes. Starting with the idea that spotting aircraft should work with heavy-gun ships, he moved from the concept of the light aircraft launched from a battleship to that of a heavier plane launched and then recovered by a special aircraft-carrying ship. From there, he shifted his perspective to aircraft-carrying ships whose planes attacked the enemy in support of their own battleships. Exactly why or precisely when he made this jump is not clear, but the surviving evidence (his letters and a lecture prepared in the period 1915–17) indicates that he made it before the United States entered World War I.

As Mustin observed, seaplanes could spot ships' gunfire, but seaplanes were "fair weather aircraft." What the Navy needed, at sea, were *real* airplanes, "the types that can operate from floating bases far from smooth water." Fighters could sweep enemy aircraft from the skies. Friendly spotters, with a flying endurance of twelve hours, could support surface ships through a whole day's engagement. Torpedo planes could strike independently of a concentrated formation of battleships. Only a special ship, designed to carry airplanes, could really bring the potential of aviation to bear at sea. This was a powerful vision. In one form or another, Mustin had been refining it and then pushing it on reformers such as Sims since 1912.

The base at Pensacola was a breeding ground for the carrier concept. Lt. Kenneth Whiting, Mustin's close associate and his successor as base commander, proposed in 1916 purchasing a railroad ferry for use as a seaplane carrier. Such ferries had two strong, open decks, and Whiting suggested using the top deck as a launching platform and the lower deck as a hangar. Once launched, the seaplanes would carry out their mission and then return, landing on the water.[10] With such a ship to get them close to their objective, seaplanes could carry large bombs. Whiting's seaplane carrier was a tool for maximizing the ordnance loads of combat aircraft.

Authorities in Washington were not voicing such advanced ideas. In testimony to the House Naval Affairs Committee in December 1914, for example, Capt. Mark Bristol, the director of naval aviation, compared aircraft to torpedo boats in terms of their independent striking power. That is, they had nuisance value and could be dangerous to damaged or anchored ships, but their primary function at sea was in his view limited to spotting for battleships.

In less than a year, however, events in Europe had convinced Capt. Bristol to change his assessment. In August 1915, he asked the secretary of the Navy for 180 planes, four kite balloons, two dirigibles, and two "aircraft ships." The General Board supported Bristol's recommendations, and Congress, in 1916, authorized a dramatic increase in funding for aircraft and for flight training operations at Pensacola. The appropriations act for fiscal year 1917 (passed in the summer of 1916) even gave the Navy permission to create a separate Naval Flying Corps and a Naval Reserve Flying Corps.

On 10 August 1916, the Navy also began negotiating its first aircraft production contract when it sent designer and manufacturer Glenn Curtiss a telegram asking him to respond to a request to build training seaplanes to Navy Department specifications. This was the Navy's first concerted, official effort to guide aircraft development. Unfortunately, it ran right into a longstanding and very bitter legal dispute over which inventor or inventors held the rights to the airplane and to its major components (such as aircraft engines and flight controls). As one student of the industry put it, "a long history of bitter litigation between the Wright and Curtiss interests made a friendly wartime union of their businesses out of the question."[11]

The Army and Navy were prepared to purchase hundreds of aircraft; the British and French thousands. The key to meeting their demands was the negotiation, among the holders of the basic patents, of an agreement that compelled every American airplane maker to pay a licensing fee on every plane manufactured. The fee was then divided between the Wright and Curtiss litigants. Because most new ideas for aeronautical technology came out of the fledgling aircraft industry, the Navy did not want that source of innovation strangled by complicated patent disputes. Neither did the Army.

The stage, then, was set for the great growth of American military aviation once the United States entered the war in Europe. Navy aviation was seen by senior Navy officers as a required adjunct to fleet operations, mainly in the roles of gunfire spotting and reconnaissance. But naval aviation also had a hand in aeronautical research (at MIT and through the Advisory Committee for the Langley Aerodynamical Laboratory); there were proponents (such as Mustin) who believed it had a greater role to play; and the aircraft industry itself was about to go through a boom that would draw enough talent to give substance to the concepts of officers such as Mustin.

World War I generated a revolution for U.S. military aviation. The aviation organizations of the Army and Navy mushroomed in size, and their personnel gained an immense amount of experience in wartime operations. On 6 April 1917, for example, the Navy had fifty-four aircraft. By 11 November 1918, it had 2,107. The aircraft industry also matured, though historian I. B. Holley Jr., in his book *Ideas and Weapons,* revealed that the military services and the American aircraft manufacturers simply could not keep up with the pace of technological change that characterized aircraft design during World War I. Moreover, despite great optimism, the military services, together with industry, were unable to produce modern aircraft in anything like the numbers that wartime operations required, even for U.S. forces. Operationally, however, aviators in both services came away from the war convinced that, in the future, military operations would be dominated by aircraft—as scouts performing reconnaissance, as observers spotting gunfire, as fighters contesting control of the air, and as bombers dropping ordnance.

THE PRIMARY STIMULUS of this expanded vision was work with Allied air forces, especially the British. In April 1917, Lt. Kenneth Whiting, already a seaplane carrier advocate from his days at Pensacola, accompanied Rear Adm. W. S. Sims, the U.S. Navy commander in European waters, to London. Dispatched to France, Whiting organized Navy aviation there. Later, in August 1917, he proposed to Capt. H. I. Cone, Sims's aide for operations (and aviation supporter since 1910), that seaplane carriers be used to attack U-boat bases.

That same month, Mustin, serving in battleship *North Dakota*, responded to an appeal from the secretary of the Navy for war-winning ideas by writing a long memo proposing combining light bombers with specially designed "sea sleds" to attack German naval bases and even the city of Essen.[12] Concerned that the United States could not build or convert ships to carriers in time to have an effect on the war, Mustin proposed that his light-draft, fast "sea sleds," each carrying one multiengine bomber, be used instead. He wanted the American automobile industry to build thousands of the sleds to launch "simultaneous operations by many large squadrons." Some sleds were actually built, and aircraft successfully launched, but the war ended before the idea could go much beyond initial tests.

Despite the delay inherent in building the "sleds" and the aircraft required by Mustin's plan, the British Admiralty had secretly endorsed Mustin's concept in December 1917.[13] In February 1918, the American Naval Planning Section in London drafted a detailed memo describing a proposed operation ("a continuous bombing offensive") against German submarine bases. The memo stressed using bombers with a heavy bombload and a "great radius of action." The British Plans Division seconded the Americans' recommendation because the Royal Navy did not have the ability to fly numbers of heavily armed aircraft from its first carriers (such as the converted cruiser *Furious*).

In the United States, the observations of American aviation personnel sent to Allied nations did not fall on deaf ears. As early as 1916, Secretary of the Navy Josephus Daniels had suggested that the Navy build its own aircraft factory (as well as factories to produce armor plate and projectiles). His goal was to have a plant that could develop small numbers of prototypes and special designs that industry could not produce profitably. When Rear Adm.

David Taylor suggested, after war had been declared, that the Navy Department construct such a factory at the Philadelphia Navy Yard, Daniels, reportedly a "great admirer of Taylor," concurred.[14] The plant opened at the end of 1917; the Navy now had a special facility under its direct control that could produce experimental prototypes as well as standard designs. The plant was also a "yardstick." Industry claims about schedules and costs could be checked against actual performance in the aircraft factory, just as the bids of shipbuilders were matched against actual construction performed in Navy shipyards.

Interaction with the Allies also benefited Navy ship designers. In late 1917, British naval constructor S. V. Goodall was sent from London to work with his American counterparts in the Navy's Bureau of Construction and Repair. He brought with him plans for the Royal Navy's first aircraft carriers. These plans were used by the bureau's designers when they completed their first large carrier design in October 1918—a ship that was not a conversion but was, instead, designed as a carrier from the start.[15]

For the U.S. Navy, this rich but varied war experience raised five crucial issues. The first was whether the future lay with seaplanes, long-range landplanes, or planes carried by ships. The second issue was the proper balance between heavier-than-air and lighter-than-air systems. German airships had successfully attacked London, and German navy airships had performed effectively as scouts for the German High Seas Fleet. The future of long-range reconnaissance seemed to be dominated by lighter-than-air craft. The third issue was whether there should be a separate naval flying corps; related to it was the question, "Should there be a separate air force?" Whether or not a separate air force were justified, how should aviators be compared with their unrestricted line counterparts for promotion? The fourth major issue was the number and location of permanent Navy airfields. The fifth was the purpose of Marine Corps aviation, and whether Marine Corps aviation needs could be and should be provided by the Navy, the Army, or by a separate Marine Corps air command.

All these issues were explored by the Navy's General Board in a series of confidential hearings held between January and June 1919.[16] War experience had suggested to a number of regular officers, even those without aviation training, that the "model" of the airplane as a kind of torpedo boat was inappropriate. But what was the proper new "model"? The British had moved from separate flying services in their army and navy to a unified air force.

Was that the way to proceed? If not, what were the alternatives? As an admiral sitting on the General Board put it to experienced naval aviator John Towers, "Look ahead five or six years. I realize your troubles, but they are our troubles too."

The members of the General Board heard Kenneth Whiting (by 1919 a commander), who had been in charge of the first U.S. naval air station in England, point out, "If the war had gone on a little longer, the bombing of Kiel, Cuxhaven, and Wilhelmshaven would have been done from airplane carriers. The *Furious* was equipped with airplanes and made an attack on Tondern, as she steamed up and down the North Sea without hindrance." Whiting's advocacy of the aircraft carrier (he had, according to van Deurs, "agitated for carriers from the spring of 1916 until . . . the *Langley* conversion was authorized") was supported by Rear Adm. Hugh Rodman, who had commanded the Navy battleship division that had served with the Royal Navy's Grand Fleet, and by Adm. H. T. Mayo, commander in chief of the U.S. Fleet during the war.

The General Board's hearings were by no means one-sided, however. John Towers, then a commander, told the board, "I don't think we can continue beyond . . . 1925 . . . in building aircraft carriers, because I think it will be quite possible that ships will all become more or less aircraft carriers and be so designed."

Despite a lack of consensus among aviators regarding the future of their new technology, the board, in its official "Conclusions and Recommendations" to the secretary of the Navy, argued, "Aircraft have become an essential arm of the fleet. A naval air service must be established, capable of accompanying and operating with the fleet in all waters of the globe."[17] Though the board supported development of all forms of naval aviation (including lighter-than-air), it informed the secretary of the Navy that "airplane carriers for the fleet [should] be provided in the proportion of one carrier to each squadron of capital ships." To implement this policy, the board requested the Bureau of Construction and Repair to prepare a carrier design soon, so that they could persuade the secretary of the Navy to put it before Congress in an effort to have it authorized for the next fiscal year. At the same time, the rapidly changing nature of aviation made the board cautious: "Construction [of aircraft] should be kept as low as possible, but for experimental and developmental work, a liberal appropriation should be included in each yearly program."

On the basis of the board's memo, Secretary of the Navy Josephus Daniels dropped his opposition to the construction of an aircraft carrier, and several influential military figures—including the Army's Brig. Gen. William Mitchell—testified strongly in support of carrier construction to the Congress. That was apparently enough for the legislators, though they did not authorize any new construction. Instead, the Naval Appropriations Act for fiscal year 1920 authorized the Navy to convert the new collier *Jupiter* to an aircraft carrier (*Langley*). *Jupiter* was chosen because of the size of her hold, which was necessary for the storage of unassembled aircraft and for the elevator well required by the equipment for moving aircraft from the primitive hangar to the flight deck. U.S. Navy officers planned to follow the Royal Navy's practice of using the flight deck to launch and recover aircraft. Aircraft would be *stored* below. *Jupiter* also had another useful characteristic: turboelectric drive. The DC motors that turned the ship's propellers could be reversed, driving her backward as well as forward. This allowed *Langley* to recover aircraft over her bow as well as over her stern. The act also authorized the purchase of two merchant ships for conversion to seaplane tenders, however, so that water-borne and carrier-borne aviation would develop side by side.

The impact of World War I on military aviation in general and on naval aviation in particular was dramatic and profound. "Air power" emerged from the realm of fantasy and was applied, with varying degrees of success, to every area of military operations. As the Navy's General Board recognized in 1919, combat aviation was essential to the fleet at sea. At the same time, however, it was not clear just how to allocate the scarce resources earmarked for Army and Navy aviation. The Royal Navy was building aircraft carriers *and* had organized a separate air force. The pressure to follow suit was great in the United States.

But war experience, though persuasive and powerful, had left a number of questions unanswered. For example, could aircraft flying from land bases successfully find and then attack, with great force, ships at sea, making surface fleets obsolete? Aviation advocates such as Brigadier General Mitchell certainly thought so. However, as the General Board learned in its 1919 hearings, the technology of naval aviation had severe limitations. The issue facing the Navy was how best to take a nascent technology and turn it into an operational force in a climate of severe fiscal restraint.

2 Great Risk, Great Achievement

THE ISSUE of the future development of the aircraft carrier was strongly affected by the dispute over whether or not the United States should consolidate all its military aviation assets in one separate air force, on the model of Britain's Royal Air Force. In 1919, this dispute began to take more and more of the time and attention of military aviators, and the publicity generated by it steadily drew more and more groups and organizations into the process by which decisions concerning aviation policy were made. The dispute itself was not settled until 1926—the same year that *Langley,* the first experimental carrier, began operating militarily significant numbers of aircraft.

Army Brigadier General William Mitchell, who had commanded all American Expeditionary Force aircraft at the end of the war, had informed the Navy's General Board in the spring of 1919 that a unified air service was inevitable. In December 1919, he testified to a subcommittee of the Committee on Military Affairs of the House of Representatives that air forces would soon supplant naval forces as the nation's first line of defense.[1] The chairman of the House subcommittee was Congressman Fiorello La Guardia, who had served in army aviation during World War I. He and other veterans had been a part of the tremendous growth of military aviation, and they welcomed the views of professionals such as Mitchell.

That same month (December), Rear Adm. W. F. Fullam, the retired former commander of U.S. Navy forces in the Pacific, published his "Battleships and Air Power" in the widely circulated *Sea Power* magazine. Fullam had already argued to the House Committee on Naval Affairs that the battle cruisers authorized by Congress in 1916 should either be converted to aircraft carriers or scrapped altogether. Like aviator Henry Mustin, Fullam saw aircraft as vital aids to accurate long-range gunnery; he also forecast in other essays published in *Sea Power* a future in which aircraft themselves would become independent strike weapons. For the next two years, Fullam would present his views, forcefully and regularly, to a wider audience in essays published by the *New York Tribune.*

In January 1920, Rear Adm. W. S. Sims, president of the Naval War College, stirred the pot still further by writing to the Senate Committee on Naval Affairs, charging that the Navy had been quite unprepared for war even by 1917 and that the responsibility for this oversight was Navy Secretary Daniels's. In response, the committee scheduled a series of hearings, which, although not specifically directed toward aviation issues, nevertheless substantiated the opinions of aviators such as Mustin that the U.S. Navy's aviation facilities and equipment had not been adequately supported until after Congress passed its major authorizations in 1916.

The congressional inquiries, along with the publicity created by aviation advocates such as Mitchell and Fullam, enlarged the audience concerned with military aviation policy in general and naval aviation policy in particular. Essays and articles by Fullam and others on the future of aviation at sea spread from specialized journals such as *Sea Power* to major national and regional newspapers. At the same time, behind the scenes, members of the General Board and influential senior Navy officers such as Rear Adm. David Taylor, chief of the Bureau of Construction and Repair, were growing convinced that aviation merited its own bureau.

The opinion of then Captain Bristol in 1913, that airplanes were like torpedo boats, had been made obsolete by the rapid growth of aviation technology and production, as well as performance, during World War I. Support for a separate aviation bureau within the Navy promised to give the new technology recognition and an organization for its management and further development. It also quieted the debate, serious even among naval aviators, over whether aviation should have a status within the Navy Department like that of the Marine Corps. Finally, it gave the Navy an answer to charges by General Mitchell and his supporters in Congress that the unification of military aviation was essential because the Navy did not devote sufficient attention or resources to its own air units.

Before the Navy got its aviation bureau, however, it would have to pass through a year of the most intense controversy and debate over "the bomb vs. the battleship." Starting in mid-October 1920, the Navy began a careful series of bombing tests using obsolete ships, anchored in Chesapeake Bay, as targets. Although the tests were conducted in secret, photographs of damage done to the old battleship *Indiana* were somehow smuggled to the *London Illustrated News* and published in England in December—the month before the House Appropriations Committee was to hold scheduled hearings on the future of Army and Navy appropriations at the end of January 1921. A week before Brigadier General Mitchell was scheduled to appear to testify, newspapers, including the *New York Tribune* and the *New York Times*, published photos of the wrecked *Indiana* and called for a "free and thorough discussion as to the effect of new weapons upon naval warfare." Brigadier General Mitchell seized the opportunity to minimize the role of the Navy in his testimony on January 28, saying, "Give us warships to attack and come and watch it."

The fight was on. According to historian Ashbrook Lincoln, Mitchell's "spectacular speech was discussed extensively in the press and went far toward awakening the public." Congress was already deeply involved. Both the House and the Senate naval affairs committees held detailed hearings on aviation and the Navy in January and February 1921. On the Senate side, Sen. William Borah, an outspoken Republican from Idaho, became a vocal champion of new naval technology. He thoroughly read the available literature (from England as well as from the United States), and he forced the Senate Naval Affairs Committee to address the question of how best to bring the new technologies of the submarine and the airplane into the Navy.

In response Navy Secretary Josephus Daniels (the Harding Administration had not yet taken office) ordered the General Board to draft a defense of the 1916 authorizations, which included battleships and battle cruisers that Daniels had pledged to complete. Daniels knew that the members of the board would support his own view that battleships were the fleet's primary fighting arm. Even during the war, when extraordinary measures had been taken to construct large numbers of merchant ships and convoy escorts, the board had pressed for completion of the heavy ships of the 1916 program. Indeed, in October 1918, the board had proposed to Daniels that the 1916 authorizations be supplemented "to establish," as historian George Baer noted, "far and away the world's strongest sea force." Hence the board's position in 1921, expressed in a memo to Daniels, was predictable: "It would be the height of unwisdom for any nation possessing sea power to pin its faith and change its practice upon mere theories as to the future development of new and untried weapons."

The board's position was countered by testimony and public statements from reformers such as Rear Admiral Sims and retired admirals such as Fiske and Fullam. The latter told the Senate Naval Affairs Committee, for example, that "the Navy Department utterly neglects the future," and in a speech he argued, "Lacking carriers, we lack landing fields. And lacking these, . . . [o]ur air force, so-called, evaporates." Under oath, of course, the reformers could not say that airplanes and submarines had driven surface ships from the sea. Rear Admiral Sims, for example, told the House Committee on Naval Affairs on 4 February 1921, "I would not abandon battleships altogether." Yet he also insisted that "an opinion is no good at all until you have the evidence." So on 7 February, Navy Secretary Daniels wrote the secretary of war and said that the Navy would welcome the Army's participation in a series of bombing tests. On 28 February, the Joint Army and Navy Board approved a program of joint tests for that summer.[2]

In the weeks leading up to the tests, participants in the debate over the merits of air power vs. sea power had a field day making extravagant claims. Army fliers went so far as to claim that they could sink the ships even if the ships defended themselves with antiaircraft guns. According to historian Ashbrook Lincoln, former Navy Secretary Daniels was supposed to have declared that he would "stand bareheaded on the deck of a battleship and let Brig. Gen. Mitchell take a crack at him with a bombing airplane."

Thus was the issue of whether or not the nation should have a unified air service turned into a raucous public debate. Behind the public mudslinging, however, cooler heads prevailed. Rear Admiral Sims, for all his public posturing, had initiated in 1919 a process whereby the potential of aviation *with the fleet* could be established systematically and rigorously through tactical and strategic simulations at the Naval War College. The simulations addressed the issues of how aviation should be used, how it should be based and supported, and how it *might* be used, given the anticipated developments in aeronautics. War College faculty corresponded regularly with Navy aviation officers, to stay aware of the lessons gained from operations. On 24 May 1919, for example, Capt. T. T. Craven, then the director of naval aviation, had noted in a letter to a Naval War College faculty member that "mobility is the prime requisite in so far as Air Forces are concerned." One consequence of this constant communication was a growing consensus among navy officers that the Navy had to defeat Brigadier General Mitchell's campaign to unify all military aviation under a separate service. In a letter to the chief of naval operations on 1 February 1921, Rear Admiral Sims went so far as to say that he was "absolutely opposed to any measure whatsoever looking to the amalgamation of the U.S. Army and naval air services."[3]

In other words, the Navy's air-minded reformers wanted more aircraft and a better organization of aviation *within the Navy.* They did not believe unification with army aviation would help them. Neither, however, would they consider abandoning the surface navy as useless. As one of Senator Borah's colleagues pointed out to the Senate Naval Affairs Committee, "having called Admiral Sims and Admiral Fiske at the suggestion of the Senator from Idaho, we were advised by both of them that it was not expedient or advisable or sound policy to suspend the [1916] building program or to abandon it." Accordingly, the Senate committee was not willing to reject the recommendations of the General Board and the secretary of the Navy.

Hence the bombing trials, though the center of the public debate (and definitely front-page news), were in fact a distraction from the truly important streams of activity. What mattered for the Navy was, first, the ongoing simulations at the Naval War College, which helped define the proper shape of naval aviation. Second, the General Board had gradually realized that aviation needed its own bureau—that aeronautics was as rich and complex technically as ordnance, ship design, and power-plant development. Third, the War Plans Division of the Office of the Chief of Naval Operations assumed the presence of large, built-for-the-purpose carriers in its 1921 planning cycle. And fourth, the new Republican administration was committed both to naval arms limitation *and* to the creation of a new bureau of aviation for the Navy.[4]

The actual bombing trials began on 21 June 1921 and reached a climax on 21 July with the sinking of captured German dreadnought *Ostfriesland.* However, in the midst of the publicity over the bombing trials, Congress (on 12 July) created a Bureau of Aeronautics for the Navy, giving, by this one act, naval aviation a level of institutional support that Army aviation lacked. Nine days later, the Navy's General Board recommended to the new secretary of the Navy that he ask Congress for funds for three thirty-nine-thousand-ton carriers. On 10 August, the secretary signed an order specifying that the new Bureau of Aeronautics have cognizance of "all that relates to designing, building, fitting out, and repairing Naval and Marine Corps aircraft." The next day, Navy investigators at Hampton Roads, Virginia, directed by Lt. (later Admiral) A. M. Pride, conducted the first test of an aircraft arresting gear for eventual installation in the experimental carrier *Langley.* By early November 1921, the same group (advised by pioneer aviator Lt. Cdr. G. Chevalier, who had observed landing operations on the Royal Navy carrier *Argus*) had developed the basis of the system that was later fitted to *Langley.* So despite the public furor over the bombing tests, and despite the claim by Brigadier General Mitchell and his supporters that the sinking of ships by aircraft had shown that surface fleets were obsolete, Navy aviation was actually growing stronger institutionally.

On 20 August 1921, the Joint Board of the Army and Navy, chaired by Gen. John J. Pershing, accepted the Navy's view of the implications of the summer's bombing tests against ships. This was a reverse for Brigadier General Mitchell. So, too, was the Harding administration's call for a naval disarmament conference, which shifted the attention of the public and Congress away from unifying the Army and Navy's air services and toward a limit on all navies' fighting power. The administration's policy also made it unlikely that all the battleships and battle cruisers then building (from the 1916 authorizations) would ever be completed. In response, the head of the Preliminary Design Division of the Navy's Bureau of Construction and Repair had his naval constructors begin plans for converting one of the large, but mostly incomplete, battle cruisers to an aircraft carrier. The *place* of naval aviation (if not its role) was assured.[5]

THE HISTORY and strategic consequences of the Washington Conference are well known. Historian George Baer summed up the consequences for the Navy as a whole when he noted that the agreements reached at the conference "gave the Navy a radically changed national policy and a new framework for force planning." That new framework for force planning, set out in the Treaty for the Limitation of Armament, had important implications for naval aviation, especially carrier aviation. The treaty imposed both a quantitative and a qualitative limit on U.S. Navy carriers. A ceiling on overall carrier tonnage was set at 135,000 tons, *Langley* excluded (on the grounds that she was experimental). With exceptions (especially the battle cruisers that both Japan and the United States would convert to carriers), no carrier could be larger than twenty-seven thousand tons, and without exception no carrier could carry guns larger than eight-inch. The "treaty lifetime" of a carrier was twenty years, and no more than three thousand tons could be added to any aircraft carrier during modernization. In effect, the Navy emerged from the

Washington Conference with just three carriers: the experimental *Langley* (commissioned in 1922) and the yet-to-be-completed converted battle cruisers *Lexington* and *Saratoga.*

This outcome was not exactly what the Navy's fliers wanted. *Langley* was too slow and small. *Lexington* and *Saratoga* were too large (thirty-three thousand tons each). Once the two converted battle cruisers were commissioned, they would eat up nearly half of the carrier tonnage allowed the United States. Studies at the Naval War College were already suggesting that the potential of aviation at sea was maximized when aircraft were launched quickly from a number of smaller carriers, so it appeared to some officers that the conversion of the battle cruisers was a mistake. What the aviators and Rear Admiral Sims's war-gamers needed to resolve this dilemma was experience with carriers at sea. What they got, unfortunately, were delays. Congress did not authorize the conversion of *Lexington* and *Saratoga* until 1 July 1922, the first plane did not land on *Langley* at sea until 26 October 1922, and *Langley* did not officially join the fleet until the end of 1924.

Fortunately for the advocates of carrier aviation, the link among the Bureau of Aeronautics, aviators in the fleet, and the Naval War College remained strong. In 1919, Chief of Naval Operations Adm. W. S. Benson had ordered that "[t]he College should be constantly supplied with the fleet doctrines on tactics, strategy, and other subjects of interest." To effect this coordination, Benson had appointed Capt. (later Admiral) Harry E. Yarnell (who would, as a captain, command *Saratoga*) to serve as his liaison officer with the War College. This connection guaranteed that the War College classes would receive the latest "war instructions" from the commander in chief of the fleet. In 1922, for example, the section of the fleet's "war instructions" dealing with aircraft noted that "as a rule, the enemy aircraft carriers or air bases will be the principal objective of attack by our aircraft squadrons."

The ties with the Bureau of Aeronautics were just as strong. For example, Cdr. A. C. Read, who had commanded the seaplane NC-4 when it became the first aircraft to cross the Atlantic by air in 1919, told his Naval War College audience in the summer of 1922 that "probably every member of the [previous] class was thoroughly convinced of the great advantage to a force of having an adequate supply of aircraft." Moreover, he continued, "the captains of ships no longer regard the airplanes assigned them as a nuisance, nor the aviators as red-headed step-children." That same summer, the tactical manual entitled "Aircraft in Battle," used as a guide for war gaming, noted,

"Carriers . . . can always meet their enemy no matter where the attack comes from, and in addition, can accompany the Fleet and attack as well." The emphasis on the offensive striking power of carrier-borne aircraft at so early a date is both significant and remarkable. Existing tactical instructions directed carrier aircraft to gain command of the air in order to facilitate unimpeded gunfire by battleships employing air spotters.

Communication between Newport and Washington was made easier because of the quality of the staff that Rear Adm. Moffett, first chief of BuAer, put together in his offices in the main Navy building on Constitution Avenue. Henry Mustin (now a captain) was his deputy. Cdr. Kenneth Whiting, soon to take command of *Langley,* headed the Plans Division. Jerome Hunsaker (now a commander) directed the Material Division, Lt. Cdr. Patrick Bellinger was chief of the Flight Division, and Lt. Cdr. Bruce Leighton ran the Engine Section. This was an outstanding group of officers, and Moffett made certain that they appeared at the Naval War College. On 6 April 1923, for example, Leighton read a lecture prepared by Moffett to the War College class of 1923. The lecture was a review of Navy accomplishments, an attack on the claims of Brigadier General Mitchell, and a preview of technical developments that held great promise for the future of naval aviation. Quite sophisticated technically and tactically, it assumed that those listening to it knew both the history of the issues surrounding the development of naval aviation and the practice and technology of flying. For example, consider this discussion of the trade-offs involved in increasing aircraft speed:

> The lift of an airplane wing varies approximately as the square of the speed. But the resistance and hence the thrust required also varies as the square of the speed. And since power is the product of thrust times resistance, the power required varies as the *cube* of the speed. . . . In other words, with increase in speed, the weight of the engine and fuel increases much more rapidly than does the lift of the wings.

Though Moffett admitted that "the most important Naval function that the aircraft has to perform today is that of observing gunfire for the main line ships of the Fleet," he also discussed the potential of aircraft as strike weapons. As he noted, the fact that there would be only two large carriers in service by 1927 limited what aircraft could do. In short, the Washington Conference, coupled with a reduction in spending on the Navy, had slowed down the pace at which aviation could be brought to bear on naval forces *at sea,* out of the range of land-based aviation.[6]

The result was a forced reliance on the war games at the Naval War College. As Rear Adm. Clarence S. Williams, president of the War College, stated in a 1923 letter to the commander of the fleet's aircraft squadrons, "Air tactics are of utmost concern to the college, and only from actual work done in the field can we hope to formulate definite and sound ideas concerning them." As the president argued in another letter, "In operating aircraft in chart maneuvers and game board exercises, various rules are applied which must of necessity be in close agreement with actual conditions, if the true value of aircraft to the Fleet is to be appreciated." By delaying the introduction of large carriers into the fleet, however, the Washington Conference agreements also limited the validity of the war games at Newport.

But what were these games like? Rear Admiral Sims had overseen the rigorous refinement of two kinds of games. The first, the strategic, called "chart maneuvers," was created to explore the major problems posed by a Pacific war between the U.S. and Japan. The strategic games covered topics such as the best route across the Pacific and the kinds and locations of bases the U.S. Navy would need to capture or build in the course of such an advance. The second kind of game, the tactical, was called a "board maneuver" because it took place on a specially inscribed wooden table measuring 200 by 308 inches. The tactical games were designed to compare the military value of different tactical formations, different attack and defensive techniques, and different force mixes.

Both kinds of games were developed to familiarize officers with the formal decision process called the "Estimate of the Situation." This was an "orderly process of reasoning by which [officers] may reach decisions and . . . also a method of formulation of either plans or orders which express the will of the Commander to his subordinates." Officers were trained in this process to improve tacit coordination among commanders and to standardize staff preparations for battle amid the anticipated confusion of wartime military operations. But the tactical games were also designed to explore, on a game board, ideas that could then, if successful, be used as the basis for fleet exercises or for warship designs.

In 1922, for example, Cdr. Chester Nimitz (later Fleet Admiral) developed for a game a novel cruising formation for the fleet that, when introduced in actual practice in 1923, was a success. Two other officers developed the concept of the mobile advanced naval base in 1921—a concept that, when implemented in 1944, would sustain the carrier fleets of that future era in waters once dominated completely by the Japanese.

Similarly, tactical games using carriers gradually showed that it was essential for carriers, once in range of an enemy, to strike immediately, with all their attack aircraft, at enemy carriers in order to gain air superiority over an enemy fleet. As a 1923 tactics manual put it, "the first step of any air plan should be to get control of the air." This was already the view of the Plans Division of the newly created Bureau of Aeronautics. The Plans Division, under the direction of Cdr. Kenneth Whiting, was responsible for formulating the military characteristics of naval aircraft, and members of the division used the War College games as a check of their own ideas. Indeed, the games eventually showed that the model of battleship effectiveness—Lanchester's "n square" law—did not apply to carriers, which delivered ordnance in great pulses rather than steady streams.

But there was a risk inherent in building a navy on game-board results. As Rear Admiral Sims told the chief of naval operations in 1922, "If the rules of the game are not right, . . . the conclusions drawn from maneuvers are sure to be erroneous." To strengthen the games, Sims, in 1922, directed a revision of the rules governing the effects of naval gunfire in tactical simulations. Though application of these more detailed rules lengthened the time any game-board "move" took, it also made the tactical games a more reliable indicator of how future systems and tactics would perform in combat. The "Maneuver Rules" promulgated in 1922, for example, contained very detailed tables with notional and actual aircraft characteristics, plus a special chart that allowed "players" to compute the time it would take to launch planes and squadrons.

The spark plug for this improvement in the sophistication of the War College's war games was Capt. Harris Laning, a surface line officer who had served under Sims before World War I. Laning took over the Tactics Department in September 1922. Sims respected Laning's pamphlet, "The Naval Battle," so much that he made it the standard "text" for the tactics course. However, as Laning noted in his memoirs, "a group of the cleverest tacticians among the students came to me and said that . . . they all believed there were better methods and they intended to find them." Instead of being offended, Laning backed them. As he recalled, "In investigating aircraft we gave the officers commanding miniature fleets a rather free hand in the use of aircraft . . . the only restriction being that planes had to operate in accordance with the capabilities and limitations as established by aviators familiar with planes."

The next step, as Laning reported it, was crucial: "I wrote to my friend in

Aeronautics [the Bureau] giving him a summary of our deductions." Then, "you can imagine my surprise a few weeks later to receive dispatch orders to appear before the General Board of the Navy for a hearing on naval aviation." The board was considering what kinds of aircraft to procure. The aviators in the Bureau of Aeronautics, influenced by what Laning had conveyed to them, had received a cold reception from the General Board, whose members were suspicious of "untried [untested] visions." Laning, in short, was asked to explain the methodology of the War College board games. He was a success: "I think the Board was antagonistic to me when the hearing started but as it went on the conclusions the College had come to seemed to be axiomatic." The end result was greater interaction and discussion among the aviators in BuAer (who saw they could use the War College gaming), the General Board (which needed more from BuAer than "untried visions"), and the war-gamers at Newport.[7]

After 1923, the inferences drawn from the games were often tested in the formal fleet problems—massive maneuvers lasting approximately two weeks, followed by careful discussions of the results. The problems themselves were based on scenarios proposed first by unit and force commanders, including the commander in chief of the Battle Fleet and the commander of the Scouting Fleet. Then these proposals were reviewed by the staff of the commander in chief of the U.S. Fleet, under whose auspices the rules for the exercise were distributed, once one had been accepted. However, various sources, including the Naval War College and the War Plans Division of the Office of the Chief of Naval Operations, suggested scenarios, and the scenarios approved for fleet problems usually were derived from the basic strategic mission of taking the offensive against Japan. For example, Fleet Problem I, staged in 1923, simulated an attack upon the Panama Canal by "enemy" forces using a simulated aircraft carrier. Fleet Problem II (1924) simulated the movement of U.S. forces, including fleet support ships, into waters contested by the Japanese. *Langley* participated for the first time in Problem III, representing a large aircraft carrier accompanying enemy forces bent on attacking the Panama Canal.

These exercises gave senior officers the chance to test the inferences drawn from games against actual operations. In games, it was difficult to quantify the effects of weather, or of personalities, or of weak intelligence, but these factors could and did have an impact on the outcome of fleet problems. The real challenge facing those planning the fleet problems, however, was drawing up rules for hits and damage. Just as unrealistic rules could produce spurious and misleading results on the game board, unrealistic damage calculations could (and did) reduce the value of lessons learned from the fleet problems. Before 1930, umpires stationed on the major warships were allowed to use their "professional judgement" in deciding whether a ship had been hit, and how badly. Results were not known until after a maneuver had been completed, which meant that "damaged" units went on playing their parts until the exercise was over. In Fleet Problem IX (1929), for example, observers on the ships involved were instructed not to "impose such drastic penalties or casualties as would vitiate carrying out the general plan of the problem." This was particularly important for carriers. There were so few of them that they had to play on, despite any "damage" received.

Umpires did not impose the consequences of "damage" on ships while mock battles were under way until 1930. As a result, the early fleet problems were often contentious affairs, as "opposing" commanders argued about which of their units had been disabled, and when. According to aviators, later problems were plagued by damage rules that did not recognize the destructive power of accurately delivered large bombs. As one recalled, "We came in from 22,000 feet, effected complete surprise with . . . roughly 54 half ton bombs. . . . The Chief Umpire, going by War College rules, slowed one BATDIV [battleship division] two knots!!!"

Nevertheless, the improved validity of the tactical war games at Newport, once coupled to the fleet problems, created a means of testing new carrier concepts, new carrier designs, and even new concepts for carrier aircraft. This "back-and-forth" between games and major exercises substituted for actual wartime operations as a breeding ground for new concepts and tactics. Admiral Laning's memoirs imply that the cycle of games-to-exercises-to-games was an almost accidental creation. The result, however, was the kind of institutional arrangement that Admiral Sims had wanted and then supported. Another Sims protégé, Rear Adm. William V. Pratt, who held the presidency of the Naval War College for the academic years 1925–27, was very conscious of the value of this round-robin relationship and acted to sustain it while he was at Newport and then, later, when he joined the fleet. In a paper he wrote in 1927, Pratt argued that the chief of naval operations and the commander in chief, U.S. Fleet, needed "an organization beneficial in the framing and testing of problems before they are executed in the Fleet."

Pratt, promoted to vice admiral, went from Newport to command first a battleship division and then the battle fleet itself. While in command of the latter, Pratt informed Adm. H. A. Wiley, commander in chief of the U.S. Fleet, that he intended to "increase the interest of the Battle Fleet in aviation matters." He did so by supporting the needs of Rear Adm. Joseph M. Reeves, then in command of the fleet's carrier aviation (which by 1928 included *Lexington* and *Saratoga,* as well as the experimental *Langley*). Reeves needed more pilots to fill out the squadrons that were being commissioned for his two new large carriers, and Pratt agreed that the way to get those pilots was by reducing the number of pilots then assigned to the battleships' catapult float planes. Pratt also worked to set aside ample time for aviation exercises. Pratt's understanding of the complementary roles of the War College and the fleet problems was especially important because the Washington Treaty had deliberately limited the number of carriers that could be used for testing new concepts and tactics. Arms control is usually thought of as a means of limiting weapons, but this case shows that it can be just as important in limiting the ways military forces learn about, and learn how to use, new systems. The games-exercises combination, stimulated by information sent to the War College by BuAer, was a workable (if imperfect) alternative to having numbers of active carriers.[8]

In March 1925, for example, the secretary of the Navy asked the General Board "to consider whether or not it is feasible to combine the qualities of a scout cruiser and an aircraft carrier in a new type of ship." The board passed the request to the Naval War College. In his response, the president of the Naval War College argued that "it would appear unwise to attempt to develop a vessel which will combine the two qualities of a cruiser and an airplane carrier." His position was "based largely upon experience gained by the War College Staff in games played in the Department of Tactics." This case illustrates how the War College games were used to analyze questions that could otherwise have been answered only through experience—experience that the Washington Treaty had denied the Navy.

The usefulness of the games-exercises-games cycle, which linked the War College with the fleet and with BuAer, was not appreciated outside the Navy. Even many officers within the Navy did not realize that this cycle was a means to frame questions, highlight unknowns, and generate evidence to answer those questions and solve those unknowns. The great value of the games-exercises-games cycle is illustrated by an incident in 1924. The secretary of the Navy wanted a thorough examination of "the development and upkeep of the Navy" before he drew up his budget proposals for fiscal year 1926 (which would start in July 1925). He asked the General Board to consider the status of aircraft and the future value of the battleship. As part of its hearings, the board asked a panel of distinguished aeronautical experts (including the head of research for the National Advisory Committee for Aeronautics, or NACA) to forecast the evolution of aircraft performance. The experts, one of whom was retired Rear Adm. David Taylor, then secretary of the NACA, said that aircraft "maximum performance . . . may be increased about thirty per cent by future developments." Their projection was significantly less than that produced by the Bureau of Aeronautics for the Naval War College in 1923. But which estimate was more accurate?

The answer to that question mattered a great deal. Given a mere 30 percent projected increase in the militarily relevant performance of aircraft, the General Board had little choice but to affirm the importance of the battleship as the principal means of delivering ship-killing ordnance at sea. After all, the new sixteen-inch-gunned battleships of the *Maryland* class were shooting accurately beyond twenty thousand yards. With the aid of spotter aircraft in 1927, these ships fired accurately over the horizon to ranges over thirty thousand yards. In 1924, by contrast, the Navy had no operational carriers, no operational carrier bombing squadrons, no effective high-level bombsight so that bombers could target ships without enduring the ships' antiaircraft barrages, and not even the beginnings of dive bombing. And no one could say just how effectively carrier aircraft would perform in a few years' time. The potential of the battleship was predictable. That of the carrier and her aircraft was not. The General Board could not gamble on an unknown and ignore the performance of existing battleships.

Despite the board's justifiable pessimism about the future of aircraft performance, the chief of naval operations, Adm. E. W. Eberle, recommended a progressive, steadily funded aircraft building program, completion of battle cruisers *Lexington* and *Saratoga* as carriers, and authorization of a new, twenty-three-thousand-ton aircraft carrier. Rear Adm. Moffett, chief of BuAer, had argued to Eberle that BuAer's projections of aircraft performance —the projections used by the Naval War College—were just as accurate as those of the panel that had advised the General Board.

Our point is that the continuing interaction among the War College, the fleet, and the Bureau of Aeronautics had not conclusively proven its value by 1924; that is, Newport's war-game predictions had not been shown to be true in the few actual fleet problems run by that time. As a result, the General Board could not rely exclusively on war-game data in its hearings. But, rather than reaffirming the dominance of the battleship, the General Board simply recognized again that the evidence was ambiguous and thus that aircraft had an uncertain future as strike weapons.[9]

In any event, Rear Admiral Moffett, chief of the Bureau of Aeronautics, also had a more serious problem to deal with: Army General Mitchell's efforts to form a separate air service.

In the spring of 1924, a Select Committee of the House of Representatives, chaired by Rep. Florian Lampert, had begun an eleven-month investigation of national aviation policy. Mitchell had told the committee, "It is a very serious question whether air power is auxiliary to the Army and the Navy, or whether armies and navies are not actually auxiliary to air power." It was Mitchell's attacks on the Navy's interest in and support for aviation that prompted Navy Secretary Curtis D. Wilbur to set the General Board and the chief of naval operations to work investigating and projecting the status and future of naval aviation. It was Mitchell who enlarged the circle of participants in the discussions over the future of naval aviation, and it was Mitchell's stridency that turned many of the participants into partisans and the discussions into a fierce debate over the import of the available evidence.

In the fall of 1923, Capt. Joseph M. Reeves began the senior officers' course at the Naval War College. After completing his year as a student, Reeves was appointed head of the Tactics Department, where he supervised the games of 1924–25. In the summer of 1925, Reeves completed the aviation observers course (a catch-up course on aviation and flying for older officers) at Pensacola, and, in September 1925, Chief of Naval Operations E. W. Eberle appointed Reeves Commander, Aircraft Squadrons, Battle Force. This assignment was the key to the success of carrier aviation in the U.S. Navy.

It would be a mistake, however, to focus only on Reeves. Rear Admiral Moffett, appointed to a second term as chief of the Bureau of Aeronautics in March 1925, fought the "political" battle with Mitchell and the latter's supporters in Congress. Moffett's tactics, described in detail by several writers, brought to bear what one called his "formidable political muscle and powers of compromise." His role is significant in that he was very effective in shielding Reeves from interference, so that the latter could bring about a revolution in carrier warfare.

Turning *Langley* from an experiment into a warship was no easy task, however. Though *Langley* and her aircraft had performed impressively in Fleet Problem V in March 1925 (the commander in chief, U.S. Fleet, observed that "operations of *Langley* with the Fleet have been of marked advantage to officers in the higher commands"), and though Navy seaplanes and airships were also gaining praise for work with the fleet, Moffett felt that it was vital to keep Navy aviation in the public eye. To that end, he approved a risky non-stop flight by two patrol seaplanes from San Francisco to Honolulu, scheduled for the end of that August. He also scheduled the new airship *Shenandoah* for a round of visits to state fairs in the Midwest. Both demonstrations blew up in his face. On 1 September 1925, the one seaplane that had not had engine problems was lost at sea; two days later, *Shenandoah* crashed after being torn apart in a thunderstorm over Ohio. Mitchell promptly accused the War and Navy departments of "incompetency, criminal negligence and almost treasonable administration of the national defense."

In response, President Coolidge created the President's Aircraft Board, headed by the prominent lawyer Dwight W. Morrow, which began public hearings on 21 September. The Morrow Board's mandate was to consider the whole future of aviation and government involvement in it. Moffett and his staff at the Bureau of Aeronautics were preoccupied by their testimony before Morrow and his colleagues. For help, they drew in senior aviators such as John Towers and Jerome Hunsaker. Their efforts paid off. The Morrow Board rejected the call for a unified air service and for a single aircraft procurement agency. It also recommended that only naval aviators (pilots, not observers) be given command of aircraft carriers and naval airfields. Finally, the board called on Congress to pass a five-year, thousand-plane procurement authorization to sustain the aircraft industry and furnish the Army and Navy with modern aircraft.[10]

Through the latter half of October 1925, while the Morrow Board and the Lampert Committee were hearing witnesses and the Army was preparing a court-martial against General Mitchell, Captain (temporarily Commodore) Reeves was watching aviation operations on *Langley.* The commander in chief, Battle Fleet, had told Reeves to focus on developing "Strategy and Tactics of the air in its relation to the Fleet." Reeves's grant of authority was therefore broad. In early November, he called *Langley*'s aviators and crew together in an auditorium at the naval airfield at North Island, California, and informed them that he planned to increase the experimental carrier's complement from eight to at least fourteen aircraft and then to even more.

According to Eugene E. Wilson, later Reeves's chief of staff, *Langley*'s aviators had seen too many of their comrades injured and killed in operations with *Langley*, and they resented having a nonpilot tell them that they would increase the tempo—and hence the danger—of their landings and takeoffs. But Reeves had learned at the War College that numbers of aircraft mattered in combat at sea. It was important to place as many aircraft as possible in the air with the fleet, especially aircraft that did not have to land on the water after they completed their missions. To increase the number of planes operating from *Langley*, Reeves proposed to carry more aircraft *and* to shorten the interval between landings and takeoffs.

The real danger came when aircraft were landing. It was essential to get a recovered plane out of the way of the next plane waiting to land as quickly as possible. Current practice was to lower the recovered plane to the hangar deck, so that the next plane, if it missed the arresting gear, would then not pile into it. But lowering a plane from the deck to the hangar took time. In early 1925, it took two minutes, ten seconds to clear *Langley*'s deck and then another two minutes for the next plane to land. Reeves understood that this slow process had to change; another means had to be found to shield the planes that had landed already from any that missed the carrier's arresting gear.

November 1925 was a key month. Reeves had to lead the crew and aviators of *Langley* in a concerted effort to change their aircraft launch-and-recovery processes. Moffett and other naval aviators were trying to persuade the Morrow Board to accept their ideas. And Rear Adm. William V. Pratt, President of the Naval War College, was preparing to testify in the court-martial of General Mitchell. Prior to his actual sworn testimony, General Mitchell had informed newspaper reporters that the war games conducted at the Naval War College had shown that the battleship was obsolete. Rear Admiral Sims, then retired, had supported Mitchell's claim. Pratt knew that Sims was wrong, that the games held when Sims was president did not show that the battleship was useless when supported by aircraft. Indeed, as Pratt had been informed, the newer battleships improved both the range and accuracy of their shooting with air spotting. Moreover, Pratt learned when he became president of the Naval War College that the games had shown that carriers had many weaknesses. The short range of attack aircraft, for example, meant that carriers had to get dangerously close to an enemy formation to launch planes, and then the carriers had to stay close in order to recover those aircraft at the end of their strike. Carriers were not yet the weapon that better aircraft would make them. Pratt had to make this point without at the same time opening carriers to attack.

Reeves's efforts to get more striking power (through more aircraft) from *Langley* were the answer to carrier critics. If successful, Reeves's innovation would then set the stage for changes in the rules governing future games at Newport. Reeves had his first success on 18 December 1925, when ten aircraft were launched from *Langley* in one minute, thirty-eight seconds. Landing the same ten aircraft took much longer: thirty-five minutes. But at least Reeves had made his point: more aircraft could be launched and recovered faster than anyone had anticipated.[11] Brigadier General Mitchell's charge that the Navy would and could not develop aviation at sea was wrong. His court-martial removed from official circles a strident critic of naval aviation.

For *Langley*'s aviators and crew, 1926 was a hectic year. But by midyear the commander in chief, U.S. Battle Fleet, could say in his annual report that "[t]he feasibility of carrier operations is believed to have been very well demonstrated." By mid-June, *Langley* had an aircraft barrier which, when lifted amidships, shielded planes parked forward from any landing aircraft whose tailhook might miss the athwartship arresting gear located farther aft. Photographs taken of *Langley* at this time show both fore-and-aft and cross-deck arresting wires. The latter stopped the plane. The former, which caught hooks on the axle of the plane's landing gear, could keep the plane from bouncing left or right. The fore-and-aft wires also slowed down the planes (which had no brakes on their landing-gear wheels). But there was always the chance that a plane would not catch properly. The barrier was a kind of safety net, not only for the pilot of the landing plane, but especially for the aircraft parked forward.

Thus was born the deck park, a key element in improving the carrying capacity and operating efficiency of aircraft carriers. Once a plane landed and stopped, the flight-deck crew pushed it forward, over the barrier wires, which were flat on the deck. Then the barrier was raised behind it, and the next plane landed. Once all the planes were aboard, they were moved aft, refueled and rearmed, and then were ready for action again. By August 1926, *Langley*'s crew could launch aircraft every fifteen seconds and recover them every ninety seconds. But Reeves was not satisfied. He kept pushing. On 9 August, fighter squadron 1 (VF-1) completed 127 landings in a single day, and Reeves then "recommended that her official status as an experimental ship be changed to that of a full-fledged combatant, believing she could double her aircraft component to twenty-eight machines." Though aviators such as John Towers (*Langley*'s executive officer) were worried about accidents, Reeves persevered, and he was supported in his efforts by the Bureau of Aeronautics.[12]

He was also aided by a new tactical innovation: "a combined attack using light bombs in conjunction with machine gun fire." As Reeves's successor noted, "in one case . . . an attack of this kind coming from an altitude of 10,000 feet to 400 feet or less produced an accuracy of 100%." Indeed, as Reeves himself observed, "about three months during the summer and early fall of 1926 . . . was devoted to intensive study by practical operations of aircraft tactics." These exercises laid the foundation for the tactics that were used so successfully against enemy aircraft and ships during World War II. The report describing these exercises shows clearly, for example, that aviators learned quickly the need for simultaneous torpedo and bomb attacks on a ship armed with antiaircraft guns. In more ways than one, 1926 was a revolutionary year for U.S. Navy carrier aviation.

New, more powerful aircraft, such as the 400-horsepower Curtiss F6C Hawk and the 435-horsepower Boeing FB-1, could withstand the stresses of powered dives and were powerful enough to carry what was a significant bombload for that time. Although these aircraft were powered by in-line, water-cooled engines, their performance was impressive. On 22 October 1926, Reeves had a squadron of such aircraft carry out a simulated attack on the battleships of the fleet outside San Pedro, California. Reeves had already warned the commander in chief, Adm. C. F. Hughes, that an attack would occur, and when. The battleships were nevertheless taken by surprise, and afterward Hughes became a strong supporter of naval aviation. This stunt was followed up in December by systematic exercises showing that this form of attack was indeed a promising technique.[13]

The early attack aircraft were followed by planes (such as the Curtiss F11C) powered by air-cooled radial engines. These high horsepower-to-weight engines, produced by private manufacturers, had been built to performance specifications developed by BuAer's Engine Section, headed first by Lt. Cdr. B. G. Leighton and then by E. E. Wilson. As Leighton put it, "the power plant has been the heart of the airplane." Under Leighton and Wilson, private firms like Pratt and Whitney were encouraged to invest in air-cooled radial engines, and the effort paid off.

Reeves's revolution in carrier operations came just in time. In the fall of 1926, the War College staff was asked to comment on discussions between the Bureau of Construction and Repair and the Bureau of Aeronautics concerning aircraft carrier design. Once the designs for the alterations to *Lexington* and *Saratoga* had been completed, the naval constructors in the Bureau of Construction and Repair had, at the request of the General Board, turned their attention to a new, built-for-the-purpose carrier. But in their testimony to the General Board, in hearings held that spring, the bureaus had differed in specifying what such a carrier would require; there was "no general consensus of service opinion." As the commander in chief of the U.S. Battle Fleet observed in June 1926, there was a "lack of Statistical Tactical Data in connection with Aerial Operations and . . . of any system or well-defined doctrine for the employment of Aircraft in major operations." The board asked the War College, which now had a junior course as well as a senior one, for help.

At the beginning of December 1926, Lt. Forrest Sherman, USN, a member of the junior class of 1927 and a future chief of naval operations, prepared a commentary on the differences in the viewpoints of the bureaus of Aeronautics and Construction and Repair with respect to carrier specifications. Surveying the progress of both British and American carrier operations, Sherman argued that it was essential that any future U.S. carriers have the capacity to arm and service planes on deck (versus in the carrier's hangar). He also noted that the British had shifted from an enclosed hangar deck to one open and "highly ventilated," so that aircraft engines could be run there without generating excessive exhaust fumes. Finally, after a careful analysis of a number of design factors, he recommended construction of "large high speed vessels, probably of 23,000 tons and 33 knots." His analysis drew on the experience with *Langley* in 1926—experience that the War College had plowed back into its games.

Reeves's work on *Langley* strengthened the link among the War College, the fleet, and BuAer. Denied a free hand to build whatever types of carriers it chose by the Washington treaty, the Navy relied necessarily on games and simulations to select its first true carrier design, *Ranger* (CV-4). It also had to rely heavily on the War College for help in deciding what kinds of aircraft to put on *Lexington* and *Saratoga.*

In March 1927, Lt. Sherman reported to the president of the War College that he and others had placed scale-model aircraft on similarly scaled models of the flight and hangar decks of *Lexington* and *Saratoga* in order to determine how best to store aircraft on the nearly completed carriers in the course of various games. Sherman's analysis, plus the commentaries of other officers, was included in a package that the War College's president, Rear Adm. W. V. Pratt, sent to the chief of naval operations in April. Pratt noted, in his cover letter, that the issues that had divided the bureaus of Construction and Repair and Aeronautics a year earlier were put to the test in the major operations game held that winter (1926–27). He also observed that the game players had stuck "rigidly to the times allowed in the rules for the various phases of airplane operations from carriers." These times were those established under Reeves.

Thus did Reeves force his changes on *Langley* at an optimal time. The trial of Brigadier General Mitchell made clear just how contentious the issue of military aviation was. Though Rear Admiral Moffett directed the campaign against Mitchell from the Bureau of Aeronautics, the pressure to show results with *Langley* and to move her from experimental to operational status fell on Reeves. That he was successful is shown clearly by comparing *Langley*'s aircraft complement from 1926 with that from 1927. In August 1926, *Langley* officially (and official data lagged behind actual practice by as much as a year) carried fourteen aircraft of nine different designations. Her "air group" was an experimental hodgepodge. Of the four full land-based squadrons under Reeves's command, only two had anything close to uniform aircraft complements. One year later, however, the picture was very different. *Langley*'s own utility aircraft numbered just seven, and all four of the combat squadrons under Reeves had uniform aircraft complements. As the Annual Report of the Commander, Aircraft Squadrons, Battle Fleet, pointed out at the end of June 1927, "Commander Aircraft Squadrons believes that he can operate in time of war 48 planes from the carrier."

In recognition of this achievement, Reeves's position (Commander, Air, Battle Force) was made a rear admiral's post in September 1927. Unfortunately, Reeves left no personal papers; his motives can only be inferred from his actions. But it seems fair to infer that his pioneering work on *Langley*, which kept officers such as ship's executive Towers and flight officer Mark Mitscher busy "day and night," was intended to show results in time to feed the Naval War College game for the class of 1927.[14]

Reeves was also racing against another deadline. Secretary of the Navy Wilbur had decided in June 1926 to postpone further carrier construction pending actual exercises with *Lexington* and *Saratoga.* BuAer chief Moffett had objected to Wilbur's decision on the grounds that such a delay would place the U.S. Navy in a position of distinct inferiority to the British and Japanese. As Rear Admiral Pratt had told the chief of naval operations, "planes *in the air* [his emphasis] at the critical time" were what mattered, and more carriers could loft a larger initial strike. But the Navy secretary still refused to change his mind. Two developments eventually brought him around to Moffett's position, however. The first was the development of the steep dive attack, using light bombs and machine gun fire. After the December exercises had demonstrated its accuracy, the steep dive attack seemed to obviate the need for torpedo planes, which, even with folding wings, took a lot of deck and hangar space. The steep dive attack also seemed to make the smaller (under twenty thousand tons) and cheaper carrier militarily attractive. The second persuasive development was the insights from the games carried on at the Naval War College in 1926–27. Though Rear Admiral Pratt had admitted to the chief of naval operations that "due to faulty conceptions frequently results were obtained from which faulty lessons were derived," Moffett was not deterred. With the materials from both the War College and the fleet in hand, Moffett could approach both the General Board and the secretary with systematic arguments, not just the opinions of aviators.

To weigh all this new evidence, the secretary of the Navy established a special board of review headed by Rear Adm. Montgomery M. Taylor in 1927. Rear Admiral Moffett persuaded Taylor to accept, as members, himself and captains Reeves and Harry E. Yarnell (the latter would be the first commander of *Saratoga* [CV-3]). Moffett's views on the future of aviation in the Navy had run into opposition from the General Board. The latter, for example, had opposed Moffett's program to construct huge aircraft-carrying airships, and both sides got the chance to present their views to Rear Admiral Taylor and his fellow review board members.

The really important issue before the Taylor Board, however, was that of aircraft types. The Morrow Board of 1925 had recommended that Congress authorize the Navy and Army to begin five-year aircraft construction programs. Congress had accepted that recommendation and passed, in June 1926, enabling legislation authorizing the Navy to begin a five-year, thousand-plane program. But what were the proper types of aircraft to procure? The Taylor Board rejected the concept of the multipurpose scout-fighter-bomber and instead endorsed the following priority of aircraft development: first, fighters; then spotters for cruisers and battleships; third, reconnaissance planes; fourth, dive-bombers; fifth, level bombers; and sixth, torpedo planes and patrol seaplanes. The emphasis on fighters and gunfire spotters shows that carrier aircraft were perceived as aids in gaining air superiority in the skies over two fighting battleship forces. But the rejection of multipurpose aircraft also shows the wisdom of the thousand-plane authorization. Within that number, there was room enough for all the specialized types that Moffett and his subordinates at BuAer wanted to build. As the instructions to the Taylor Board put it, "It is . . . necessary to assume certain risks in the purchase of new equipment, and be willing to assume these risks if we expect to advance."[15]

Once experience with *Langley* had made clear what carriers could do, the next question was how to employ *Lexington* and *Saratoga.* The two converted battle cruisers would be placed in commission at the end of 1927, and Captain Reeves wanted to practice employing them together, as the centerpiece of a fast striking force. It is not clear if his view was based upon the 1926–27 games at Newport, but that was certainly one inference drawn from those exercises by Lt. Forrest Sherman, who had been one of the participants. What is striking is Reeves's insistence on placing numbers of aircraft in the air; he grasped, first intuitively and then analytically, the necessity to deliver a knockout blow against enemy air power in the opening minutes of any confrontation between opposing carrier forces. He also understood how critical this insight was. In a letter to Moffett dated 4 October 1928, for example, Reeves explained how he had hidden *Langley*'s true air strength from visiting Vice Admiral Fuller of the Royal Navy: "Of course I did not tell Admiral Fuller that we operated not 24, but 36 and could operate 42 and possibly 48 airplanes from the *Langley.*"

Unfortunately, it took all of 1928 to prepare *Lexington* and *Saratoga* for normal operations with the rest of the fleet. The delay was another of a series of embarrassments connected with the conversion of these ships from battle cruisers to carriers. The conversion process itself had taken almost twice as long as originally estimated and had cost nearly twice as much as planned. But there still remained unanticipated obstacles to turning these ships into effective military units. For example, when hydraulic shock absorbers replaced the rubber cord type on carrier aircraft in 1927, *Langley* was stripped of her fore-and-aft arresting gear wires, and the number of crashes during landings dropped off. Planes with the rubber cord shock absorbers had bounced around a lot, like a bungee cord jumper. The fore-and-aft wires were needed to keep the early planes from flopping around on the deck. Unfortunately, the fore-and-aft wires themselves proved a hazard; planes sometimes missed the cross-deck wires but became ensnared in the fore-and-aft array. Given the experience gained in *Langley,* it was thought that the cross-deck wires on the two converted battle cruisers would work satisfactorily.

But the rotary brakes used to tighten the arresting gear wires on *Saratoga* and *Lexington* did not pull proportionately when a landing aircraft hooked an arresting gear wire off the center line. The result, at first, was an increase in damaged aircraft. There were all sorts of other details to be worked out, too: fire-fighting arrangements, safe refueling on the hangar and flight decks, loading ordnance, and learning to move large numbers of aircraft around on deck in all kinds of weather and at night. *Saratoga* even served briefly as a floating base for the rigid airship *Los Angeles* to test the possibility that the big carriers might help extend the range and the effectiveness of the Navy's airships.

By the end of 1928, however, the two big converted battle cruisers were ready for their first major test, Fleet Problem IX (23–27 January 1929, off Panama)—the first real test of multiple carriers launching significant numbers of aircraft. On her departure from San Diego, *Saratoga* carried 110 planes and one hundred pilots—almost one-third of all aircraft capable of going to sea and almost two-thirds of all the aviators experienced in carrier operations. She and *Lexington* were a world away from *Langley* in terms of size, speed, and facilities. One reason their alteration from battle cruisers to carriers had been delayed (and made more expensive) was that Moffett had insisted that they have facilities on their flight decks to rearm and refuel their aircraft. The development of the deck park by *Langley*'s crew in 1926 and 1927 had shown the value of such facilities, but it still took time, in 1928, to develop routines for their proper use.

Charles Melhorn, in his book *Two-Block Fox,* argued that the exploits of carrier *Saratoga* in Fleet Problem IX were revolutionary. In making this argument, he was following the lead of E. E. Wilson, who had been Reeves's chief of staff. As Wilson put it in his memoirs, "the Navy had created the first American strategic air force." In brief, in the climax to Problem IX, *Saratoga,* under the command of Reeves as commander of the "enemy" force, left the main force of battleships and, accompanied by one light cruiser, made a high-speed run from the west in order to launch a seventy-plane strike against the locks of the Panama Canal from the range of 140 miles. On her approach, *Saratoga* used her own aircraft to scout, and her light attack planes dove on the canal's locks from an altitude of ten thousand feet. They caught "defending" forces by surprise, thus demonstrating—supposedly—the potential of carrier aviation.

Yet the records in the National Archives show that *Saratoga*'s swift strike was not part of the original plan; she was detached from her battleship escort because the battleships' destroyer screen did not have the fuel to stay with her. It is true that Rear Admiral Reeves favored clustering cruisers and destroyers around the big carriers to form a striking force (or forces), but it is also true that Admiral Pratt, commander in chief of the U.S. Fleet, did not think that he could draw any major lessons from Fleet Problem IX because, in his view, it was not realistic enough.

However, the available records indicate that the actions of the carriers boosted the morale of their personnel and gave credibility to carriers as *operational* units. After Problem IX, the commander in chief of the U.S. Fleet presided over a formal critique held in a theater in Panama. Approximately seven hundred officers (including some from the Army) attended, and many officers made formal presentations. Attendance was required of all force commanders, all commanding officers of ships larger than minesweepers, all senior officers of battleships, carriers, and cruisers, and all the formal observers. Junior officers were also encouraged to attend. At the critique, the commander of the force that included *Saratoga* noted that "when we learn more of the possibilities of the carriers we will come to an acceptance of Admiral Reeves's plan which provides for a very powerful and mobile force . . . the nucleus of which is the carrier."

After Fleet Problem IX, carriers were accepted fleet units. They were not, however, accepted as independent strike platforms outside the naval aviation community. As then Cdr. John Towers told the General Board in October 1929, "We can't drop a 500 pound bomb on a battleship." Aviators flying from carriers had simulated such an attack, and they had actually dropped five-hundred-pound bombs on targets ashore, but they had only one squadron trained and equipped for this kind of strike. The problem they faced in 1929 was complex: "fighting" planes equipped with five-hundred-pound bombs could not climb as fast or maneuver as well as planes without such a load.

But what was the primary mission of the aircraft? If it was to gain control of the air, then "fighting" planes had to be fighters first and bombers only secondarily. But if having bombs gave these same planes the chance to knock out an opposing carrier, then some reduction in their performance as fighters was acceptable. As historian Thomas Wildenberg has shown, this question divided Reeves from Towers. Towers wanted to fight for the air first. Reeves wanted to attack "enemy" carriers first. This dispute shows that carrier development was diverging from aircraft development. Carriers were becoming *multimission* ships, able to scout, attack submarines, protect the battleships, and attack enemy ships. Aircraft, on the other hand, were becoming increasingly specialized. The fighter-bomber was beginning to look as though it could not be effective in either role. Yet only so many aircraft could be operated from a carrier, so carriers needed multirole or multimission aircraft. The solution was for the Navy's Bureau of Aeronautics to produce a multirole scout bomber, the Curtiss SBC.

A senior naval aviator, reviewing the results of Fleet Problems IX, X, and XI, told the Naval War College class at Newport in August 1930, "Carriers combine great power with extreme vulnerability." Lacking armored flight decks, crammed with volatile aviation gas and munitions, carriers could be put out of action by enemy bombers in minutes. Carriers were also vulnerable to submarines: "[O]perating four 18 plane squadrons, the carrier is constrained to a windward course for about 18 minutes while launching her planes, and for about 50 minutes while recovering them." The combination of great striking power with potentially devastating vulnerability made carrier warfare very risky and highly leveraged; the fleet with the carrier force that struck first was almost always the winner in later fleet problems.[16]

3 Fleet Carriers—or Fleets of Carriers

After Fleet Problem IX in 1929, the question was not "Should the United States Navy have a force of carriers?" but "How should that treaty-limited force of carriers be employed in concert with the rest of the fleet, including the other forms of naval aviation?" As Professor Wayne P. Hughes Jr. of the U.S. Navy's Postgraduate School has pointed out, the second question could be put in another way: "What was the correct tactical model of carrier warfare, and what were its implications?"

The leaders of U.S. Navy aviation, such as Rear Admiral Reeves, realized by 1929 that the proper tactical model for carrier warfare was not the same as for surface ship engagements, but they could not anticipate, from the evidence, what the new world of carrier warfare would be like. In particular, they were hampered by the problem of carrier vulnerability. Because there were even fewer carriers than battleships, the loss of only one carrier could have dramatic effects on the course of any future fleet engagement with their professional counterparts in the Imperial Japanese navy.

The U.S. Navy worked through the 1930s to find the correct model for battles between carriers. After the war, carrier advocates argued that not enough was done fast enough—that the U.S. Navy missed its chance to develop the concept of a strategically mobile, aggressive fleet of fast carriers. But we agree with Wayne Hughes that the "air power zealots . . . foretold too much too soon." This chapter will explain why.[1]

The offensive potential of a body (or fleet) of aircraft carriers was predicted by a few officers in the U.S. Navy as early as 1921, when Capt. William V. Pratt (later chief of naval operations) advised the assistant secretary of the Navy that the aircraft carrier was "the possible capital ship of the future." Ten years later, Rear Admiral Moffett, still chief of the Bureau Aeronautics, argued to the members of the Navy's General Board that "the primary function of the main body of carriers is certainly to increase the major attack power of the fleet." Though he acknowledged that the "use of heavy attack planes from carriers is comparatively undeveloped," he also insisted that future development would place "fleet carriers in exactly the same category as battleships for improving the striking power of the battleline."[2] Considering the linkage among BuAer, the fleet, and the Naval War College that had led to the spectacular results of Fleet Problem IX, Moffett assessed the situation correctly. Yet historian Clark Reynolds, author of *The Fast Carriers,* would charge almost four decades later that Navy aviation was as unprepared for World War II as it had been for World War I. Was *he* correct? If indeed he was, then why was the "carrier revolution" delayed?[3]

Reynolds aligned himself with the Navy's aviators in pointing to the influence that nonaviators held in the highest levels of the Navy Department. For example, the chiefs of naval operations who immediately followed Adm. William V. Pratt were all nonaviators: Adm. W. H. Standley (1933–37), Adm. William D. Leahy (1937–39), and Adm. Harold R. Stark (1939–42). And of the six fleet commanders from 1933 until the end of 1940, only one —Adm. Joseph M. Reeves (1934–36)—was experienced in the command of carrier aviation forces. In his postwar memoirs, Adm. Frederick C. Sherman, a contemporary of Adm. William F. Halsey Jr. and, like Halsey, a carrier admiral, castigated these senior members of the so-called "gun club"—officers such as Leahy who had commanded battleships at sea and had held senior posts in the Bureau of Ordnance ashore. Sherman argued that these non-aviators simply did not grasp aviation's potential. However, the *Navy Register* of 1 July 1937 reveals that seven of the total of forty rear admirals (the highest permanent rank possible then) were qualified as aviators or as aviation observers. That's 17.5 percent of the total, a far cry from the situation then existing in the Royal Navy. What Frederick Sherman was really complaining about was the lack of true aviators—pilots who were fervent in their faith in the power and potential of carrier aviation.

Clark Reynolds developed a different but related argument: that officers such as Capt. (later Admiral) Raymond Spruance, who were senior instructors at the Naval War College in the late 1930s (Spruance taught in the operations department from 1935 to 1938), believed that a naval war in the Pacific would climax with a great fleet engagement, where carriers would support battleships. Reynolds has argued that their focus on preparing for a fleet engagement crowded out studies of the effects of multicarrier forces acting independently of battleships.[4]

Common to the criticisms of both the "zealots" like Sherman and historians such as Reynolds is the assertion that senior officers in the Navy failed to learn from the experience of prewar exercises—that they ignored the facts because of ignorance or prejudice, or that they failed to draw the proper inferences from those facts because their methods of analysis were flawed. We believe that the truth was far more complicated than this. Our view is that the "evidence" of the potential effectiveness of carriers was ambiguous.

Four factors worked together to obscure the potential of large, mobile carrier forces. The first was the small number of carriers. *Ranger,* the first carrier designed as such, did not commission until June 1934 and operated with the fleet only at the end of that year. *Yorktown* and *Enterprise,* successors to *Ranger,* did not work as fleet units until January 1939. This meant that there were a maximum of three first-line carriers through almost all of the 1930s. *Langley,* the first—but experimental—carrier, was far too slow to operate with the three real carriers (*Lexington, Saratoga,* and *Ranger*). So it was difficult to test any new idea that called for more than three carriers in maneuvers and fleet problems. The assumption was, apparently, that carrier air power would scale up linearly as the number of carriers increased. This was correct, but, as Wayne Hughes has shown, it had implications for the use of carriers that no major navy realized clearly before the war.

Officers in the U.S. Navy and in other major navies were familiar with an accepted model of surface ship combat. This model assumed that opposing surface forces would pump shells at and into one another at the greatest possible range in an effort to wear each other down. The first side to lose ships would find itself in a dangerous situation. Its firepower would start to erode faster. It would find its losses mounting without being able to inflict similar losses on the other side. The validity of this model is what prompted the U.S. Navy to develop gunnery fire control systems (with centralized directors linked to the guns via servomechanisms) that would allow U.S. surface combatants to hit first. But the 1930s fleet problems of the U.S. Navy showed that the model for carrier warfare was different. As Hughes has put it, carrier firepower was "best represented as one large pulse . . . unleashed upon the arrival of the air wing at the target." In this model, it was possible for opposing carriers to send off, simultaneously, roughly equal pulses of power. The result would be a one-for-one exchange, assuming each carrier launched its strike aircraft at about the same time. In 1929 and through the 1930s it was not possible for a carrier to defend itself against such a wave of enemy aircraft attacking all at once. Hence the dream of a carrier commander was to find the opposing carrier before it found him. There was a strong chance that the carrier that struck first would sink or at least disable its opponent without suffering any damage in return. In Fleet Problem XX (1939), *Ranger*'s air group did exactly that, "sinking" *Enterprise* after communications specialists on *Ranger* were able to detect the presence of *Enterprise* through the use of high-frequency direction finding (HFDF).[5] Such exercises suggested strongly that carriers would not last long in battle because they simply could not defend themselves from one another.

A second important factor working against the concept of a carrier fleet was the growing range and ordnance load of seaplanes. By the mid-1930s, they seemed to have the capability to displace carrier aircraft as the real prime movers of ordnance. A third factor was the growing power, weight, and size of carrier aircraft. The Bureau of Aeronautics continued to encourage American industry to build faster carrier fighter aircraft and bombers that could carry heavier ordnance loads greater and greater distances. Industry responded, but the trend lines for aircraft weight, physical size (wingspan, for example), and particularly for landing speed were up—steeply, especially in the late 1930s. There was a real chance that aircraft would outgrow the carriers intended to hold them.

The fourth factor—perhaps the key factor—however, was that U.S. carriers were vulnerable, especially to attack by aircraft from other carriers. Lacking radar, carriers counted on concealment, covering fighters, and striking first for protection. But these devices were not enough. As the commander in chief, U.S. Fleet, noted in his report on Fleet Problem XV in 1934, "Under actual war conditions it is quite possible that all of the carriers engaged . . . [will be] lost or put completely out of action. With opposing air forces of equal efficiency this is by no means an impossible result of the opening movements of a naval campaign."[6] Added to this vulnerability was the high attrition rate for carrier aircraft and the need of carriers and their escorts for underway replenishment. After all, carriers were only one element of the massed carrier fleet concept. Just as important were the fast oilers and the ammunition ships that resupplied the carriers and gave the carrier forces of 1944 their great mobility. As Thomas Wildenberg has shown in his *Gray Steel and Black*

Oil, the Navy simply did not have such replenishment ships in the early and mid-1930s, nor could it therefore have a clear understanding of how such auxiliaries would change the operations of formations of carriers.

In the case of the carriers, the devil was indeed in the details. This is not an argument unique to us. In December 1950, for example, historian Henry M. Dater, who had served as head of aviation history in the office of the deputy chief of Naval Operations (Air) during World War II, listed three factors that he thought had limited the Navy's appreciation of the potential of massed carrier forces in the years before the war. The first factor was the lack of "sufficient numbers of carriers to form an effective task force." The second was radar: "In carrier aviation it radically altered the division between offensive and defensive effort." The third factor was "the refueling of ships at sea."[7] We believe these were indeed key factors, not resolved until just before or even during the war. We also believe that senior Navy aviators themselves were aware of these factors, and that senior nonaviators were, too. In fact, the evidence suggests that the role of the aircraft carrier was thoroughly explored in the 1930s within the U.S. Navy and that the reasons for not exploring the role of the carrier *fleet* were very understandable ones.

Restrictions on total aircraft carrier tonnages set by the Washington Treaty were not considered severe in the 1920s. The U.S. Navy was allowed 135,000 tons of carriers by the Washington Treaty. The only problem with that upper bound was the size of the battle cruiser conversions *Lexington* and *Saratoga*—thirty-three thousand tons each, leaving just sixty-nine thousand tons for the remaining ships of the carrier force. Accordingly, in 1927, the General Board, acting on the information given the Taylor Board, recommended to the secretary of the Navy that he ask Congress for five 13,800-ton carriers. He did, but Congress authorized only one (which became *Ranger*). Influential members of Congress could see no reason to increase significantly the number of carriers while the major naval powers were trying to negotiate further limits at a disarmament conference then meeting in Geneva.[8]

The Geneva Conference of 1927 failed to resolve the problems not covered by the earlier agreements in Washington, but the Hoover administration, in 1930, successfully negotiated an extension of the Washington Treaty, and the new agreement (the London Naval Treaty of 1930) continued the ceiling on aircraft carrier tonnage. It also changed the definition of "aircraft carrier" to *any* warship whose purpose was to launch aircraft, *regardless of its tonnage.* The negotiators took this step to keep the major navies from creating "auxiliary" carriers—cargo ships or liners that would not be classed as carriers but would have the facilities to launch and recover aircraft. The London Treaty also forbade the signatories to place carrier decks on existing battleships and battle cruisers. This move was designed to forestall the kinds of proposals that Moffett and his bureau had already made to turn cruisers into aircraft-carrying warships.[9]

Though President Hoover "had stated in his 1928 presidential campaign that he would build the Navy to treaty strength," he did not ask Congress for the necessary authorizations, including those that would have allowed the Navy to complete the aircraft procurement program authorized by the Congress in the Air Corps Act of 1926. His decision had serious implications for carrier aviation in the U.S. Navy. The first and most obvious was that the Navy lacked carriers. It had three when it might have had seven. Lacking carriers, it also lacked carrier squadrons, and that limited the amount of ordnance that the carriers' aircraft could deliver in a single strike. Just as important a limitation was the inability to experiment with multiple carrier formations and multiple carrier operations. How should groups of carriers be maneuvered together? How should the attacks of their squadrons be coordinated, and how could the carriers themselves be defended against retaliation? These critical questions came up again and again in the 1930s fleet problems, and the answers were still uncertain when Japanese forces attacked Pearl Harbor.[10]

In April 1932, for example, Capt. Ernest J. King, then commanding carrier *Lexington,* argued to the Commander Aircraft, Battle Force, that "Joint Army and Navy Exercise Number 4 clearly showed the necessity of operating aircraft carriers as a division—more extensive operations of carriers by divisions should be continued and carrier division doctrines developed with respect to distribution of aircraft within the carriers." Later, in August, Rear Admiral Moffett appealed to the chief of naval operations to make available fiscal year 1934 funds for altering *Lexington* and *Saratoga* so that each carrier could rearm full squadrons of eighteen scout bombers on its flight deck at the same time, thereby increasing the ability of these two carriers to send off multiple offensive strikes in the course of an engagement. As Moffett noted, the efficiency with which *Lexington* and *Saratoga* rearmed their aircraft was significantly less than that assumed in war games, and this inefficiency was holding back "further development."[11] Despite Moffett's best efforts to remedy this and related deficiencies, there were still problems with the carrier concept. In 1934, for example, in testimony to the General Board, a representative of BuAer described the performance of the largest carrier-based bombers then deployed (TG-2) as "very poor." As he admitted, "They have an endurance of about three hours. . . . When they go out with 1000 pound bombs they can just about make a big circle and come back."[12] Matters were already improving with the introduction of the smaller though longer-range BM, and they would advance even more with the introduction of the TBD-1 in 1937. However, in 1934, just how much improvement there would be was not clear.

There was also another issue: should carriers be armored against air attack? *Saratoga* and *Lexington* did not have armored flight decks, though they both possessed some of the heavy inner armor (and underwater) protection that had been built into them when they were still battle-cruiser hulls. But *Lexington* and *Saratoga* were clearly exceptions to the rule—accidents of naval arms control. The ship to watch was *Ranger* (CV-4), the first true carrier in the U.S. Navy. *Ranger,* however, was designed before Fleet Problem IX was even held, and her initial drawings—showing a full flush deck and an aircraft elevator in the stern to facilitate the rearming of aircraft—were strongly influenced by the need to have relatively small ships that, when operating together, could launch and recover large numbers of aircraft. *Ranger,* in short, was a "treaty ship," designed with the Washington Treaty's tonnage ceiling in mind. When she was authorized, BuAer believed that having more and smaller carriers was a better alternative to having a few large carriers. The larger ships were clearly better able to withstand attack, but what mattered was not defense but offense: the ability to get lots of planes in the air swiftly. And there a large number of smaller ships held the advantage. Given the tonnage ceiling, however, carriers with either armored *or* unarmored flight decks were a gamble. *Any* design was risky, because the Washington and London treaties forbade navies from building an operational carrier that could be experimented with and then thrown away if the experiment failed. As a result, Navy carrier commanders were still arguing about the value of carriers with armored flight decks as late as 1939.[13]

Admiral Moffett's vision of carriers as attack platforms with the same role as battleships was deliberately thwarted by treaty and by the justification the treaties gave for not increasing naval authorizations and appropriations. This should come as no surprise. The Washington agreements were deliberately designed to restrict both capital ship construction and technological progress. The Great Depression, though, threatened to exterminate Moffett's vision altogether. Eugene E. Wilson, who had left the Navy to head Hamilton-Standard, the propeller manufacturer, and who in 1931 was president of Chance Vought Aircraft, recalled that "an earthquake hit American aviation" in 1933. Military business almost melted away. There was no new "1,000-plane" program. Instead, the new administration of Franklin Roosevelt at first promised to carry on the previous administration's reduction of naval forces.

Carrier aviation was saved at the last minute by two initiatives. The first was the passage of the National Industrial Recovery Act in June 1933, which made it clear that the new administration had changed its mind about its fiscal policy. It would support *increased* spending on the Navy. The second was the passage of the Naval Parity Act (Vinson-Trammell Act) of 1934, in which the Congress authorized the administration to build the Navy to "treaty strength." The appropriation authorized by the National Industrial Recovery Act allowed the Navy to begin design of the next two carriers, *Yorktown* (CV-5) and *Enterprise* (CV-6), and more carriers meant more aircraft. The aircraft industry, however, left without firm production commitments for another year, was saved only by the passage of Vinson-Trammell in 1934. This law authorized the construction of over one hundred warships and more than a thousand naval aircraft over a period of five years. As historian George Baer put it, "The Navy's revival in the 1930s began not because of its war plans or security forecasts, but because of the connection between arms and jobs, because of the effort to pull the country out of the Depression."[14]

Yet that revival (such as it was) brought new problems. One was the apparent renaissance of the battleship. The existing battle line, composed of twelve first-line battleships, was neither homogeneous in terms of armament (some ships mounted fourteen-inch guns, others sixteen-inch) nor as fast as that of its likely opponent (the Japanese). Studies done in the mid-1920s for the General Board showed that when these ships grew too old in treaty terms they could be replaced with warships that were much more powerful but not much faster. New developments in steam power plant design in the early 1930s, however, promised to allow as yet unbuilt battleships, even those designed to treaty limits, to steam at higher speeds and still have the great range required by a Pacific campaign. Advances in gunnery also promised to give these ships the capability of firing at very long range with significantly greater accuracy. Given such progress, the Navy had no choice but to invest limited funds in new battleships if the opportunity arose. Until then, the existing ships had to be modernized at considerable expense.[15]

A SECOND potential problem was the challenge that long-range seaplanes posed to the attack role that Moffett had wanted to give to carrier squadrons. In the 1920s, Navy aviation had five primary divisions: carrier air, lighter-than-air rigid airships and nonrigid dirigibles, land-based bombers, catapult floatplanes carried by battleships and cruisers, and sea-based patrol planes. To Moffett, aviation in support of the fleet meant all five groups. Aviation *with* the fleet meant mainly the carriers. The airships would conduct long-range reconnaissance. The land-based bombers would guard fleet anchorages and their approaches. Floatplanes catapulted from battleships and cruisers would scout and spot gunfire for the ships that carried them. Patrol seaplanes would serve as the eyes of the fleet, scouting ahead of the fleet's movements. That left attack in the hands of the carriers. But after the London Treaty, large seaplanes became an *attack* alternative.

There were two reasons for this. One was the development, particularly by the airlines financing aviation pioneers such as Igor Sikorsky, of seaplanes with great range, payload, and reliability. The other was Carl Norden's invention of a series of bombsights for high-flying planes. With these bombsights, accurate high-level (from ten thousand to twenty thousand feet) bombing became possible; now large seaplanes could both scout and attack. The military promise of large seaplanes convinced Moffett and his successors in BuAer that naval offensive aviation at sea had two wings: one operating from carrier decks in direct support of the fleet and the other operating from tenders to extend fleet reconnaissance and air attack over great distances. The progress of seaplane technology moved even more of Navy aviation to sea. In 1931, for example, the chief of naval operations and the chief of staff of the Army signed an agreement giving responsibility for air defense of naval bases to army aviation. The land-based attack role was abandoned in 1931 by the chief of naval operations as a fiscal expedient and to convince Congress that the Navy was not threatening Army aviation. But the CNO, Admiral Pratt, took this controversial move because of the confidence Navy leaders had in the growing force of large seaplanes as an alternative to land-based bombers.

The contract for the first *Catalina* PBY flying boat, the prototype of a whole new type of seaplane, was signed in October 1933, and the first models were delivered to the Navy in 1936. Its delivery ushered in a change in the composition of naval aviation. In 1934, for example, BuAer estimated that it would field 643 carrier aircraft by the end of fiscal year 1936. In 1938, with the addition of two more carriers (*Yorktown* and *Enterprise*), the number of carrier aircraft would increase to 718. That number was not projected to go any higher unless the agreement signed at London in 1930 (and scheduled to be renewed in 1936) lapsed. Similarly, Navy cruisers and battleships were scheduled to carry 228 aircraft by the end of fiscal year 1936; by the end of fiscal year 1940, that number was supposed to rise to 258 and then level off as treaty levels for cruisers were finally reached.

By contrast, the number of seaplane patrol bombers was projected to nearly double—from 218 in 1936 to 423 in 1941. As Rear Adm. E. J. King, Moffett's successor as chief of BuAer, told the General Board in 1934, "Patrol planes are powerful striking force [*sic*]; they are not limited in number by Treaty as are carrier planes." The desire to slide around the constraints of the treaty also explains the commitment by BuAer to an expensive lighter-than-air program that produced only two large, aircraft-carrying airships. The loss of one in 1933 (with Rear Admiral Moffett aboard) and the other in 1935 to accidents did not lessen the appeal to the General Board of airships as very long range scouts, despite the steady increase in the effective range of seaplanes. But in the fall of 1937, Rear Adm. Arthur B. Cook, Chief of BuAer, revealed the logical successors to the lost airships. He informed the General Board that seaplanes then planned would weigh as much as fifty tons, have a range of eight thousand miles, and remain in the air for as much as three days. Instead of simply supplementing existing fleet units, these large seaplanes "might possibly replace certain surface ships and replace the outer screen in a fleet and very much augment the effective scouting radius from the main body."[16]

The development of a large seaplane patrol force and the continuing interest of BuAer in a substantial lighter-than-air program shows how closely strategic concerns and treaty limits were intertwined in the 1920s and 1930s. Numbers of carriers, and numbers of carrier aircraft, were limited by treaty, but board games at the Naval War College and the annual fleet problems showed that *numbers* of aircraft mattered. The force that could get more, and better, aircraft into the skies *faster* could overwhelm its opponent. The General Board called this characteristic the "effective air effort," and recommended to the secretary of the Navy that larger carriers be built as follow-ons to *Ranger* (CV-4) because they were better on paper than *Ranger* at sustaining this "effective air effort." Yet fewer large carriers meant that there would not be enough carriers for all the work that they were needed to do: shielding U.S. battleships, conducting antisubmarine patrols, scouting, and attacking enemy carriers. If long-range aircraft-carrying airships and seaplanes could carry some of this burden, then so much the better.[17]

Carrier aircraft complements were expensive. In 1931, for example, the General Board estimated that replacing a carrier's air wing every three years would, over the carrier's lifetime, cost as much as the carrier itself. In 1937, the head of the War Plans Division of the Office of the Chief of Naval Operations (OPNAV) testified to the General Board that the total cost of naval aviation (carriers, aircraft, training, etc.) in 1935 had come to about 30 percent of all naval appropriations.[18] The fiscal implications of this military necessity were not lost on Congress. Not until 1938, after Japan had already refused to renew the London Treaty, would Congress, in a special Naval Expansion Act, authorize the Navy to construct two new carriers and have on hand "not less than" three thousand naval aircraft. Thus the expense of carrier aircraft squadrons had to be added to the other *demonstrated* drawbacks of carrier aviation: (1) the inability of carrier aircraft to attack targets at night and in bad weather, (2) the difficulty of getting enough aircraft *to* the carriers to replace operational losses as they steamed across the Pacific, and (3) the inferiority (in terms of speed and rate of climb) of carrier planes to their land-based counterparts. All these factors had to be considered as Navy planners tried to improve their aviation forces within the constraints set by treaty and finance.[19]

The Depression also stunted pilot training. In 1932, Congress halved the number of Naval Academy graduates—the primary source of pilots—who could be commissioned. In 1934, the Navy's Bureau of Navigation required all Naval Academy graduates assigned to flight training at Pensacola, Florida, to first spend two years at sea. At the same time, however, the Vinson-Trammell Act also authorized the Navy to commission all the 1934 graduates of the Naval Academy and those graduates who had been denied a commission in 1933 but still wanted one. In April 1935, at the urging of BuAer, Congress approved the Aviation Cadet Act to overcome the persistent shortage of officer pilots. The new law allowed the Navy to offer flight training to recent college graduates. In return, these prospective pilots would serve three years' active duty in the fleet after one year of training. At the end of the four years, these cadets were to be commissioned as ensigns or second lieutenants and then placed in the naval reserve. The aviation cadet program was apparently a "complete success" in terms of the number and quality of pilots it produced, but it did not offer its graduates any future in naval aviation, thereby restricting access to higher command to Naval Academy alumni.[20]

Still another vexing problem was the rapid increase in the capability and weight of carrier aircraft. Though deliberately fostered by BuAer, progress in aircraft performance was a mixed blessing. Stronger, more reliable, and higher-output radial engines did indeed hold out the promise of effective carrier *attack* aircraft, especially when such engines were coupled with variable-pitch propellers (for high-altitude flight) and cowl flaps (for more effective engine cooling), but the aircraft themselves grew larger and heavier, and carriers could hold fewer of them. As Eugene Wilson noted, "Large airplanes could not be carried on the flattops in the same numbers as could the smaller, more compact fighters; number was an important factor."

Behind the numbers issue was another—the switch from biplanes to monoplanes. Biplanes were light, maneuverable, and responsive and had relatively slow landing speeds. The last feature was especially important for carrier pilots. As Rear Admiral Cook, chief of BuAer, noted to the General Board in 1937, the bureau tried to hold landing speeds for carrier aircraft to "65 miles an hour."[21] Yet the more powerful engines, driving controllable-pitch propellers, "paved the way for low-wing monoplanes with their high wing loadings" and better combat performance—and greater landing speeds. Compare, for example, the Grumman F3F-1 of 1935 (wing loading of 13.53 psf) with the Grumman F4F-4 of 1941 (wing loading of 26.07 psf). The latter was heavier, better protected, better armed, and faster in a dive than its biplane predecessors, but it was less maneuverable and had a slower rate of climb than the F3F-3 of 1938. It was, however, one of the first of a new breed of monoplanes produced in response to the military requirements that BuAer was imposing on American aircraft manufacturers. It was superseded quickly by even heavier, more powerful, and quite maneuverable fighters, such as the F6F "Hellcat."

Some representative numbers indicate the success of the bureau's effort with attack aircraft. In 1929, the F8C-4, used as a bomber, was powered by a 450-horsepower engine, had a gross weight of 4,020 pounds, flew at 146 miles per hour, and had a range of 720 statute miles carrying two 100-pound bombs. The SBC-4 of 1937 had, in comparison, a 950-horsepower engine, a gross weight of 7,632 pounds, a maximum speed of 237 miles per hour, and a range of 590 statute miles carrying a 1,000-pound bomb. The monoplane SBD-2 of 1941 could carry 1,200 pounds of ordnance 1,100 miles. The ability to attack targets with 1,000-pound bombs made carrier dive bombers real ship-killers—especially *carrier*-killers—in themselves. In Fleet Problem XV, for example, umpires assumed that any 1,000-pound bomb that struck a carrier's flight deck would blow a hole fifteen feet in diameter in the deck, penetrate the hangar deck below, and start major fires. By 1937, umpires in Fleet Problem XVIII were told that three such bombs would wreck (though not sink) a carrier such as *Ranger* or *Enterprise.*[22]

This was a major improvement over the situation in the late 1920s, when both bombers and torpedo planes had to attack the same targets in order to be sure of inflicting enough damage to knock a ship—especially another carrier—out of the fight. The T4M-1 of 1928 did carry a 1,750-pound torpedo, but the airplane was very slow (maximum speed of 114 mph) and therefore extremely vulnerable both to defending fighters and antiaircraft fire. Moreover, both *Ranger* and *Wasp* (CV-7), the smallest of the prewar carriers, were too small to carry the innovative torpedo bomber TBD-1 of 1937, so the development of more advanced dive bombers (such as the BT of 1938) that could drop one-thousand-pound weapons was essential if these two ships were to continue to have the significant offensive potential given them by early dive-bombers such as the BM-1 and BM-2.

The increase in range for scout bombers also added to the offensive strength of U.S. carriers because it meant that one plane could serve two purposes simultaneously. Fleet problems showed that aircraft that could both scout and attack were very valuable. Though such scouts could carry only a five-hundred-pound bomb while searching for the enemy, they could perhaps cripple an enemy carrier without having to wait for reinforcements. But to do that, they needed range and a heavy ordnance load. The policy of BuAer was to give scout bombers precisely those characteristics. Thus a policy developed to compensate for a lack of aircraft and carriers caused by a treaty agreement actually improved the striking power of the carriers that *were* built. But the strike role of these carriers was that of *ambush,* especially of other carriers, *not* of sustained attacks against enemy forces on land and sea across a wide area of the Pacific. The revolution in naval warfare that U.S. Navy task forces initiated in 1944 was *strategic* in character. Japan's military plan in 1941 and 1942 was to gain so much territory that the U.S. would hesitate to reconquer it. The Japanese, after all, would have interior lines of communication, and they hoped to keep the initiative as U.S. forces tried to penetrate Japanese-controlled waters. As historian Clark Reynolds pointed out, the combination of numbers of fast carriers *and* mobile supply ships and fast oilers gave the U.S. Navy the strategic initiative, forcing the Japanese to stretch their forces thinly across a huge area and giving the United States the chance to mass overwhelming strength against selected objectives. This was not forecast in the 1930s fleet problems.

The advances in bombers were paralleled, as noted above, by those in fighters. The F4B-1 of 1929 was powered by a 450-horsepower engine, had a gross weight of 2,750 pounds, a maximum speed of 176 miles per hour, a range of 371 statute miles, and a rate of climb of 1,724 feet per minute. The F3F-3 of 1938 was much improved, with a 950-horsepower engine, a gross weight of 4,795 pounds, a maximum speed of 264 miles per hour, a range of 980 statute miles, and a rate of climb of 2,750 feet per minute. The F4F-4 of 1942, a monoplane, had a maximum speed of 318 miles per hour and a service ceiling of almost 35,000 feet. The famous F4U Corsair, the prototype of which first flew in 1940, had a gross weight of over 11,000 pounds, an engine of 2,250 horsepower, and a speed of over 400 miles per hour.

But why the move to ever heavier, ever more powerful fighters? Two reasons are apparent. First, the experience of World War I had shown that fast, rapidly climbing fighters had the tactical advantage. Aviators such as John Towers were firm in their insistence on developing fighters for aircraft carriers that could fight on equal terms with land-based opponents. As an early (1927) BuAer manual on aircraft tactics put it, "Risk is never to be avoided." That is, plane-on-plane engagements went to the bold, but boldness was worthless without power (especially for climbing) and maneuverability, and power was a function of engine output. The second reason was that carrier aircraft, especially fighters, would inevitably encounter land-based Japanese aircraft, based on Japanese-held islands, as the fleet moved across the Pacific. Because so little was known in the 1920s and 1930s about the performance of Japanese aircraft, BuAer matched its own requirements against those of the Army. The lesson drawn from that experience was that U.S. Navy fighters needed to meet the highest possible standards for engine power.[23]

Yet rapid technological progress had an operational price: it placed a premium on development over production, and so kept BuAer from building up a large inventory of aircraft. In October 1937, at a General Board hearing to determine the requests to Congress for aircraft for fiscal year 1939, the director of the War Plans Division of the Office of the Chief of Naval Operations (OPNAV) argued *against* high levels of production for carrier aircraft on the grounds that such aircraft grew "obsolete quickly." He was right, but if there were no reserve of carrier aircraft, then the Navy's carriers might find themselves out of combat-ready aircraft after just an initial campaign. More serious would be a shortage of trained pilots—pilots not recruited and trained because there were no planes for them to fly.[24]

Despite these problems, progress before World War II was significant. Experience showed the way to a standard, robust carrier design (the *Essex* type of twenty-seven thousand tons and as many as one hundred aircraft). Aircraft designs were satisfactory, if not superior to those fielded by the Japanese, and they were backed up, ultimately, by the huge production potential of the American aircraft and automobile industries. Pilot training was standardized, and new sources (reserves and aviation cadets) of pilots were tapped.

There was even an effort to spread awareness of aviation's potential. In 1925, for example, Adm. R. E. Coontz, commander in chief of the U.S. Fleet, had strongly recommended to the CNO "that all students at the U.S. Naval Academy be given a course in aeronautics." Coontz knew that "all graduates may not be able to qualify as Naval pilots, and fewer still as Naval aviators, [yet] the great majority can . . . become familiar with . . . the offensive and defensive employment of aircraft."

Coontz's recommendation was heeded. Indeed, by 1931, the Bureau of Navigation, responsible for Navy training and for standards of promotion, required unrestricted line officers eligible "for promotion to the rank of captain and below" to pass an examination on the uses of naval aviation and the characteristics of aircraft. The possible examination questions included, among many others, these: "At what height will bombing probably be attempted from air? How will bombers attack? When will they attack? What is the best defense against such attacks?" An officer able to answer all the questions on the list would have had to learn and think seriously about naval aviation. The existence of the examination is evidence of an effort to indoctrinate unrestricted line officers in naval aviation's principles. (The effort was not necessarily successful, but that is another issue.) The program of indoctrination indicates an important institutional commitment.[25]

THERE WERE other indicators of a commitment to naval aviation as well. In 1935, for example, one member of the General Board argued that any conflict with Japan in the Pacific would be decided by battles between carrier air forces, *not* by a gunnery duel between opposing lines of battleships. If any new battleships were built, they would escort and support the carriers. This was not the conventional view, yet it was a position put forward often, and it was not dismissed out of hand. Nevertheless, the level of uncertainty about the future role of carrier aviation remained high in the years before World War II. This uncertainty provoked a series of running discussions and debates.

One ongoing discussion concerned the need for "auxiliary" carriers, or combined cruiser-carriers. In November 1938, the director of the War Plans Division in OPNAV sent a memo to the CNO arguing that the Navy needed two kinds of carriers—one for the fleet battle (to gain command of the sea) and another to exploit the results of that battle (to exercise command of the sea). Given the treaty restrictions, the Navy had no choice but to devote its carrier tonnage to the larger, "heavy" carriers. But there was a need for a smaller carrier to work with cruisers and other units in protecting and covering convoys, in hunting down enemy surface raiders and submarines, and in supporting amphibious forces. In effect, War Plans was recommending that the Navy build a "high-low" carrier force: larger, better protected ships for fleet engagements, and smaller, cheaper, less protected ships for other work where tactical aircraft were needed but not in great numbers. The concept foundered, however, on the requirements laid down for the "scouting" or "auxiliary" carriers. War Plans wanted fast ships that could keep up with cruisers. The Bureau of Aeronautics wanted ships that could hold, launch, and recover an adequate number of aircraft safely and efficiently. Such requirements drove up cost and size, and Congress would not authorize the building of such ships.[26]

A more important issue was the vulnerability of carriers to air attack. In July 1939, then Rear Adm. R. L. Ghormley, head of the War Plans Division, told the General Board that "the vulnerability of our carriers constitutes the Achilles heel of our Fleet strength." Later that year, in November, Capt. C. M.

Cooke Jr., also speaking for War Plans, said, "Ordinarily when we advance the fleet [in war games] into enemy controlled areas . . . we are concerned about the vulnerability of our large carriers." Both War Plans and BuAer wanted to use carriers aggressively and in force. Ghormley, for example, noted that "too much" emphasis had been placed on the carrier as an offensive weapon in the initial phase of a war in the Pacific. He wanted more stress laid on the importance of "*continued* offensive air power." Similarly, Rear Adm. John Towers, then chief of BuAer, stated, "I am convinced that carriers must be considered, not as individual vessels, but as part of a striking force." And an officer in the Intelligence Division of OPNAV made the point that "in our studies at the War College we have all come to the conclusion that the isolated carrier is pretty much a thing of the past."[27] But the desire for aggressive use of the carriers ran afoul of carrier vulnerability. Unless carriers could be better protected, "more carriers" did not translate into "more power."

Historian Henry Dater described in 1950 the changes that would make the solution of this problem possible: the combination of radar plus suitable aircraft interceptor tactics, both under the control of specialists riding in a carrier who had studied and learned from the experience of the British in the Mediterranean in 1940. But there had to be someone pushing these developments. One such "someone" was then Rear Adm. W. F. Halsey, who commanded Carrier Division One of the U.S. Fleet in 1940. That January, Halsey argued to his colleagues in a formal critique written after a joint Army-Navy exercise that "a carrier, with suitable airplane complement, constitutes a powerful threat against shore based aircraft and establishments." Nothing particularly striking there, at least to naval aviators. The Army was another matter altogether, however. But Halsey went on to say that "defending pursuit, even though in small numbers, are highly effective in reducing accuracy of attack, even by larger groups." *This* was new, and audacious as well. Halsey underestimated the vulnerability of carriers to the kind of attack such as the Japanese could organize, but he apparently did so because he believed so strongly in the offensive capability of carriers.[28]

In the fall of 1940, technology began to vindicate Halsey's confidence. Carrier *Yorktown* emerged from a Pearl Harbor overhaul in October 1940 with a CXAM radar. Halsey saw it as the key to a new level of carrier effectiveness. His instinct was correct. In July 1941, further exercises with carrier task forces equipped with radar demonstrated the potential of carrier defense.

Halsey noted that the exercises showed the need for (1) an automatic "identification, friend or foe" system, (2) a "fighter directing ship" with radar and adequate, multichannel communications enabling it to monitor attacking groups and "coach" defending interceptors against them, and (3) radio silence on the part of carriers and their escorts unless and until they were attacked. This was the beginning of the revolution that allowed carriers to use their mobility to strategic advantage.

But it hinged on information from the Royal Navy. As Halsey himself admitted, "[I]t had been planned for these exercises to place full control of the combat patrols with the senior pilot in the air." But reports from Navy observers with the Royal Navy stressed placing control of intercepting aircraft with the "fighter directing ship," and so the plans were changed. Halsey was encouraged by the July exercises, although "experience in the Pacific Fleet in coordination of RADAR [*sic*] and disposition defense against aircraft had been meager" and the results raised as many questions as they answered. Halsey and his staff were analyzing the information from the exercises, and the admiral himself listed the new questions that had been raised by the very positive results of the realistic simulations. The placement of available air-search and height-finding radars in a formation of ships was an issue, as was the location of combat air patrol stations. Exercises in August 1941 confirmed the results obtained in July and showed the urgent need for an "identification, friend or foe" (IFF) transponder, for improved short-range communications, and for "a systematic, well trained, radar plot organization."[29]

Japan's attack on Pearl Harbor put an end to further exercises and tests. From then on, it was "trial and error" with a vengeance. As Henry Dater observed in 1950, however, the foundation for the fast carrier task forces with their strategic potential had been set in place *before* the United States entered the war. The prewar exercises had produced the demand for an IFF transponder, for effective short-range multichannel radios, for improved radar displays, and for a command and control doctrine to take advantage of this technology. Once all these pieces were available, the organization—the officers and enlisted personnel who manned and led carriers and their planes—put them together to create a potentially powerful *strategic* force.

But it was a near thing, almost missed, if only because of logistics problems. After 1934, when the Vinson-Trammell legislation granted the Navy a blanket authorization to build its combat forces to treaty levels, few auxiliaries—

oilers and supply ships and tenders—were constructed, despite continuous pleas from successive CNOs. In his secret "Annual Estimate of the Situation" for the fiscal year 1935, for example, CNO Adm. W. V. Pratt stated, "The material readiness and condition of the Merchant Marine today is the material readiness and condition of the augmented naval auxiliary service the day war is declared." This was in March 1933. Pratt wanted all auxiliaries—and all likely auxiliaries drawn from the merchant marine—to steam at no less than fifteen knots. In 1935, Pratt's successor, Adm. W. H. Standley, repeated the call for faster auxiliaries: "[I]t is important that the Navy's influence be exerted toward a shipping policy which will bring about the constant replacement of existing vessels in the United States Merchant Marine with modern ships of gradually increasing speed capabilities."[30] Though this was eventually done (as historian Thomas Wildenberg describes in his *Gray Steel and Black Oil*), it was not done soon enough before the war to have made a difference in the prewar fleet problems.

The lack of fast and mobile oilers and of a fast, large, and modern "fleet train" of supply ships and tenders rooted U.S. Navy logistics to "substantially a system of continental support." That is, naval task forces were dependent upon fixed bases for support, and those bases, even when established in forward areas, were dependent in their turn upon a line of supply reaching back to the United States. In his *U.S. Naval Logistics in the Second World War,* Duncan Ballantine, who served as a historian with OPNAV during the conflict, argued that it took two years (1942 and 1943) to establish an effective logistics supply system in the Pacific theater and another year again to develop effective underway replenishment groups. As he noted, "[T]he exploitation of Japanese weaknesses as they developed required some means of furnishing support to task forces more rapidly and more flexibly than was permitted by base development." War games and prewar fleet exercises had shown the need for logistics support, "but until the close of 1943 the facilities had not been available." Over the course of 1944, the Pacific Fleet established a mobile "service squadron," consisting of five "major" units "located at various strategic points in the Pacific and comprising hundreds of vessels." By the end of 1944, the fleet had created a "Logistics Support Group" that actually "formed part of the task force itself," moving as the fleet's task forces moved, rendezvousing "for refueling, rearming and reprovisioning."[31]

The point here is that improvements in carrier defenses, added to an increase in the number of large, fast carriers, did not produce a weapon with *strategic* impact. Logistics mattered just as much, and the logistic support for a large force of carriers and other ships simply did not exist until 1943. *Mobile* logistic support would not be ready for another year. Moreover, if Ballantine's analysis was correct (and we believe that it was), then the mobile support of late 1944 was not something that had been foreseen before the war began. Prewar chiefs of naval operations and their staffs had pressed for more and faster auxiliaries, but the authors could find no evidence that Naval War College simulations were used to explore the possible implications of forming truly mobile support forces.

Throughout the 1930s, both war games and fleet problems assumed that the "fleet train" would move with the combat ships across the Pacific to some distant objective. There the auxiliaries would form the beginnings of a base. This concept of an advanced forward base, built under the cover of the fleet, was an essential element of prewar planning. But there is no evidence that fast oilers and replenishment ships were tied conceptually to far-ranging carrier task forces to form a formidable strategic force. As historian George Baer put it, "sustained mobility" of carrier forces was the key to victory in the Pacific.[32] The need for a fleet support force had been demonstrated in the War College war games, yet the ability of a mobile force to multiply the power of a carrier task force in the face of Japanese defenses was not so clear before the war.

It is not clear why this "force multiplier effect" was not foreseen. Historian Henry Dater offered explanations such as the limited number of aircraft carriers allowed by treaty and the apparent strategic effect of the development of large, long-range seaplanes. But two other factors may have mattered, too. One was the change in the Naval War College program under presidents W. V. Pratt and Harris Laning. In the 1920s, the War College classes had—as we have already shown—examined tactical issues in the field of aviation that could be dealt with systematically in no other way. In the 1926–27 academic year, however, Rear Adm. W. V. Pratt (later commander in chief of the U.S. Fleet, and then chief of naval operations) altered the course of study at the War College so that the members of each class could both assist the fleet "in the staging and solution of the latter's practical sea problems" and study the elements of *national* strategy, such as the proper relationship between the Navy and the nation's industrial, scientific, and human resources. It was Pratt who supplemented the War College's formal, individually written thesis requirement with games conducted by groups of officers working as high-level command staffs. Pratt's goal was to develop a curriculum that would prepare a generation of senior officers for the highest levels of command.

Pratt's concept was embraced by Rear Adm. Harris Laning, president of the War College from 1930 to 1933. Laning created a special research department to collect information about the capability of naval weapons and the plans and tactics of potential enemies of the United States. He wanted to make the war games and command exercises held at the War College as realistic and as useful as possible. His goal was to give the Navy an analytical base for its tactical doctrine, and so he emphasized the study of "fleet battle tactics," meaning the use of the fleet against that of "Orange" (Japan). The operations department of the college crafted the game board problem, members of the class participated in the game, and the faculty of the operations department wrote a critique of the game after it was over.

The problems were afterwards criticized for being focused too often on a great fleet engagement between surface forces (as at Jutland), but Jutland was used as a case because it posed a particularly important dilemma: Could a fleet commander, at sea, control his whole force and wield it as a single weapon? Or was a fleet best divided and then distributed among separate commanders who were directed (not commanded) from shore? Did Jutland spell the end of the time when an individual fleet commander controlled a huge force at sea (a critical question)? But other, equally interesting issues were also considered. The critique of Operations Problem IV in 1933, for example, noted the "tremendous influence of air operations . . . in all our games." It also recalled that "[l]ast year a BLUE CV [a U.S. carrier] accompanied one CA [heavy cruiser], fueled at KISKA and then made a bombing raid on TOKIO [*sic*], finally rejoining the fleet unhurt." The author of the critique noted, "We cannot evaluate such a raid in our games, but the effect might be far-reaching." Indeed![33]

Yet later, in November 1939, the head of the strategy department at the Naval War College observed, "The only reason for the formation of a fleet is to provide battle power. Therefore, the chief strategic function of the battle fleet is the creation of situations that will bring about decisive battle under conditions that will ensure the defeat of the enemy." This was not new thinking. The mechanism for exploring the value of a fleet of carriers existed at the Naval War College, but it was apparently not used for that purpose in the 1930s. It is, however, hard to say why. The surviving evidence provides no clear answer.

In his biography of John Towers, Clark Reynolds argued that the reason was the presence, in Newport, of individuals such as Raymond Spruance, who served in the War College's operations department in the late 1930s. But one of Spruance's contemporaries in that department was Capt. Richmond K. Turner, an aviator and "one of the college's most effective leaders on naval strategy." Of course Turner himself noted in his memoirs that he left the field of naval aviation because he believed his chances for promotion would be greater if he served in the general line, so his presence at the War College is not proof that the study of aviation was properly institutionalized there. But it would be wrong, in our view, to lay the blame for the oversight (if indeed that is what it was) at the Naval War College on the shoulders of a few officers on the staff. Individuals can and do make a difference in institutions, especially in small ones, but it is wise to look for other influences on policy, too. Besides, Spruance was no novice in the use of aviation to achieve the goals of the "Orange" war plan against Japan. His direction of the U.S. carriers at Midway is proof of that.

Alternatively, historian Ronald Spector has argued that the Naval War College was—paradoxically—its own worst enemy: "The very . . . innovations which in the short run led to great improvement in the training and subsequent performance of naval officers, in the long run resulted in the decline of the College as a center of original research." That is, the better the War College became at training officers for high command, the less suited it was as a center for the generation of novel ideas. Once it found the "right" method, it taught officers how to use that method to marshal and command large forces. It did not *use* its classes to explore new forms of warfare at sea; there was no time for that.

Spector and others have also noted that fleet expansion in the 1930s drew away many of the better officers, who were needed to command the new ships being commissioned in that decade. In addition, the president of the Naval War College ceased to sit as an ex-officio member of the General Board in 1934, and that same year the War College was "placed under the administrative jurisdiction" of the Bureau of Navigation, whose chief, Rear Adm. F. B. Upham, believed that the War College was "primarily a technical school for the training and education of line officers."[34]

Still, "[t]he interwar years saw the Naval War College maintain its closest contact with the fleet. Not only did the College administration suggest problems to be considered by fleet commanders in the annual fleet exercises, but the results achieved were often returned to the College for additional assessment." So the explanations offered by historians for what happened at the Naval War College to keep its classes from exploring the potential of fleets of carriers linked to a mobile supply force seem inadequate. The link between the War College and the fleet appears to have been strong. The correspondence between the president of the War College and the senior officers of the fleet continued, though the content of that correspondence is hard to infer from the scraps that remain. Perhaps the link between BuAer and the Naval War College weakened after Rear Admiral Moffett died in the crash of airship *Akron* in the spring of 1933. Even without Moffett, however, BuAer remained an innovative organization. There was no obvious barrier to close cooperation. The link between the War College and the General Board also weakened, perhaps because the president of the Naval War College ceased to sit (after 1934) as a nonvoting member of the General Board. The available evidence, however, does not provide a firm answer to the question, "Did the productive relationship among the War College, the fleet, and BuAer that led to innovation in the 1920s dry up in the 1930s?"

Maybe "dry up" is the wrong phrase to describe what happened. Perhaps the relationship grew rigid and formal and lost spontaneity. Naval analyst Michael Vlahos suggested as much in 1980, when he wrote that the Naval War College became, before World War II, the spiritual guardian of the fleet's mission. The college's war games, according to Vlahos, became over time solemn rituals of mock combat, giving substance to what was essentially a dream—the dream of American naval sway in the Pacific. In his *The Blue Sword,* Vlahos considered the ritualistic side to the activities of the Naval War College, and he suggested that in the years before the war the "fleet engagement" between Japanese and American forces became enshrined and even celebrated as the Navy's great drama and its *raison d'être.* In July 1932, for instance, Rear Adm. Harris Laning, then president of the college, told the General Board, "In all forms of naval warfare, aircraft will exert a decisive influence. . . . For this reason our naval air forces must be developed to the maximum." But, as noted already, Laning still considered the "battle line action" as "the final decisive phase of the war." Vlahos regarded such repeated assertions as a kind of incantation, as a sign that careful analytic thinking had been displaced by ritual assertions of a kind of dogma, or faith. The fleet action—the inevitability of which justified the board games—was also justified by them, so that, conceptually, the War College program became trapped in a circle that the games themselves could not break out of. The games were the tool to study possible fleet actions and the ritual acknowledgment of a kind of naval determinism.

Meanwhile, as the war approached, the uncertainty of carrier-vs.-carrier engagements that Wayne Hughes highlighted was still an issue to be resolved. At the battle of Midway in June 1942, for example, four Japanese carriers fought three of the United States. Had the ships engaged been battleships of roughly equal firepower, the Japanese would have held the initial advantage. Admirals from both navies would have anticipated this. They were all trained on the war gaming boards. But the actual result was quite different and *typical* of carrier engagements in prewar U.S. Navy fleet exercises: three U.S. Navy carriers sank four carriers of the Imperial Japanese Navy with a loss of only one of their own carriers. The reason for this lopsided victory was that the Japanese carriers were bunched together when the primary pulse of attacking firepower from the American carriers showed up. Massed carriers could deliver a great pulse of firepower. Pearl Harbor showed that. But such a formation of carriers was also very vulnerable until (for the U.S. Navy at least) radar provided advanced warning and carriers could mass defensive fighters against attacking enemy aircraft. In 1942, carriers were still best suited for offensive operations; a Japanese or American carrier could not really defend itself if attacked first by the air strength of another carrier. This made carrier operations very risky indeed, and officers in the American and Japanese navies were apparently well aware of this risk. What their exercises and simulations did not reveal was the best means of reducing it.

Though conscious of the risk, senior aviation officers in the U.S. Navy nevertheless pressed for a stronger organizational role for aviation forces—a role they saw as commensurate with the growing tactical influence of naval aviation. This was part of a more general effort to make command of the Navy's combat forces more effective. The commander in chief of the U.S. Fleet in 1928 and 1929, Adm. Henry A. Wiley, had proposed that "type commanders" (for ship types and aircraft) be responsible for training the fleet while "force commanders" direct the major units of the fleet in operations. Wiley's successor, Adm. W. V. Pratt, also recommended to the chief of naval operations that the fleet be organized into "type" commands and that, for operations, "task forces" should be formed from the units under the command of the type commanders.[35] What these officers were after was a peacetime organization that could move swiftly and smoothly to wartime operations. Of course, the question was whether aviation, one of the major "types," deserved the same organizational status as battleships, the primary "type."

In short, the future organizational standing of carrier aviation in the fleet could not be separated from the larger issue of how best to organize the whole fleet *before* war for action *in* war. The first senior aviator who had the chance to come to grips with this problem was Adm. J. M. Reeves, appointed commander in chief of the fleet in 1934. Eugene Wilson pointed out in his 1950 memoirs that Reeves had wanted, when he was fleet air commander in 1929, to give command of all the carrier squadrons to Commander, Aircraft Squadrons, Battle Fleet, and not to the carrier captains themselves. If Wilson is to be believed, Reeves was the first senior operational commander to advocate central command of all the carrier aircraft, with Commander, Aircraft Squadrons, subordinate only to Commander, Battle Fleet. As the new fleet commander in 1934, Reeves picked up where Pratt had left off. He wanted a "type commander" for fleet aircraft. Type commanders "prescribed or recommended" shipboard organization, training requirements, inspection standards, personnel complements, material allowances, and "other administrative matters." They served as subordinates to the commander in chief of the U.S. Fleet. They were not operational commanders like the commanders of the battle and scouting fleets, but they possessed seniority and high rank, and they reported directly to a senior operational commander. Their job, basically, was to guarantee the operational commanders that the units of the fleet—its ships and aircraft—were ready for war.[36]

Reeves's proposal ignited an intense controversy among the senior officers of the Navy. As Reeves himself said, "The present organization of the Fleet is neither suitable nor adequate for the accomplishment of its primary war mission." His point was that the use of task forces such as the Battle Force and the Scouting Force in peacetime was worse than useless: "In all Fleet Problems which simulate actual war conditions, the Battle Force and Scouting Force inevitably and naturally disappear." Better, argued Reeves, to rely on the type commanders in peacetime and create task forces as the need arose in wartime. Not so, responded the General Board and the chief of naval operations. As Adm. Thomas Hart, writing for the members of the General Board, informed the secretary of the Navy in April 1937, "the performance of duty as a task force commander is of the highest importance and . . . the provision therefor [*sic*] in the chain of command is essential for a well organized and efficiently prepared fleet." That is, the only way to prepare officers for command of large task forces was to have such forces already organized in peacetime. Type commanders, because they were not operational commanders, would not be prepared to step into task force commands in the event of war.

But which task force commands should exist in peacetime? Adm. A. J. Hepburn, commander in chief of the U.S. Fleet, had written to the General Board in October 1936 and sided with his predecessor Reeves. Hepburn put it bluntly: "The correspondence on this subject from the senior flag commanders in the fleet shows an almost unanimous consensus of opinion . . . that it is illogical if not absurd to adopt a permanent Task Force organization for administrative purposes before one knows what tasks are to be executed." Hepburn's argument was that no one knew just what form the next war would take. Would there be a grand fleet engagement? Perhaps. But perhaps not. Why then organize as if such an engagement were inevitable? In specific terms, why make the chief deputy to the fleet's commander an officer skilled at maneuvering the battle line when the clash of battle lines might never take place? As Hepburn remarked, "I am convinced that in time of war the distinction between Battle Force and Scouting Force would disappear with no other effect than to leave the commander in chief with his next two senior officers, who should be his greatest assets, more or less in the position of fifth wheels." This is exactly what happened on 7 December 1941.

The arguments went back and forth for almost two years. In the summer of 1934, in response to Reeves's proposal to abolish the task-force commands, Rear Admiral King, then head of BuAer, proposed to make Commander, Aircraft, equal in rank to the commanders of the Battle Force and the Scouting Force. That is, there would be an aviation vice admiral directly under the fleet commander in an operational position. Subordinate to this vice admiral would be four rear admirals—two carrier division commanders and two commanders of seaplane forces (one in the Atlantic and one in the Pacific). These five flag officers in operational commands would be in addition to the admirals serving as type commanders. The argument put forward to support this proposal was that there were not enough senior operational commands for naval aviators. The law required carrier and seaplane tender captains to be aviators, but then where could they go? The head of BuAer was a rear admiral, and the head of aviation forces in the fleet was a rear admiral, but King wanted to alter the organization of the high command so that aviators could hold an *operational* vice admiral's post on a regular basis. The rear admiral's positions would be necessary as preparation for the vice admiral's billet, and would give the fleet commander enough candidates from which to select the aviation vice admiral.

Reeves's position was more subtle than this. Instead of proposing that aviators get more of the scarce operational flag officer billets, Reeves suggested eliminating the peacetime task-force structure altogether. As Admiral Hepburn, concurring, explained in his memo to the General Board, "my principal objection to the Battle Force–Scouting Force organization is its psychological effect in limiting the imagination and breadth of view of the whole service as to the wide variety of operations which will constitute the overwhelming activity in any war." *Psychological effect:* This is precisely what Reeves had been after—changing the psychology of the officers of the fleet so that they were mentally prepared for whatever war might throw at them. Chief of Naval Operations Standley was strongly opposed to such a change, and one reason he gave for his opposition is revealing. As Standley wrote to the General Board, "Carriers are a type that do not lend themselves to *tactical* [his emphasis] organization for all purposes into divisions like other types." Put another way, "the very nature of the ships makes their operations individual—that is they cannot fight in a formation." Hence a carrier type commander could not be prepared to assume command of a task force composed of surface ships. He would understand how to maneuver and direct a carrier and its escorts, but not standard formations of battleships and cruisers, and certainly not the fleet in concentration.

Whereas Reeves wanted to break the existing psychology of fleet officers, Standley wanted to protect the highest levels of operational command from officers whom he did not regard as suitably prepared to assume such posts. Allowing the Reeves proposal to stand—throwing aside the existing task force commands—would open the highest positions to aviators, but in Standley's mind the aviators were simply not trained to handle the fleet or its major components. Carriers were raiders and bushwhackers. The officers commanding them needed that sort of mentality, not the kind of thinking needed in a fleet commander. Of course Reeves completely disagreed. The president of the Naval War College and the members of the General Board sided with the chief of naval operations, and the issue died when Reeves retired. As Clark Reynolds has shown, however, Reeves was prescient. Admiral Reeves had taken his case to the General Board because he needed their support if his proposal were to have any success with the secretary of the Navy. He knew the members of the board might be hostile. Despite its history of support for aviation (since 1919), the board had always opposed the creation of a separate naval air force. Reeves had tried to allay the possible suspicions of the members of the board when he testified before them: "The aircraft of our Fleet is an integral part of our Fleet under this organization. It doesn't even tend one inch toward a separate air corps or separate organization." He had made no headway, however. As one of the members of the board told him, "The present organization of the Fleet, which we are all familiar with, is based on what is considered the primary, the first and outstanding, functions that our naval forces must perform in war."[37] But Reeves had a point. The "fundamental administrative pattern" of the U.S. Fleet "was built about type commands," yet the "aviation forces assigned to the fleet were not placed under a unified command but were . . . assigned to the various fleets . . . [T]here was no unified fleet administration [for training, safety, maintenance, etc.] short of the Bureau of Aeronautics."[38]

John Towers, once appointed vice admiral and aviation type commander in the Pacific in the fall of 1942, went on to do just what Reeves had proposed: develop a new concept of carrier operations while acting as the direct subordinate of the fleet commander.[39] As Towers understood, a single type command for all aircraft in the fleet would place a senior aviator in a singularly influential and visible position. A skilled individual could use such a position to influence how aircraft and carriers were used, as well as how they were supported and maintained.

In the minds of aviators such as John Towers and Frederick Sherman, senior naval officers committed a grave error by not taking this step before the war. It meant that aviation was always integrated into the fleet, instead of the surface forces being integrated with a growing and powerful aircraft carrier force. The absence of an aviation type command also limited the number of high command positions *in the fleet* available to aviators. There could be one aviator (rear) admiral subordinate to Commander, Battle Fleet, and another heading BuAer back in Washington. In case of war and the inevitable need then to expand naval aviation rapidly, there would only be two rear admirals available for promotion to three-star rank. Officers like Sherman and Towers—particularly the latter—anticipated the growth in both the size and the effectiveness of carrier forces in the event of war, and they feared that the fleet would lack officers adequately prepared to wield this new weapon.

Once Towers became the aviation type commander in the Pacific, for example, he pressed the Pacific Fleet's commander, Adm. Chester Nimitz, to appoint a deputy commander for air operations and an operations officer for air planning.[40] It was not just, in Towers's view, that such officers were needed; it was also necessary to prepare senior aviators for the highest command positions.

It is ironic that Reeves's proposal was finally adopted only because the early war administration of naval aviation in the Pacific could not handle what American industry could produce in such great numbers. Before the war, BuAer had planned for the development of aviation, standardized aviation training, and supplied aircraft to the various organizations which together made up the U.S. Fleet. By the summer of 1942, the prewar process, based in BuAer, had broken down. It had proved incapable of "steering" the many aircraft beginning to pour out of industry to the right places to have the optimal military effect in the Pacific theater. The creation of the Pacific aviation type command, then a similar command in the Atlantic, and finally, in August 1943, the deputy chief of naval operations for Air [DCNO(Air)] was aimed at organizing the rapidly growing air arm of the Navy. These new and powerful positions were also signs that carrier aviation had become the center of the Navy's striking power. The General Board's position of 1919 had been vindicated.[41]

Waldo Heinrichs, a skilled and thoughtful historian, once argued that the prewar Navy was innovative in the 1920s but "conservative, complex, and political" in the 1930s. For Heinrichs, carrier aviation, initially a field of great innovations, was incorporated in the 1930s within "an existing framework of compromise and consensus."[42] Our view is different from his. The possibility of placing carrier aviation at the center of the U.S. Fleet was neither ignored nor somehow bargained away. The vulnerability of carriers was the rock on which the ambitious dreams of the Navy's aviators broke. This problem had no apparent solution until the experience of the Royal Navy's carriers in 1939 and 1940 showed that carriers could, in fact, defend themselves. As Adm. E. J. King, then commanding the Atlantic Fleet, argued to the chairman of the General Board in the summer of 1941, "considering the accelerating importance of air power," the "current scheduled rate" of aircraft carrier construction was "wholly inadequate."[43]

In short, even in the late 1930s, the amount of uncertainty surrounding the future of carrier warfare was so great that no one could say with confidence that the traditional battle-line concept could be abandoned. In the face of great uncertainty, the Navy covered its bets, spreading scarce resources among a variety of systems and producing what was then called a "balanced fleet." This was indeed a sensible approach to the problem of uncertainty, and it was, as Heinrichs argued, a kind of compromise among different—and opposed—views of the future of naval warfare. But the compromise was forced, not by an unwillingness to experiment or by some sort of bureaucratic obfuscation, but by the nature of the problem. Before the war (and certainly during the first year of the war against Japan), U.S. Navy carriers *were* highly vulnerable. Until that problem could be dealt with, they could not be sent into the teeth of enemy defenses. Before the war, carrier mobility was tactical, *not* strategic, because there were no fast oilers and replenishment ships available to sustain a free-ranging carrier force. Until they gained strategic mobility, carrier forces could not take advantage of their ability to mass aircraft against weak points of the enemy. Finally, there just weren't enough carriers early enough in the 1930s to suggest what multiple carrier formations could do. Given this uncertainty, it was rational—as well as understandable—for the Navy's senior officers to compromise.

Still, the question remains: Why didn't the Naval War College at least consider the possibility that there was a revolution coming in naval warfare? Why did the War College staff not push the bounds of accepted doctrine by making some assumptions (that carriers could be protected, for example) and then exploring the consequences of doing so in games? We do not know for sure. But we do know that the conditions that led to the gaming in the 1920s did not exist in the 1930s. As we have shown in earlier chapters, there was a widespread commitment within the ranks of senior naval officers after World War I to a stronger role for naval aviation. Admiral Sims, in launching a kind of educational revolution at Newport, had the support of many of his peers—support based upon what they had all seen the Royal Navy doing with aviation. It was "catch-up" time. But there was no one to catch in the 1930s. The U.S. Navy was ahead of its main model and rival, the Royal Navy, and naval officers were well aware that their service would need more aircraft carriers were it to wage offensive war against the Imperial Japanese Navy in the western Pacific. So what was left to be done? Better aircraft were coming along steadily. More carriers were being built—certainly all that arms limits would allow. There was no example to follow, and no imperative to spur drastic experiment. When the example (the Royal Navy) and the imperative (Japanese naval aviation) appeared, the U.S. Navy's responses were sensible and prompt, and they were based on all that had happened before.

In September 1941, the Naval War College prepared a confidential study comparing a "balanced" navy against a "carrier" navy. The study, submitted in the name of Rear Adm. E. C. Kalbfus, president of the War College, was designed to counter the "political elements" then pressing for the construction of more aircraft and more carriers. One of these political elements was probably President Roosevelt. The study was scathing in its criticisms of the advocates of aviation. In just over twenty pages, it stated again the weakness of carriers, the need for existing surface ships such as cruisers and destroyers, and the unwillingness of potential enemies such as Japan to gamble on the ascendancy of a strictly carrier fleet.[44] But while this study was being prepared, Admiral Halsey and his carrier forces in the Pacific were working out the techniques that would eventually refute Kalbfus's arguments. Did the War College know about those exercises? Could the War College, through its simulations, have stimulated such exercises? Would no progress have been made without information from the Royal Navy? There is no one, certain answer.

Yet the evidence of progress in the U.S. Navy is inescapable. One indicator of that progress is improvements in aircraft carrier design. The U.S. Navy commissioned three types of "pure" carriers in the years from 1930 through 1940: *Ranger* (1934, one ship in the class), *Yorktown* (1937 and 1938, two ships in the class), and *Wasp* (1940, one ship in the class). *Ranger* and *Wasp* were roughly the same size, with standard displacements of approximately 14,500 tons. *Ranger* had been built "small" because her size seemed optimal at the time. Though she lacked the speed, range, and protection of the much larger *Lexington* and *Saratoga, Ranger* carried about as many aircraft. *Wasp,* on the other hand, was smaller than desired because of treaty limits. There just was no more tonnage that the Navy could put into her. But *Wasp* had 20 percent greater steaming range (at fifteen knots), a larger flight deck, a somewhat larger hangar, catapults for launching aircraft (*Ranger* had none), and almost 20 percent more aviation gasoline for her air wing. *Wasp*'s flight deck was also 35 percent higher above the waterline than *Ranger*'s.[45] Without question, the trend in the U.S. Navy was toward greater carrier displacements. *Yorktown* was twenty thousand tons standard; the *Essex* type, authorized in 1940, was twenty-seven thousand tons standard. But the differences between

Wasp and *Ranger* indicate the progress made in carrier aviation over the span of just six years or so: the aircraft are heavier and more powerful, and so even a "small" carrier must, to operate them, have catapults, more aviation gasoline stowage, a larger flight deck, and a flight deck that is higher off the water. These improvements are, in miniature, an expression of the progress made in U.S. Navy carrier aviation in the decade before World War II.

4 The Fleet Air Arm: A Failed Revolution?

Aviation was the key to three dramatic developments between the two world wars: carrier aviation, blitzkrieg, and strategic bombing. This chapter is about the first and the second, but particularly, in connection with carrier aviation, the first: the failure of the Royal Navy to match the carrier and other naval aviation achievements of Japan and the United States. However, the course of British interwar politics makes it impossible to detach the story of the Fleet Air Arm from those of other nascent or realized developments involving aircraft. In the U.S. case, the Army and Navy proceeded along separate roads once the issue of a separate, independent air force had been put aside. In Britain, by contrast, a central question facing the Royal Navy and the British army was how much the creation of the Royal Air Force (RAF) might stunt the growth of naval aviation and air-to-ground support and thus abort the naval and army versions of the airplane-led military revolution.

The RAF, the world's first independent (of army and navy) air force, was created on 1 April 1918 out of the air branches of the British army and navy, the Royal Flying Corps, and the Royal Naval Air Service. Each had been created mainly to support its parent service. During World War I, however, both were charged with, among other things, the aerial defense of Great Britain. The Germans raided Britain, first with Zeppelins and then with large bombers. There was a public outcry; surely the British government could do something to stop the raids. An inquiry, headed by Field Marshal Sir Jan Smuts, suggested that decentralized design, production, and operational control of aircraft was a major reason for the failures.[1]

In effect the formation of the RAF was a statement of belief in an organizational form that could deliver and then use airplanes in ways that would best capitalize on the new technology. The RAF was created on the assumption that the revolution built around the airplane was fundamentally different from traditional forms (on land and at sea) of warfare. By implication, its creators assumed that the surface (army and navy) elements of the aviation revolution could not be dealt with by the army and the Royal Navy. British writers tend to blame the failures of the Fleet Air Arm on this one event. They argue that, once the RAF was formed, it inevitably assumed functions that it could pursue without reference to (or domination by) the other services: independent bombing (i.e., strategic bombing, when applied to a major war, and "air policing," when applied to the problem of imperial peacekeeping). The argument goes on that, because the RAF effectively controlled British air resources, it was well placed to deny the Royal Navy the aircraft types the latter needed to survive World War II. The general perception is that the interwar years were characterized by an essentially political struggle between the RAF and its sister services and that the RAF won that struggle, to the detriment of the British army and the Royal Navy (leaving the latter with, for example, the obsolete Swordfish biplane torpedo bomber). The general perception is off the mark, but it will take some explaining—in this chapter and the next—to show why that is so.

THE CREATION of the RAF was an act of faith, since in 1918 aircraft technology could not justify the sort of strategic air operations its creators envisaged. To maintain this new kind of service, devoted entirely to air power, required considerable salesmanship, particularly in a period of deep retrenchment after World War I. Any deviation by RAF officers from the central faith in bombing would have had very serious fiscal consequences; even after 1918 many in the army and navy resented the new service's inroads into their budgets (not to mention its near-total indifference to their air needs) and would have seized on any skeptical remarks by senior RAF officers.

In theory, the RAF was intended to cooperate with the senior services; its Coastal Area was to work with the Royal Navy. But the RAF could never admit that its primary role was providing air support to the two existing services, because in that case it could not have justified its separate existence. The RAF's founder and chief ideologist, Sir Hugh Trenchard, went so far as to block the Admiralty from direct contact with the senior ex-naval RAF officers who were, in theory, responsible for cooperation with the Royal Navy. Presumably he feared that the RAF might be reduced to serving as the technical support service for aircraft operating with and for the two senior services, particularly the Royal Navy.

In effect, the British jumped before all the evidence was in. The subsequent need of the RAF to justify the decision that created it blinded the RAF to evidence that would have enabled it to fulfill its initial potential. This is indeed ironic. Aviation desperately needed an interactive institutional setting, like the relationship among the U.S. Navy's Bureau of Aeronautics, the Naval War College, and the U.S. Fleet. Such a setting provided the means to experiment and discover errors. The RAF failed to develop this setting, which would have encouraged the RN's development of an air arm of its own.

The RAF did quite the reverse. Because the *roles* of the two senior services still clearly existed, the RAF came to see itself as a less expensive *replacement* for them, a doctrine called "air substitution." Thus it was willing to buy airplanes that might seem to replace conventional army and navy forces, even though they were not the favored heavy bombers. For example, as Secretary of State for Air in 1919, Winston Churchill published a white paper advocating substitution of air forces for ground forces; aircraft actually replaced army units in Iraq in 1921. The RAF repeatedly claimed that its shore-based torpedo bombers could defend Singapore, the key Far East naval base, far better than conventional fortifications or, for that matter, ships or submarines permanently based there.[2] Similarly, its big flying boats were designed to attack surface ships but not to provide reconnaissance support for the British fleet. The RAF saw them as an alternative to a surface navy.

To justify its concentration on bombing, the RAF staff had to rely on the relatively weak evidence of the feeble British and German strategic bombing campaigns of World War I. Thus, in the face of considerable criticism from the army and navy (who claimed that RAF statistics had been doctored), the RAF asserted that, in any future war, bombers would inflict very serious damage on unprotected British cities. Its calculations do seem to have been heavily biased. The RAF also claimed that effective air defense was impossible: "The bomber will always get through," in Prime Minister Stanley Baldwin's famous 1932 words. The only way to avoid the destruction of Britain was to build up a sufficiently frightening British bomber force. Because the British had a limited aircraft manufacturing capacity, any other call on that industry, such as that made by the navy, had to be opposed.

Reliance on deterrence also led the RAF to denigrate active air defense, at least until 1937. Evidence suggests that it was the British *Treasury* that forced the RAF staff to emphasize fighters in 1937–38. Until the Inskip defense policy review of early 1937, the senior permanent civil servant in the Treasury, Warren Fisher, had supported the RAF's demand for bombers. After the review, Fisher changed his mind, and that led the RAF, in turn, to change its position.[3] In any event, once fighters were wanted for home defense, they had to be crash-produced, leaving little aviation industry capacity for such roles as fleet air defense.

The RAF's resistance to the naval support role clearly enraged the Admiralty, and the latter, throughout the interwar period, waged more or less open war to recover control over the aircraft and the pilots flying from its ships. Unquestionably, the wartime Fleet Air Arm lacked the resources that its counterparts abroad enjoyed. Our point is that the RAF did exert a pernicious effect on the Fleet Air Arm, but the effect was more subtle and much less intentional than is usually imagined. The very existence of the RAF meant that the leaders of the British armed forces interacted in a setting very different from that of the U.S. services. This different setting, like the stage background in a theater, affected the "play"—that is, the development of RN aviation—at multiple levels. One example was the lack of British carrier captains trained as pilots. A second example is the way in which British carrier aircraft complements were set, both in terms of types of aircraft and numbers of aircraft. A third example was the problem the Fleet Air Arm had in getting adequate (to say nothing of good) publicity. This is why the account that follows pays more attention to the details of RAF development than may seem immediately relevant to the history of the Fleet Air Arm.

One other point is very important. The naval military revolution was the rise of naval air power, *not* merely the rise of aircraft carriers. During World War II, entirely land-based air forces, such as those of Germany and Japan, exerted enormous effects on navies largely by using long-range torpedo bombers. Japan and the United States combined carrier-borne aircraft with large forces of land-based bombers and seaplanes. Though the U.S. Navy had ceded control of the mission of land-based sea patrol to the Army in 1931, it got it back at the end of 1942. Britain, by contrast, was unique. Her World War II navy owned aircraft afloat, but the big land-based types were still owned by the RAF (though the limited number of coastal-patrol aircraft were under naval operational control).

The Royal Navy invented the aircraft carrier during World War I because it already had an interest in seaborne aircraft. In 1914, for example, the Royal Navy converted three small liners to seaplane carriers in order to strike at the German fleet in its anchorages. These ships conducted the first naval air strike

—on Cuxhaven, in 1914. But the rough North Sea hampered seaplane operations, and so the Royal Navy turned to ships that could launch and recover wheeled aircraft. During the war it commissioned the world's first true carrier, HMS *Argus,* and began construction on two more, HMS *Eagle* (a converted battleship) and HMS *Hermes* (of cruiser size). Many other ships, including two cruisers (*Furious* and *Vindictive*), were converted into more or less satisfactory carriers. Specialist naval aircraft, including the world's first shipboard torpedo bombers, were developed.

Moreover, the Royal Navy was unique, in World War I, for actually operating carriers, both with the main fleet and in independent operations. A lot of what was learned from these operations was lost, partly because Rear Adm. Murray Sueter, who effectively founded the Royal Naval Air Service, deliberately edited the papers of the service after the war to show that the Admiralty was *not* innovative in the field of aviation. His motive was apparently revenge. After being forced out of the Royal Navy, he became a strong proponent of the RAF. The papers, now in the Public Records Office, that form the documentary history of the Royal Naval Air Service were organized, edited, and summarized by Sueter, but they do not adequately cover Sueter's own efforts —supported by his Admiralty superiors—to convert liners in 1914 or experiments with the converted cruiser *Hermes* in 1913. Late in the war, a Royal Navy constructor (naval architect), Stanley Goodall, helped to sketch the first U.S. carrier while on a special assignment with the U.S. Navy's Bureau of Construction and Repair in Washington. American naval airmen studied and initially copied British operating practices, and many American aviators turned to the British for models of what they wanted their own aviation forces to become. A 1921 British naval mission effectively established the Japanese naval air arm. British advice shaped the single French carrier, *Bearn,* which was built after World War I.[4]

Yet by 1939 the Royal Navy seemed far behind its major rivals, the U.S. and Japanese navies. It had a large carrier force, but the ships seemed outmoded. Much more importantly, British naval aircraft seemed far behind those in service in the U.S. and Japanese navies. The British position was symbolized, perhaps, by the standard torpedo bomber, the biplane Swordfish with its open cockpits. Although it had been designed in the mid-1930s, the Swordfish seemed more reminiscent of World War I. The Fleet Air Arm entered World War II using cast-off RAF biplane single-seat fighters. Later, when it needed high-performance shipboard fighters (none of which it had in 1939), it had to adapt RAF Hurricanes and Spitfires, with indifferent results (particularly with the Spitfire). During the war, the British Fleet Air Arm seemed to survive and thrive mainly because it adopted U.S. naval aircraft to replace its apparently inferior British-built types. Surely this is the story of an unrealized military revolution.

The Fleet Air Arm did achieve some remarkable successes, however, even before it adopted American aircraft. In April 1940 its Skuas made the first successful dive-bombing attack on a ship in wartime, sinking the German cruiser *Königsberg* at Bergen. That November the archaic-looking Swordfish struck and crippled the Italian battle fleet at anchor at Taranto, in an attack that some feel inspired Pearl Harbor. The plan for that attack dates from at least 1936. It is described in detail in the Mediterranean Fleet 1934–39 battle orders file in the Public Records Office. But the notion of attacking a fleet that had taken refuge in a harbor dates back to World War I, when the first carrier (HMS *Argus*) was built to carry planes that would launch torpedoes against Germany's anchored battleships and battle cruisers, and the concept did not die with the creation of the RAF. About 1928, for example, a Harbor Attack Committee was formed, and one of its recommendations was that a carrier fighter direct, by radio signals, a large battleship-killing semisubmersible. Seven years later, HMS *Eagle*'s aircraft carried out a mock dawn attack from over the horizon against ships anchored in Singapore. In 1924 and 1927, respectively, Royal Navy tacticians considered the possibility of flying torpedo bombers from carriers at night and then (in 1927) providing aid to them on their return flight so that they could find and successfully land on their home carriers. The idea that carrier aircraft might strike an anchored fleet and then withdraw, *without* leading enemy bombers back to their own carrier, was neither new nor unusual in the Royal Navy's Fleet Air Arm in 1940.[5]

Taranto in particular showed a flair and an understanding of the role of naval aviation that belies any claim that the Royal Navy had lost sight of its air heritage. Yet British naval aircraft really were far outperformed by their foreign rivals. How could British naval air technology lag so far behind Royal Navy air-mindedness? One obvious answer is that the Royal Navy emphasized aspects of performance, such as low stall speed, that limited other aspects of aircraft performance (and hence employment). But why did the RN do that? The answer is that the Fleet Air Arm lacked the institutional support, gained through interaction, that sustained the U.S. Navy's aviation development.

Certainly lack of funding, due to a lack of political support or any concern on the part of senior officials, does not explain the lag. The 1940 operations show that the British Admiralty was very interested in (and even in advance of) exactly the sort of naval aviation its contemporaries practiced. Neither does the notion that the British aircraft industry could not produce modern naval aircraft. In 1939 the RAF had some of the best combat aircraft in the world. Another possible explanation is that a dominant RAF reserved all modern aircraft to itself, leaving the unfortunate Fleet Air Arm with castoffs. Yet, with one exception (the Fairey Fulmar), the naval aircraft with which the Royal Navy began World War II were unrelated to RAF types and met specifications laid down by the Admiralty.

It turns out that the Admiralty made a series of unfortunate decisions, some of them actually consequences of its enthusiasm for naval aviation, as expressed in a demand for very large numbers of aircraft to support the fleet. The British failed to link some extremely good thinking about how to use carriers with a series of technical choices about which kinds of aircraft to develop. Some British historians would argue that the juxtaposition of good tactical thinking with a disastrously bad developmental process is symptomatic of larger problems in British society. In any event, the result, for the RN, was a failure of its version of the carrier revolution in naval warfare.

In reviewing the history of the Fleet Air Arm, it is difficult to avoid the thought that being first in a technical revolution often is not best. Technological development often follows an S-shaped curve. At the beginning, progress is extremely difficult. Quite limited capability may be very costly. Then, just as enormous investments have been made to secure relatively little, development may move on to the near-vertical part of the S. Generations of equipment succeed each other at a dizzying pace (consider, for example, the rapid development of the armored surface ship in the second half of the nineteenth century). The initial investment becomes a barrier to adopting later equipment, or at least enough later (that is, better) equipment to maintain a modern force. Put another way, initial investment in one level of technology is an opportunity cost. It constrains future options. Resources are often exhausted before the curve of technological development flattens out again.

Airplanes in the interwar period followed exactly this pattern, except that the early ones, bought in great numbers during World War I, were not terribly expensive. For the British, it was important (but somewhat unfortunate) that the upper knee of the curve for piston-engine aircraft was reached about 1942. In mobilizing for war, they had frozen many of their designs at the 1938–40 state of the aeronautical art. They had begun rearmament in 1934, so the 1938–40 aircraft succeeded large numbers of 1934–35 aircraft. The combination, plus the strain of war itself, precluded full production of the next generation. The United States mobilized later, so in effect 1938–40 types (such as the Grumman F4F Wildcat and the P-40 Warhawk) were her first wave. She still had the capacity for the second wave, which included the very high-performance wartime carrier aircraft (such as the Grumman F6F Hellcat and TBM Avenger, as well as the F4U Corsair). Fortunately for the Royal Navy, these airplanes were available through Lend-Lease. Note that this explanation makes no reference whatever to the sins of the RAF, though it will later be clear that the RAF did hurt the Fleet Air Arm.

More generally, in the course of a military revolution, those who come later often build on the ideas of the pioneer, and they may well avoid costs and errors. Too, the pioneering service may forget just why particular decisions were made and, thus, under which circumstances those decisions should be reversed. In the British case, very early decisions on carrier operating practice (the rejection of early versions of arresting gear, for example) had profound effects that were not shared by other, later, carrier operators. The British also seem to have suffered from mirror-imaging, the besetting military sin: they imagined that all seaborne aircraft inevitably suffered from the limitations that their own operating practices had imposed. That assumption, in turn, protected them from the unhappy realization that their aircraft, and even some operational concepts, were inferior, until they met superior aircraft and concepts in combat.

As it happens, enough prewar intelligence publications are now available in more or less public archives to show that, beginning in 1931, the Admiralty staff had abundant evidence to support alternative choices that would have led to very different consequences. The annual (except for 1933 and 1936) "Progress in Tactics" classified booklet included a section on foreign tactical developments. It provided an extremely clear account of U.S. practice, for example.[6] Yet we can only infer that the part of the Admiralty tracking foreign developments did not communicate with the section drawing up carrier aircraft requirements. The requirements officers probably lacked easy access to data that would have shown how to overcome the limits imposed on them that resulted in low-performance airplanes. In his *Air Power and the Royal Navy,* for example, Geoffrey Till notes that there just were not enough RN officers with aviation experience in the period (late '20s to early '30s) to staff all the critical posts *necessary* for the RN's Fleet Air Arm to mature as a specialty.

The British were also extremely unlucky: some of their central assumptions, which seemed perfectly rational in the mid-1930s, were entirely overturned by the advent of radar a few years later. Radar had even more profound implications for naval air war at sea (particularly for air defense) than it had on land. It changed interception from a very difficult and unlikely proposition to the usual state of affairs. The first mention of radar (then called RDF) in the "Progress in Tactics" series comes in 1939, where it is described as a means of providing early warning of air attack. It could detect a bomber approaching at ten thousand feet at forty to fifty nautical miles, with an accuracy of about half a mile (fifteen degrees of bearing). This description did not contain any discussion of the possibility of using RDF as the basis for a fighter air defense system.[7]

The British situation was complicated in that the Royal Navy had several carriers designed during World War I, before the facts of carrier operation were much understood. Once the British Admiralty had decided, during World War I, that it wanted carriers, it invested very heavily. The Washington Naval Arms Limitation Treaty of 1922 limited overall British carrier strength, leaving only enough tonnage for a single postwar ship (which did not materialize because of the economic slump). The two best existing ships were virtually impossible to alter; a third, HMS *Furious,* was rebuilt to her final carrier configuration before very much operating experience had been gained. By the early 1920s, the only way to modernize the British carrier force would have been to scrap recently built ships, to provide the tonnage required for new ones.

The British delegation to the Washington Conference understood this problem. They demanded enough tonnage for six fleet carriers and persuaded their American and Japanese counterparts to accept *Argus, Eagle, Hermes, Furious* (as then configured), and *Vindictive* as experimental ships, like the U.S. Navy's *Langley. Furious* was indeed rebuilt, but her aircraft capacity was only half that of the similar *Glorious* and *Courageous,* both of which were converted from cruisers under the terms of the Washington agreements. *Vindictive* was converted back into a cruiser. The others lived on as, essentially, obsolete carriers. The British had managed to have the treaty written so as to allow scrapping them—they certainly knew the ships would soon be obsolete—but politics and postwar economics precluded any such program.[8]

The Admiralty was already well aware of how valuable carriers could be. Indeed, it had staged actual carrier operations earlier than other navies, including that of the United States. Even after the creation of the RAF, the Admiralty specified aircraft characteristics and paid for the aircraft and their crews, even though both came under RAF control. For example, it was British delegates at the Washington Naval Conference of 1922 who demanded large tonnage allowances for carriers, even though aircraft carriers were a decidedly experimental proposition at the time. There was, however, a limit, which for Britain and the United States equated to six fleet carriers each. Total tonnage limitation survived to 1936. Battleships retained their dominance in all the interwar navies partly because carriers, which were cheaper initially to build, could not be built in sufficient numbers to make a difference.[9] In the case of the RN, there was another problem—the financial and human resources to man and operate more carriers simply did not exist in this period.

The Royal Navy reached the treaty limit earlier than its competitors because it began the interwar period with substantial carrier tonnage built or begun during World War I. Aware that its existing ships were obsolete, the Admiralty began ordering new carriers as soon as the tonnage limit lapsed in 1936. In 1939 its carrier building program (two of the *Illustrious* class in the 1936 program, two more of the *Illustrious* class in the 1937 program [of which *Indomitable* was redesigned], and one each of the *Implacable* class in 1938 and 1939) was larger than that of any of its rivals. The RN also placed great weight on the consequences of air attack. They alone provided their carriers with armored flight decks (actually armored hangars) and thus with the ability to survive severe air attack. *Illustrious* and *Formidible* were both severely battered by German land-based dive-bombers in 1941, yet both survived. Other armored-deck carriers survived attacks by kamikazes better than American carriers in 1945.

The case of the armored-deck carriers is an interesting illustration of the wartime impact of prewar tactical concepts. Ships such as *Illustrious* were conceived immediately after the Ethiopian crisis focused attention on the Royal

Navy's need to defend its ships against land-based air attack in the Mediterranean. Confronted by many potentially hostile air bases, the Royal Navy could not hope to gain air superiority through early attacks; there were just too many airfields ashore. If enemy bombers could not be attacked on the ground, and if they could "always get through," then the Royal Navy's carriers would have to suffer (and survive) their attacks; hence the armor. The operational "price" of armor was an aircraft capacity half that of a carrier, such as *Ark Royal,* with an unarmored hangar, and so the armored carriers were designed to carry only bombers.

Ironically, the armored carriers were completed just as radar entered service. With radar, a carrier could launch interceptors in time to break up raids by attacking bombers. However, to exploit the advantage of radar, a carrier needed more aircraft (both fighters and bombers). Here, the Americans and Japanese, whose unarmored or lightly armored carriers fielded more aircraft, had the potential advantage.

As it happened, the Royal Navy suffered very heavy losses early in World War II. Of its three best prewar carriers, it lost one each in 1939 and 1940 (*Courageous* and *Glorious*), and the third (*Ark Royal*) in 1941. The two best British pre-Washington carriers (*Eagle* and *Hermes*) were lost in 1942. British capacity to build new carriers was very limited, at least partly because the yards were hard pressed to replace other war losses. Because carriers were complex, they were difficult to complete in wartime, and ships ordered by the Royal Navy in wartime served mainly postwar (no new carriers were ordered after 1945, and none ordered after 1943 was ever completed). The effect of all these shortfalls was to make the Admiralty appear much less air-minded than in fact it was, both before and during the war.

Britain emerged from the Washington Treaty with by far the largest carrier fleet in the world and thus, thanks to the treaty, the least room for subsequent new construction. However, her situation was not altogether unique. In all the major fleets, naval aviation was shaped by carrier design decisions made long before much operating experience had been acquired. The early carriers were terribly expensive and quite durable; all of the first-generation carriers served in World War II. None of the aircraft first carried on board those ships survived nearly as long. They were cheap and short-lived—appropriate qualities for craft whose technology was changing very rapidly. Their characteristics were always shaped to some extent by the earlier carrier design decisions. Moreover, the desire of successive British governments in the interwar period to hold down military spending meant that it was relatively difficult to finance reconstruction to overcome design errors made years earlier.[10] The British were quite strapped until after 1936. As the official *History of the Second World War* put it, "the policy since 1930 was to lay down one ship every three years. . . . In fact, only one ship, the *Ark Royal,* had been laid down by 1935."[11]

Unlike an airfield ashore, the carrier itself, by its design dimensions, profoundly affects the characteristics of the aircraft operated from it. Hangars have limits: length, breadth, *and* height. So do elevators and flight decks. In the British case, hangars were relatively small because they were fully enclosed within hulls; their dimensions severely limited aircraft length and folded width. Every increase in airplane size drastically reduced hangar capacity. As it happened, the Admiralty associated the capacity of each carrier with the capacity of her hangar deck (the U.S. Navy did not). The early British carriers had very small hangars and were so designed that enlargement would have been difficult or impossible. Based on its World War I experience, the Admiralty badly wanted large numbers of naval aircraft to operate with the fleet; it concluded, though, that they would have to be accommodated outside the carriers. It was in the interest of the Air Ministry (RAF) to agree that the carriers' capacities were very limited, because that limited its investment in naval aviation.

Carrier structures imposed other physical limits as well. Elevator size limited airplane dimensions, and both elevators and flight decks could accommodate only limited weight. Too, aviation gasoline was quite dangerous. Special tanks were needed to accommodate it. They could not easily be enlarged, short of major reconstruction. Total aviation fuel capacity determines how many airplane flight-hours a given carrier can support, quite aside from how many airplanes she can carry. During the 1930s, advancing airplane technology was associated with advancing aero-engine technology, which meant thirstier engines. None of these physical limits was easily breached, as the Royal Navy's ship designers knew.

The Admiralty staff did not realize, however, how high a price they had paid for not solving the organizational problem of illuminating the "unknown unknowns": the unexpected, difficult-to-predict problems that dog any effort to master a new and rapidly advancing military technology and the tactics associated with it. Carrier aviation had many "unknown unknowns." One was how to protect carriers from air attack. With fighters? With guns? Or passively, with armor? Another "unknown unknown" was how to employ carriers in battle. As independent task forces, each organized around one carrier? As a massed striking force of carriers operating together? Under the cover of the guns of a navy's battleships? A third "unknown unknown" was what kind of aircraft to develop. Multimission types? Specialized types? A fourth was the attrition rates for aircraft and aircrew in battle. Did the Fleet Air Arm need a substantial reserve of pilots and aircraft? The RN and the Fleet Air Arm did not have an effective experimental process for finding reliable answers to a majority of these important questions.

The Royal Navy's organizational and institutional arrangement limited the exploration of the RN's options in other ways, too. For example, the design of a carrier imposed several limits on aircraft performance. Aircraft had to take off by rolling down the flight deck (catapulting from carriers was rare until World War II).[12] Because piston-engine aircraft had to warm up before taking off, typically they were parked at the after end of the flight deck. The fraction of deck length needed to roll the first airplane off (generally into a particular wind) determined how much of the deck could be devoted to parked airplanes and, thus, how many airplanes the carrier could launch in a single strike. This consideration was common to all three major carrier navies.

One other limit is important: airplane engine power. As we noted previously, the U.S. Navy's carrier aviation program took a major step forward with the introduction of high-powered (450 horsepower and above) radial engines in the years after 1926. In England, airplanes designed in the early 1930s generally had six-hundred- to seven-hundred-horsepower engines, such as the 590-horsepower Kestrel in the Hawker Nimrod fighter (flown 1931) or the 690- or 750-horsepower Pegasus in the Swordfish. By the late 1930s they might run to eight hundred to one thousand horsepower, such as the 890-horsepower Perseus in the Skua fighter (ordered 1935) or the 1,065-horsepower Taurus in the Albacore (the Swordfish successor) or the 1,080-horsepower Merlin engine in the Fairey Fulmar (the Skua successor). Aircraft flown in 1942 often had engines of about two thousand horsepower, such as the 1,850-horsepower Griffon of the Fairey Firefly or the 2,000-horsepower R-2800 of the U.S.-supplied F6F Hellcat.

Past a certain point, extra engine power bought little more maximum speed, but it did buy other qualities of particular importance to naval operation, such as range. For example, the famous Spitfire originally had a Merlin of about one thousand horsepower. To achieve high performance, it had to be quite light, with a very compact airframe and relatively little fuel (or range). Even though the engine grew considerably in wartime, the airframe did not. Thus the Merlin-powered Seafire III (1,470 hp) achieved a combat radius of only eighty-one nautical miles at 190 knots. Its empty weight was 6,204 pounds. The Hellcat II, rated at 2,250 horsepower, had a combat radius of 248 nautical miles at 206 knots. It weighed 12,647 pounds empty. Both had comparable maximum speeds, 307 and 330 knots at medium altitude (about twelve thousand feet). The Royal Navy bought Skuas and Fulmars rather than "navalized" Spitfires in the 1930s, not because it had some sort of prejudice against modern high-performance aircraft but because, for its kind of naval tactics, long range was the first virtue, not mere high speed. Ironically, high-performance interceptors became useful only just as World War II began.[13]

To many British naval officers the clearest proof of the Admiralty's lack of air-mindedness was a string of losses of surface ships to air attack, from the 1940 Norwegian campaign on. British destroyers lacked dual-purpose guns, and the standard British antiaircraft fire control system was grossly ineffective.[14] This was ironic, because the prewar Royal Navy had by far the best existing medium-range machine cannon, the multiple barrel two-pounder. On the other hand, the Royal Navy, unlike the U.S. Navy, did not develop dual-purpose gun directors or dual-purpose main guns for its destroyers in the 1930s. The Royal Navy decision to adopt what turned out to be the wrong antiaircraft fire control system seems analogous to the failure, around 1912, to adopt an effective surface fire control system. The December 1941 loss of the *Prince of Wales* and *Repulse* to Japanese bombers off Malaya seems to have been the last straw. In its wake, a special Future Building Committee was formed. Its mandate was essentially to remake the Royal Navy in the modern image suggested by the U.S. Navy in the Pacific. Like the U.S. Navy's General Board nearly a generation earlier, the Future Building Committee emphasized carriers, and it included naval aircraft specifications in its deliberations.[15]

Our argument should be clear: the conventional explanation of the Royal Navy's apparent failure, the surrender of the Fleet Air Arm to the RAF, is probably far too simple. The RAF's effects, particularly during the formative period of the 1920s, were subtle and indirect. There is no evidence at all to support the common view that the Fleet Air Arm was crippled because the RAF gave it only castoff aircraft designs. There is every evidence that the aircraft the Royal Navy had in 1939 exactly fitted the Royal Navy's own ideas on air operations at sea. That some of those ideas were faulty, by the standards of the U.S. and Japanese navies, reflects the more subtle effects (at all three levels of analysis—individual, organizational, and institutional) of the RAF. As Geoffrey Till pointed out, the use of its Swordfish seaplane (flown by an enlisted pilot and commanded by an officer observer) by battleship *Warspite* in the second battle of Narvik (13 April 1940) was "as good an example of the Navy's pre-war personnel policy in operation as it [was] of its expectations about the tactical uses of naval air power."[16]

IT WOULD SEEM that the "standard" explanation of the Royal Navy's travail applies much more to the British army. This point might appear to be an irrelevant departure from our primary argument about the Royal Navy, but it is not. Both the British army and the British navy had to decide what the next war (assuming one occurred) would be like. The range of possible alternatives was large—from another war with Germany in France, to a conflict with Italy over North African colonies, to a fight with Japan in the Far East. The two services' visions of that future war shaped the aircraft requirements both services presented to the Air Ministry and Royal Air Force in the 1920s and 1930s.

During World War I, the British invented and exploited tanks. They also developed effective ground-attack aircraft (as did the Germans). British army officers, such as Brig. J. F. C. Fuller, invented the blitzkrieg attack, which combined tanks and close air support. Yet the idea eventually died in Britain. Experimental armored units formed between the wars enjoyed no semi-organic air cooperation. It was the Germans, not the British, who used blitzkrieg two decades later. The British army and the RAF had never been able to put the idea into practice. They lacked the organizational means to do so, as well as a method for keeping the idea (and its implementation) alive when funds were painfully scarce.

It can be argued that after 1918 the British army was less than enthusiastic about any future commitment to the sort of war it had just fought. It concentrated largely on its role of imperial peace keeping. For this purpose the RAF developed a family of what it called army cooperation aircraft, which were extremely light bombers intended to attack colonial insurrectionists in the field. During the early 1930s, these planes were adaptations of the existing Hawker high-performance light bombers, rather than specially designed craft. Their lineal successor was the Westland Lysander, which could carry a few bombs in a rack between its undercarriage wheels. None of these aircraft was intended to attack enemy formations that might shoot back. The policy of adapting standard light bombers for air-to-ground attacks held down production costs by increasing the production runs of certain aircraft. But it also cut off the development work begun in 1917–18 and therefore shut the door to the development of blitzkrieg-like formations and tactics.

In his history of the RAF at war, John Terraine recalls a pivotal War Cabinet meeting in May 1940, when the RAF rejected air support of the troops collapsing in France as a misuse of air power—despite the fact that air attacks on advancing German troops had appeared quite important in stopping the 1918 German spring offensive. According to Terraine, the RAF was eager to bomb the industrial targets in the Ruhr instead, and it got its way. Would it then be proper to say that the independence of the RAF led directly to the collapse of the Western Front in 1940, as well as to the victory over Germany several years later? After all, the RAF had been much better supported than the French air force between the wars, so it—rather than the French force—had the potential to intervene decisively against advancing German armored forces.

Terraine is not the only military historian critical of the RAF's position that ground support was a secondary mission. Support for carrier aviation was in some ways analogous—in the RAF's view—to support of British army ground units, and so similarly neglected.[17] After all, the RAF knew all about carrier vulnerability. The chief of the air staff (RAF) had opposed building large aircraft carriers for that reason. He regarded such construction as just a waste of overall aviation resources.

The failure of the British army to develop effective air-ground coordination is usually traced to excessive "conservatism" in the army itself. That is an argument at the first (individual) level of analysis: key individuals lacked insight. We believe the correct explanation should focus at the second and third levels within the British army and RAF and at the interaction between the two services. In effect, the potentially fruitful collaboration of tank and airplane, understood in 1918, became virtually impossible with the creation of the RAF. The case of ground attack is striking simply because it is so little remarked. The unwillingness of the RAF to buy dive-bombers (the most effective but quite specialized means of close air support available in the 1930s) is well known, but not the broken connection to the earlier collaboration between ground-attack pilots and the British army. Similarly, the early British failures in the face of blitzkrieg are never blamed on the transformation of British army aviation in 1918.

Ground Attack Aircraft of World War II, by C. Shores, gives a typical account. Shores points out that by 1918 Sopwith Camels were regularly bombing and strafing on the Western Front and that ground attack was extremely successful in the Middle East. Shores states that the postwar RAF leadership included few men with any experience of close air support. Although the French Army retained control of its air force, it had not developed ground attack to any great degree during World War I and therefore presumably did not have nearly the potential to develop the tank-airplane combination that the British Army of 1918 enjoyed. In 1939 the RAF had no ground-attack aircraft or dive-bombers. It did have light bombers (Fairey Battles), but they were intended for level rather than dive-bombing, and they lacked forward-firing weapons for strafing. In February 1934 the RAF did issue a specification (P.4/34) for a light dive-bomber to carry a five-hundred-pound bomb, but neither of the two prototypes entered production (the Fairey version became the Fulmar fleet fighter), and neither P.4/34 contender had much in the way of strafing armament.[18]

British naval aviation was spared a similar fate, not because of some analysis or experiment conducted by the RAF, but because of the early Admiralty investment in carriers. On the one hand, each carrier represented slots (aircraft, aircrew, service crew) that the RAF had to fill. If it failed to do so, it risked re-creation of a separate Royal Navy Fleet Air Arm and, thus, loss of its vital political claim to unity of air power. The RAF considered the Fleet Air Arm a peripheral activity; it did not want to support any more carrier aircraft than it had to. Thus, in 1931 it was able to veto a serious naval attempt to increase the air complement per carrier. On the other hand, even though the RAF owned the airplanes on British warships (until 1939), the Admiralty paid for them, decided their overall characteristics, and in many cases supplied their aircrew. Whatever the RAF might have wanted to do with carriers, it had limited control over aviation at sea. For example, the disastrous lack of reserves seems to have been due largely to Admiralty policy.

In 1935, the Fleet Air Arm (FAA) had only a 20 percent officer reserve; the Air Ministry claimed that the RAF could provide the difference when needed. At this time the RAF wanted a 450 percent reserve, was willing to accept 300 percent, and wanted 200 percent for the FAA. The Admiralty aimed for 100 percent, which it did not achieve. Many British writers argue that the navy's hostility toward air power discouraged naval officers who might otherwise have volunteered for FAA duty. This, rather than any explicit Admiralty policy, might have been the deadly effect of coming under RAF control and thus losing prospects for promotion. Geoffrey Till, in his *Air Power and the Royal Navy,* argued that the Admiralty deserved much of the blame, because it imagined that pilots would most likely be lost during a single climactic battle, rather than steadily in the course of a sustained war at sea. Given a lack of reserves, the effect of attrition during the 1940 Norwegian campaign was disastrous: the FAA lost about a third of its total strength (125 aircrew, one hundred aircraft), many in the sinking of the carrier *Glorious.*

Another explanation deserves some mention. Between World War I and World War II, Britain faced three quite distinct threats of war: conflict in Europe (e.g., against France, and later against Germany), conflict in the Far East against an aggressive Japan bent on seizing imperial possessions there, and minor warfare on the borders of the Empire. The RAF was most concerned with the first threat, claiming that its bombers could either deter or knock out a continental enemy before a costly World War I–style trench war got under way. The Royal Navy was mainly concerned with the possibility of war in the Far East. The army hoped devoutly that it could confine its activities to the frontiers of the Empire. Because distances in the East were so great, the RAF seems not to have entertained any real hope of mounting a strategic air offensive against Japan. It could participate only to the extent of securing Singapore and providing Fleet Air Arm and maritime patrol aircraft. Thus presumably it had to tolerate the Fleet Air Arm despite its strong doctrinal preference for heavy bombing. Once rearmament started in 1934, the RAF position was that Britain must concentrate on the European problem, appeasing the Japanese. The Royal Navy took the opposite view: that the Germans could be appeased but the Japanese had already shown in China that they could not be. No one imagined that Britain was strong enough economically to fight both Germany and Japan simultaneously.[19]

The decision virtually to eliminate close air support caused the RAF remarkably little political trouble until 1940, when it was far too late to reverse it. Close air support died partly because there was no fixed army structure, such as combined-arms divisions, requiring RAF investment. There was also no inherent threat that the army, given its focus on garrisoning Britain's empire, would somehow revive the support component of the Royal Flying Corps if the RAF failed. The British army had no permanent divisional or corps organization, and low-performance aircraft sufficed for its main peacetime role of policing the empire's borders. Experimental army formations were assembled to test armor doctrine, but they never lasted long enough to make the need for organic tactical air power obvious. On one occasion, the RAF leadership severely reprimanded a squadron commander who lent his unit to an experimental army formation for an afternoon.

It may also have been relevant that the interwar army had no obvious future large-army opponent. Until 1939, it had fervently hoped to avoid commitment to the Continent. Moreover, the army was very poor. It was lucky to have the funds to buy such obvious necessities as small tanks and modern field guns. By 1944 the RAF did have an outstanding close-air attack fighter in the Hawker Typhoon, but that was an accident (the airplane had been conceived as an interceptor). It steadfastly refused to adopt dive-bombers; the main such airplane used in wartime was the U.S. Vultee Vengeance, used mainly in the Far East.

When the Royal Navy regained full control over the Fleet Air Arm in 1939, it still had not completely reversed the 1918 surrender: its control was limited to aircraft intended to serve aboard ships. The other vital element of the old Royal Naval Air Service, the shore-based strike and long-range aircraft, remained under RAF control as Coastal Command. The RAF had imagined these aircraft mainly as an alternative to conventional naval forces, not primarily as a means of cooperating with the deployed navy. They were not considered particularly important. When war came in 1939, the Royal Navy found Coastal Command extremely weak and quite ill-prepared, and the lack of coastal aircraft had an immediate and unfortunate impact on British antisubmarine capabilities.

As in the case of ground support, this was a failing unappreciated until losses to German forces pounded home the point. Most accounts of World War I success and postwar neglect of antisubmarine warfare (ASW) emphasize the central role of the convoy strategy. However, shore-based aircraft were extremely important at the time, because they drastically reduced the mobility of the submarines. This role was probably not completely understood because the Royal Navy lost shore-based aviation to the RAF just as it was beginning to formally analyze the ASW lessons of the war. The analyses themselves are in the Admiralty Staff Histories, held by the Naval Historical Branch in London. They include elaborate mathematical studies of convoy operations. This early operational analysis seems not to have had much, if any, effect on World War II operations. In the case of coastal aircraft, analysis would have been particularly important because their role was not intuitively obvious: they sank no submarines during the war. The key was that U-boats were submersible warships that had to spend much of their time on the surface merely to make good any distance. Whenever a U-boat spotted an airplane, the submarine had to dive to avoid being bombed. Each successful evasion drastically reduced the U-boat's mobility. Only careful analysis could reveal the true value of the coastal airplanes, which was clearly recognized after World War II.

The pre–World War II U.S. Navy, because it was concerned with an offensive Pacific campaign, did not even develop a requirement for land-based ASW aircraft to support convoys, although about 1940 it did want to buy a coastal patrol airplane primarily for ASW. The neglect of the lessons learned from World War I had serious consequences for the Royal Navy. To cite just one example, HMS *Courageous,* the first British carrier lost during World War II, was sunk while carrying out ASW patrols, that is, while filling in for insufficient Coastal Command aircraft.

Coastal ASW patrol competed directly with bombing operations, because (at least until well into World War II) the main requirements, a good bombload and long endurance, were not too different. The only land-based patrol airplane available in 1939 was the Avro Anson, a small twin-engine type later widely used as a trainer. It could not patrol well beyond waters immediately around the British Isles. When U-boat patrol areas enlarged dramatically after the defeat of France in 1940, it could not reach the new mid-ocean hunting grounds.

U-boat patrol areas had been limited in 1939–40 because coastal air patrols kept boats transiting from Germany from surfacing in daylight in the North Sea and around Scotland. They could not make much net speed, so their time on patrol was limited; to maximize it, they stayed as close as possible to the Irish coast. The Anson could, at least in theory, cover the areas thus defined. As soon as the German army reached the French and Norwegian coasts, it provided U-boats with bases very close to the Atlantic. With the same endurance, they could spend their time much farther out to sea. The same logic of U-boat patrol areas had inspired the design of the corvette, a coastal escort, in 1938. The idea was that until a convoy reached about six hundred nautical miles from Britain, U-boats would not be a threat, although it did need an escort against surface raiders. However, the small corvettes were clearly ill adapted to the sort of mid-ocean convoy work required from late 1940 onward.

Long-range bombers were needed, but the RAF was unwilling to transfer them from its preferred operation, the strategic attack on Germany. As four-engine bombers (Lancasters and Halifaxes) entered service in sufficient numbers, obsolescent twin-engine Whitleys and Wellingtons joined Coastal Command, to push the area of air patrol out to the west. However, full coverage of the North Atlantic was not possible until four-engine bombers were released from the strategic air offensive to Coastal Command. That became possible only because U.S. factories produced more aircraft, particularly B-24 Liberators, than were needed for the direct attack against Germany. A similar conflict arose in the United States. Postwar, some of the British Operational Researchers would conclude rather bitterly that RAF heavy bombers used against Germany would have been much more profitably employed by the Coastal Command.

Coastal Command did have some long-range flying boats (Short Sunderlands), but they could not substitute completely for land-based aircraft, presumably because the latter could be launched in much worse weather. The flying boats had been designed primarily to patrol (e.g., against pirates in the Far East) and to attack surface units. They were very suitable for air ASW work but not for long-endurance scouting in support of the fleet. (The prewar Royal Navy complained that it could not get the RAF to provide anything like the cooperation the U.S. fleet received from its big flying boats.) Contemporary U.S. flying boats were owned by the U.S. Navy, which was interested mainly in reconnaissance to support fleet operations. The aircraft did not differ much, at least externally, but the difference in application had enormous consequences.

At least on some level, the Royal Navy grasped the difference. The foreign intelligence section of the 1931 edition of "Progress in Tactics," for example, noted that the U.S. Navy operated 137 tender-borne aircraft, and that they were under the command of the fleet commander, rather than a coastal commander ashore. The authors of "Progress in Tactics 1935" were much impressed by the support given the fleet by patrol planes during a major exercise in April 1934. Royal Navy officers could not say that there were no competing models, no alternatives.[20]

Again, it would be easy to fall back on what might be called the "accepted" explanations for the Royal Navy's problems. One, for example, is that the transfer of naval air officers in 1918 left the interwar Royal Navy without any senior "air-minded" officers and, legend would have it, thus with an antiquated outlook that emphasized battleships and therefore resisted change. This explanation supports the belief that the Royal Navy entered World War II with a grossly inadequate carrier force and with little interest in expanding it, not to mention antiquated tactical ideas and the wrong aircraft. The RAF had some of the world's best fighters (Spitfires) and an impressive force of twin-engine heavy bombers (Whitleys and Wellingtons), but the Royal Navy began the war with unimpressive two-seat fighters and, worse, with a low-speed biplane as its main attack bomber. Surely, say the pundits, such gross obsolescence reflected "evil intent" on the part of the RAF: why couldn't the navy have received something better? The contemporary U.S. Navy was introducing a monoplane fighter, the Grumman Wildcat, and already had monoplane attack and torpedo bombers. The Japanese had introduced monoplane naval fighters some years before and were about to field the revolutionary Zero.

The usual impression is misleading at best. Even after the RAF took over, many of the Fleet Air Arm flyers were naval officers; the Admiralty demanded these billets as a way of maintaining some measure of air-mindedness. A Naval Air Section (NAS) created within the Admiralty staff in 1920 expanded to become the Naval Air Division (NAD), and from 1920 a member of the Board of Admiralty was charged with special responsibility for naval aviation. Eventually the special member became assistant chief of staff (Air) and then fifth sea lord/chief of the Naval Air Service.

As described by Geoffrey Till, however, NAS/NAD was entirely separate from Rear Admiral (Aircraft Carriers), the *operational* air commander who flew his flag in a carrier. He was deliberately placed afloat to avoid conflict with NAD and with the Air Ministry's coastal aircraft command. Till, in *Air Power and the Royal Navy,* was much impressed with the Naval Air Division's technical expertise and particularly with its ability to lay out specifications for naval aircraft. However, with only twenty officers in 1936, it was often overwhelmed by staff work and thus probably unable to look beyond immediate concerns. NAD had no executive power; it was intended to advise the Naval Staff as a whole and Assistant Chief of Naval Staff (Air) in particular. Only the Admiralty Board could make executive decisions. In addition, NAD was concerned with tactical rather than with technical issues. A Department of Air Materiel (DAM) was set up in January 1938 specifically to achieve independence from the Air Ministry. Like NAD, it reported to ACNS (Air). Note that most of the British naval aircraft of World War II (and all the really bad ones) were designed or specified well before DAM was set up. DAM was unusual among Admiralty materiel divisions in that it did not report to a technical chief (as, say, naval construction reported to the Director of Naval Construction [DNC]). There was also a Rear Admiral, Naval Air Stations (RANAS) responsible for the shore and training establishments. He was not under Rear Admiral (Carriers), either.[21]

The Air Ministry, the parent organization of the RAF, gained control over aircraft technology, including the experimental establishments. As rearmament gained momentum in the 1930s, the British ran into bottlenecks in production, particularly in aircraft engines (as the United States was also to encounter later). It was clearly very much in the RAF's interest that the overall size of the Fleet Air Arm be limited, simply to avoid excessive competition for valuable engines, such as the Merlin.

To support its political assault, at the institutional level, on the Royal Navy's role, the RAF had to claim that surface ships were extremely vulnerable to air attack. The Royal Navy was forced into a somewhat defensive position, denying the vulnerability of ships instead of advocating the potential of its own aircraft at sea. Ironically, because it wanted to concentrate on strategic bombing, the RAF spent very little time or money developing techniques or weapons needed to execute effective antiship attacks. The Admiralty staff, well aware of the RAF's limitations (in reconnaissance at sea, for example), may have imagined that such limitations were inherent in land-based aircraft rather than in the RAF itself. The problem was that the Admiralty could not distinguish technological limits on what aircraft could do from limits set on their performance by the doctrine of the RAF. Unfortunately for the Royal Navy, foreign air forces, such as those created by the Germans, Japanese, and Italians, did not share the RAF's organizational processes and thus became more effective at attacking targets at sea.

5 The Fleet Air Arm before World War II

Like its contemporaries, the prewar Royal Navy concentrated on the problem of the fleet action. A fleet commander first needed warning that the enemy fleet was coming. That was generally expected to come from a submarine off the enemy's fleet base. Then the enemy fleet had to be located far enough away—say, about one thousand nautical miles—to steer the fleet into position to intercept. The British called this strategic scouting. The battle would begin, however, with contact by *tactical* scouting forces operating with the fleet. For example, during and immediately after World War I, the British planned to station a scouting line of cruisers (the "A-K line," so named after the designations of the cruisers comprising it) in the van of the fleet. As one or more would contact the enemy's cruisers, the fleet commander would guess how to maneuver.

Such tactical reconnaissance was essential; the British failed at Jutland in 1916 partly because some of the scouting cruisers did not describe the enemy disposition. Aircraft had been involved only peripherally; after Jutland Admiral Jellicoe demanded carrier- and cruiser-borne aircraft to operate with the fleet. In at least one case after Jutland, the German fleet, advised by reconnaissance Zeppelins, was able to avoid a crushing British concentration. It was generally agreed quite early after World War I that a British fleet could not force a faster enemy fleet to action if the enemy were properly served by reconnaissance aircraft. Thus the vital fleet air roles, established early on, were reconnaissance and denial of reconnaissance to an enemy.

Geoffrey Till, in *Air Power and the Royal Navy,* describes and illustrates the 1924 British fleet disposition, with two carriers (for reconnaissance and torpedo attack) just behind the A-K line and air scouts searching a sector 135 nautical miles deep and fifty to one hundred nautical miles wide ahead of the fleet. Over the next decade, much effort went into increasing scouting range and also into insuring that scouts could locate enemy forces accurately. Once the enemy fleet was spotted in the search sector, it would be shadowed until it was struck or the fleets came into contact. In the 1924 cruising disposition, the battle fleet trailed the reconnaissance carriers; it was accompanied by two carriers responsible mainly for spotting gunfire and for fleet air defense. This scheme, incidentally, explains why the Admiralty fought so hard at Washington for a large carrier allowance: it required four ships.[1]

Aircraft offered two important advantages. First, they could spot the enemy fleet well before it came into contact with any surface ships. Aircraft could, then, replace the A-K line altogether, releasing the cruisers for other duties during the battle, such as stiffening destroyer flotillas. Second, aircraft could strike an enemy fleet at a range of several hundred miles, limited only by the accuracy of air reconnaissance.

Early strikes were particularly important to the Royal Navy. It felt that it had been cheated of victory at Jutland mainly because the German fleet had managed to outrun it on the night after the battle. The fleet the RN expected to oppose in the next war, the Japanese, had faster battleships. Unless something were done to slow them down, they could approach and withdraw at will, accepting action only in favorable circumstances. Carrier aircraft alone offered the possibility of slowing the approach of Japanese battleships or of preventing their escape from superior British gun power. Thus the British were very proud that they had extended air reconnaissance as far as 164 nautical miles in a 1930 exercise. The previous record (1929) had been 135 nautical miles.

Because numbers were so limited, aircraft could not be sent out in pairs. The success of a reconnaissance flight depended on a single aircraft. If a reconnaissance aircraft missed the carrier altogether and had to ditch, the carrier would lose a valuable plane, its just as valuable crew, and the intelligence the mission had gained. Hence the importance of a carrier homing beacon, which the Royal Navy developed (Type 72). But the value of the beacon in guiding reconnaissance aircraft back to the carrier ran counter to the navy's great reluctance, in the interest of avoiding detection, to allow ships to emit signals. The beacon was worth the risk only if the reconnaissance aircraft performed well enough to make that risk worthwhile. This is why, by 1930, British naval aircraft were expected to locate an enemy force to within six nautical miles after an hour in the air on patrol. In 1931, the British believed that, although the U.S. Navy was "considerably ahead of our Fleet Air Arm in the techniques of operating aircraft from catapults and carrier decks, their efficiency in reconnaissance is not up to our current standard."[2]

The interwar U.S. Navy expected its big seaplanes to conduct strategic scouting, locating the enemy fleet at long range. For the Royal Navy, the RAF blocked that option. The British fleet depended on a combination of radio interception and direction finding for very long range location. Because there were no long-range fleet aircraft, other than those on carriers, to locate and shadow an enemy fleet, carrier air reconnaissance became more important than in other navies. British dependence on radio location reinforced a tendency, already marked, toward strict radio silence. That had significant effects on aircraft design, which we will discuss shortly.

The RAF's search for dominance had a further important effect. It became accepted doctrine that British naval aircraft would not raid land targets. Thus British carrier bombers, unlike their U.S. Navy contemporaries, did not have to compete in performance with land-based fighters. Experiments in the 1930s seemed to show that virtually any naval bomber had an excellent chance of catching a warship unawares, so maximum performance in the air was of little importance. Other characteristics, such as takeoff and landing speed, mattered more.

It can be argued that the interwar Admiralty was at least as air-minded as its U.S. counterpart, if far less well equipped, especially in terms of "hardware" (aircraft, catapult floatplanes on battleships and cruisers, and carriers) and manpower. Both navies believed that only battleship gunfire could reliably neutralize battleships (a quite reasonable belief at the time, given the ordnance capacities of early 1930s carrier bombers). The Royal Navy was far more concerned with the possibility that a faster enemy battle line might escape, as the Germans had escaped at Jutland. It therefore emphasized the creation of a long-range air striking force consisting mainly of torpedo bombers.

By the mid-1930s U.S. doctrine, as understood by the British, was quite different. The U.S. Navy defined offensive capability as superiority in surface warships. For the offensive fleet, the obvious and most efficient weapon was the gun. For the defensive fleet, the obvious weapon was air attack. The offensive fleet would not form an air striking force, as that would reduce its ability to stave off air attacks by the defensive fleet. On the other hand, "Progress in Tactics 1935" noted that the U.S. Naval War College argued that the offensive fleet should break off action if its carriers were sunk, unless it was certain that the defensive fleet's surface craft were on the point of being sunk. The defensive fleet, in the opposite situation, would put all its resources into air attacks on the offensive fleet, the carriers being the primary objective.[3] Thus, to the British, the U.S. fleet did not appear to integrate carrier aircraft into its overall fleet tactics as completely as did the Royal Navy, although it did have much better airplanes and much better operating practices on its carriers.

In 1931 the Royal Navy appointed a flag officer, Rear Admiral (Aircraft Carriers), or RAA, specifically to develop carrier tactics. "Progress in Tactics," the annual classified Admiralty publication, shows that special exercises were held to evaluate the "known unknowns" of carrier operations, and that the Royal Navy considered these ships extremely important. One sign of their rising status is that air operations were promoted to a separate chapter in 1934. In previous editions they had been split up among sections devoted to particular phases of the fleet engagement: overall tactical policy, reconnaissance, security (screening against enemy reconnaissance), contact and approach, deployment, and the battle itself. In this, the British were approximately a dozen years behind the U.S. Navy. However, both navies faced the same *organizational* problem: how to turn the results of exercises into doctrine and force structure (such as new aircraft) *despite* the constraints imposed by treaty and by a lack of funds. As noted in chapter 4, it was particularly important that the Royal Navy find a way to reveal the "unknown unknowns"—the factors that could turn out to be devastating surprises when war began.

The Royal Navy did not quite solve the organizational problem. The Admiralty's carrier aircraft did meet its requirements, but unfortunately those requirements were not generated by organizations interacting in an experimental setting. Too, the Royal Navy never had anything like the numbers its enemies and its main ally had, nor did it have sufficient aircrew. The Air Ministry adamantly refused to provide reserves against early losses, especially once the RAF itself began to expand in the late 1930s. Indeed, the Fleet Air Arm's own official history blames considerable failures in 1941 and 1942 on the loss of virtually all the trained aircrews in 1940, particularly in the Norwegian campaign.[4]

The record suggests that a chain of apparently rational (though not experimentally based) decisions was also to blame for the inability of the Royal Navy to discover the "unknown unknowns." Among warships, a carrier has the most "open" (or flexible) of architectures: it can operate the widest variety of weapons (aircraft). The Royal Navy accepted an architecture that was the reverse of the U.S. Navy's deck park and a technique of operation that placed severe limits on the aircraft its ships could operate, thus badly limiting the sorts of aircraft that it could buy—and which its planners could expect. Moreover, because the Royal Navy's decision process limited its examination of possibilities, its leaders seem to have assumed that any other navy would suffer from the same limitations. In particular, the Royal Navy assumed that, to operate from a carrier, an airplane had to suffer limited performance. That assumption had a dramatic—and deadening—effect on the Royal Navy's estimates of requirements.

From about 1920 on, the Royal Navy, like the USN, considered Japan the most likely future enemy. In its view, the war would be decided by a fleet action in the South China Sea, far from the airfields used by both combatants. The U.S. Navy, on the other hand, imagined it would have to fight its way past Japanese outposts in order to force a fleet confrontation. In the course of its journey west, the USN would therefore face lots of land-based, high-performance aircraft and would have to build its own air arm to deal with them. After the Ethiopian crisis of 1935–36, the Royal Navy also had to contemplate war against Italy in the Mediterranean. There were so many potentially threatening airfields there, however, that the Royal Navy did not believe it could deal with them all.

The Admiralty expected that these two possible wars (Mediterranean and South China Sea) would be very different. It was assumed—wrongly, as it turned out—that the Japanese battle would be a pure fleet-on-fleet encounter, because it would occur well beyond the range of land-based aircraft. British naval aircraft thus would meet only Japanese naval aircraft. To the extent that naval aircraft were limited in performance, then, they would not meet anything beyond their capabilities. Moreover, because all the Japanese aircraft would be ship-borne, early strikes against Japanese carriers would secure air superiority. This view would have been correct through most of the 1930s.

In 1933, however, Adm. Isoroku Yamamoto, who later planned the Pearl Harbor raid and who was then chief of the technical division of the Japanese Navy's Aviation Department, asked Mitsubishi to design a land-based airplane with sufficient range to maintain surveillance of U.S. naval bases in Hawaii and in the Philippines. Once designed, it was transformed into a very long range torpedo bomber intended specifically to make up for the treaty-imposed inferiority of the Japanese carrier force. This development reached fruition, in the form of the G3M bomber ("Nell"), before World War II.

The British knew about this airplane, partly because it was used in the Sino-Japanese War, but they seem not to have grasped the strategic implication of its very long range. Thus the list of Japanese naval aircraft in the standard British intelligence manual, CB.1815 ("World naval vessels and naval aircraft"), for October 1938 identifies Nell as a heavy bomber or coastal reconnaissance aircraft with a range of 723 statute miles (628 nm). In reality G3M was a torpedo bomber with a maximum range of 2,365 nautical miles in its 1941 version (G3M2). Its range when carrying a torpedo was probably somewhat shorter. Its successor, G4M ("Betty"), was designed to carry a torpedo two thousand nautical miles and had a maximum range of 3,256 nautical miles.

As for the role of such a shore-based airplane, according to the foreign notes in "Progress in Tactics" for 1938, Japan had twenty-five squadrons of naval shore-based aircraft, including light and heavy bombers, whose primary responsibility was "defence against sea-borne attack, whether by carriers or warships. Japan is particularly apprehensive of carrier-borne air attacks, and relies on her shore-based squadrons to locate and destroy enemy carriers that may have escaped her main fleet." This is mistaken mirror-imaging; the Japanese planned to use the long-range bombers to wear down an approaching fleet *before* it was brought to action. Hence the extreme range of G3M and G4M. It was not accidental that the U.S. Navy, which hoped to use its own seaplanes in the prebattle attack role, well understood that the Japanese planned to wear it down by air attacks before the big surface action. The USN's analytic process was better than the RN's in this case.[5]

It was Nell's range, about which the British were mistaken, that gave it its strategic significance. For example, in December 1941, G3Ms sank the *Prince of Wales* and *Repulse* far beyond the supposed range of Japanese land-based aircraft. The Royal Navy's shocked realization was that now capital ships would always need carrier fighter escorts: there no longer were viable havens from land-based air attack. The wartime light fleet carriers (*Colossus* class) were conceived as fighter escorts for just this mission. This is clear from documents in their Ships' Cover (No. 666) and from the papers of the Future Building Committee. Other materiel decisions in response to the loss of the *Prince of Wales* and *Repulse* included the decision to adopt power-operated dual-purpose main armament in the new "Battle" class destroyers, despite the considerable increase in size and cost entailed.

In the Mediterranean, it was a given that land-based aircraft would most probably attack the fleet. There could be no hope of destroying their many airfields with carrier bombers alone, and exercises showed that land-based bombers from these fields could not reliably be intercepted. On the other hand, the enemy fleet probably would not be able to call upon land-based interceptors, which had to trade short range to achieve high performance. As long as the RAF could be relied on to hit most targets ashore, then the Mediterranean scenario did not impose unusually high performance on naval strike aircraft.

In 1937 the Admiralty believed that the Italian air force had assigned four squadrons of thirty-six Savoia 55X twin-hull floatplanes to naval cooperation and that the three-engine S.79 land-based bomber was being adapted for ship attack, carrying a single 1,500-kilogram (3,300 lb) bomb. It was also reported in the 1938 "Progress in Tactics" that the Italians were planning to abandon torpedo attack altogether in favor of bombing, particularly dive-bombing. This was the first description of Italian shore-based antiship aircraft to appear in "Progress in Tactics," though it seems evident that Italy had been the threat leading to the adoption of armored flight decks two years before. The S.79 was known because it had just been used in Spain. In fact, the Italians concentrated on torpedo attack during the war, using the S.79 Sparviero. They also introduced the Luftwaffe to torpedo bombing, with extremely unfortunate results for the Royal Navy.[6]

As we observed in the previous chapter, British carrier design most dramatically reflected the emergence of the growing threat of attack by land-based aircraft. In 1934 the Royal Navy ordered HMS *Ark Royal,* in effect a modern version of its earlier designs. She had a double hangar, to accommodate the largest possible air group, sufficient to preemptively eliminate an enemy carrier force. Two years later, however, the orders went for armored carriers, their hangars protected against bomb hits. Unit carrier tonnage was restricted by treaty, so the weight of the armor had to be paid for—in this case, by halving hangar capacity. In each case, the navy assumed that "the bomber would get through," assuming it was still in existence by the time the carrier came within range.

In 1918 the Royal Navy had commissioned the first true aircraft carrier,

HMS *Argus.* She naturally became the experimental platform for developing naval air practices. One of the first questions to answer was, "How many aircraft could she operate effectively?" Her air group commander assumed that she would operate as the seagoing equivalent of an airfield ashore. Before an airplane could land, the deck would have to be cleared of the preceding one, which would be moved into the hangar. The landing cycle was determined by the time it took to stop an airplane, move it onto the elevator, and bring it below. The number of aircraft a particular carrier could operate was determined by the capacity of her hangar and, to some extent, by the time it took a group of airplanes to form up and land. For example, in a 1930 exercise, HMS *Courageous* launched fifty-one aircraft in a single strike, but that took an hour, and it took two hours to recover all of them. Both times were far too long for wartime (as the U.S. Navy already knew), when a large ship could never run a straight course for very long for fear of being torpedoed.

The two carriers designed and begun during World War I, the cruiser-sized *Hermes* and the converted battleship *Eagle,* had small hangars. By 1920 it was clear that neither could be altogether satisfactory. Yet it was literally inconceivable that they should be discarded before completion, nor could they be redesigned with substantially larger capacity. When the Washington Treaty was framed the following year, Britain, like the United States and Japan, had a fixed total tonnage allocation. The two unsatisfactory early carriers had to be included. *Eagle* took up a particularly large fraction of overall tonnage. The Washington Treaty allowed each signatory to convert two existing capital ships to carriers. Britain chose two large cruisers, *Courageous* and *Glorious,* which were near-sisters to HMS *Furious,* a ship partly converted to a carrier during the war.

Because hangar capacity was so important, the designers developed an unusual two-level hangar design, similar to the one adopted by the Japanese, for the converted large cruisers. Moreover, because fighters of the 1920s could become airborne after a short takeoff, these ships had two flight decks. One, just behind the bow, led right from one hangar. The other flight deck was above and behind the first. In both the earlier carriers and in these two conversions, however, the hangar was totally enclosed in the ship's hull. The enclosed hangar would have significant consequences. Because the Fleet Air Arm's process for testing such innovations was not as rigorous as that of the USN, the operational implications of the enclosed hangar were not much appreciated at the time. Piston-engine airplanes must warm up their engines for some minutes before they can take off. On a carrier, they could do so only on an open flight deck, not in an enclosed hangar. Because flight deck space was very limited, a British carrier could not launch all or most of her aircraft in a single strike, *despite* the ability to launch fighters from the short flight deck forward. The prewar Royal Navy therefore never was able to concentrate naval air striking power.

By way of contrast, most U.S. carriers had open hangars. Aircraft could warm up below decks, moving up to the flight deck once a deckload had flown off. There is evidence that at least some officers in the Royal Navy were aware by 1931 of the different technique used in the U.S. Navy, but by then the Air Ministry (the RAF) was unwilling to change the established aircraft complements of the RN's carriers.

British carriers were badly squeezed even if they could fly off their aircraft in small groups, which were not really limited by the need to warm up. In 1932, for example, fleet exercises showed that a single carrier supporting the battle fleet could not provide sufficient spotters out of her two flights of spotter/reconnaissance (S/R) aircraft. She needed three. Given limited capacity, the extra numbers had to be made up out of strike aircraft (torpedo bombers). Nothing was done at the time, because there was no money for additional S/Rs. However, the problem undoubtedly led to the design of the Swordfish, which could function both as a torpedo bomber and as a spotter/reconnaissance plane.[7] The U.S. Navy had already learned this lesson and had, accordingly, given the duty of spotting gunfire to its battleship and cruiser floatplanes, leaving its carrier aircraft free for strike missions.

Despite the improvements in the two double-hangar carriers, overall British fleet aircraft capacity was quite limited. The Admiralty could not order carriers to increase it, because of the limits imposed by the Washington Treaty and the fiscal effects of the postwar British recession. Significantly, a carrier planned for 1925 was not built. The Admiralty staff hit upon two complementary approaches to the shortage of carriers. First, some combat aircraft would be carried by surface ships—quite in contrast to the U.S. Navy's policy—and launched by catapult. Second, the requirement for overall numbers would be trimmed to meet capacity, by making aircraft multipurpose insofar as possible.

Battleship and cruiser catapults launched aircraft, of limited maximum weight, at about sixty knots. Because they might have to launch combatant aircraft (fighters and bombers), the sixty-knot takeoff speed applied to these types. In other navies with more capacious carriers (or, as in the case of the

USN, with a doctrine of operating from the flight deck), cruisers and battleships launched only specialized aircraft, such as scouts and spotters. Only the Royal Navy demanded so low a takeoff speed of its fighters and bombers. The requirement was relatively undemanding in the 1920s, but it made a considerable difference when high-powered monoplanes were introduced in the 1930s. For example, the sort of high rate of climb required for a deck-launched interceptor was not compatible with the low wing loading needed to limit takeoff and landing speeds. The requirement for a low takeoff speed was probably responsible for the decision to retain a biplane (i.e., high lift) configuration for the Swordfish torpedo bomber. As it happened, the catapult scheme was little implemented; it was painfully obvious that these aircraft could never practice, because they would not be recovered after battle. However, the RN adapted to the consequences of the sixty-knot launch speed without questioning its necessity, probably because the lack of an analytical learning process meant there was no way to prove how harmful the takeoff speed limitation was.[8]

Limited fleet aircraft capacity equated to limited naval aircraft production runs and, we think, to limited interest in developing new types. The counterargument is that, in at least some categories, the Royal Navy of the early and middle 1930s was quite on a par with others. It began to fall behind as aircraft technology moved toward highly loaded, high-powered monoplanes, which had high landing and takeoff speeds. The sixty-knot and weight limits began to make it impossible for the Fleet Air Arm to take advantage of the improvements in aircraft technology.

HIGHER AIRCRAFT performance had another consequence for the air defense of carriers. In common with other navies, the Royal Navy of the 1920s expected to launch interceptors to deal with approaching bombers. Air warning would be provided by lookouts on destroyers and cruisers well away from the carrier. For example, in a 1930 exercise (AF), destroyers were disposed ten nautical miles from the capital ships to provide sufficient warning (in this case, mainly to gun crews). In 1931 the fleet tried sector patrols by spotter/reconnaissance aircraft, which achieved good results. In good visibility, these four to six aircraft ten to twenty nautical miles from the fleet could spot an air striking force in time to direct fighters and to warn antiaircraft gunners. In eight exercises, fighter patrols achieved 67 percent success in early interceptions before bombers could reach the fleet. Standing orders called for fighters to orbit above the fleet and to attack without restriction, breaking off only when antiaircraft fire became too hot, but not coming within automatic weapon range.[9]

In theory, a combination of air and surface lookouts should have provided good warning even in heavy cloud conditions. As "Progress in Tactics 1934" warned, "It is impossible, however, to provide any guarantee that the fleet will have warning of, or air protection from, air attack. Under the worst conditions, those of heavy cloud banks combined with good visibility, it is unlikely to do so." Calculations showed that eight aircraft in forty-five-degree sectors at twelve nautical miles from the fleet provided 100 percent warning; an exercise with five aircraft provided 70 percent warning, which agreed well with the calculation. It was assumed that attackers would first sight their objective at ten to fifteen nautical miles, working around in a circle to find the appropriate course. That made the twelve-nautical-mile patrol so effective against most forms of attack. High-altitude bombers, by contrast, sometimes escaped detection altogether (but their effectiveness against maneuvering ships was a matter of dispute). Exercises, then, showed that twelve nautical miles was the minimum acceptable patrol radius and that the aerial pickets would have to fly very intensively to maintain their patrol.

The U.S. Navy adopted the picket idea briefly in 1938, using it to justify increasing the number of fighters per carrier. By 1937 the British had concluded that the air patrol intended to intercept an enemy's air striking force could be flown off only when attack seemed likely (to conserve flying endurance). The air patrol would be directed by a specified officer on board a fighter control ship, normally the carrier, who would communicate with the leader of the air patrol. This policy was adopted, albeit much more effectively, after radar appeared. Deck-launched fighters would be used to intercept and drive off enemy reconnaissance aircraft, because standing patrols could not possibly be maintained continuously. These duties were quite apart from the important role of defending British spotting and observation aircraft while denying the airspace above a surface battle to those of the enemy.[10]

Exercises in 1933 had shown that such spotters could cue fighters on standing patrol over the fleet. Unfortunately, carriers had limited fuel supplies, so they could not hope to maintain fighter patrols for very long. The higher the performance of the fighters, moreover, the greater their thirst for gasoline, and hence the less time a given ship's aviation fuel reserves would last. "Progress in Tactics 1934" concluded that the fleet at sea could not rely on fighters to protect it and hence had to depend on its own resources in the form of antiaircraft guns. Radar changed the situation, because fighters could be held on deck until attackers were detected. A 1933 exercise showed that a carrier could keep her fighters on deck if she could be provided with fifteen minutes' warning. That amounted to a warning range of about twenty-five nautical miles for a hundred-knot bomber (like a Swordfish), which was within the capacity of the standing air patrol, but it would have meant fifty nautical miles for the two-hundred-knot bomber of the late 1930s. Intercepting the faster bomber turned out to require radar. "Progress in Tactics" also pointed out that the air patrol could be ineffective in bad weather.

Moreover, carriers' capacity for aviation fuel was limited because aviation gasoline (especially the higher-octane, more volatile types) was so dangerous; it had to be carried in special double tanks. The danger of explosions and fires was very real, as war experience would later demonstrate. The World War I carriers were intended to carry their gasoline supplies in standard cans rather than in bulk stowage. In 1938 a generational change in British naval aircraft led to a demand for much increased gasoline stowage, which was extremely difficult to meet. The theoretical requirement was sufficient fuel for a month's operation (sixty hours for a torpedo/spotter/reconnaissance aircraft, forty-five for a fighter)—hardly continuous patrolling, as later experience would show. The crisis came when the theoretical hourly rate rose from thirty to thirty-five gallons.[11]

As aircraft performance improved, deck-launched interceptor schemes became less and less practical. Lookouts would provide too little warning time, and aircraft might fly over clouds. The common land tactic of mounting standing patrols was ruled out by limited carrier aviation fuel supplies, limited fighter endurance, limited fighter numbers, and the slow British deck cycle. Like the other carrier navies, the Royal Navy came to have little faith in the ability of carrier-borne interceptors to deal with fast bombers. The universal solution was to try to find and hit the other navy's carrier before being attacked. Thus the prewar Royal Navy placed enormous emphasis on very long range scouting and virtually none on high-performance carrier-based interceptors. It saw fighters mainly as strike escorts, to counter any possible enemy fighter opposition near the target.

Signals intelligence was another important technical factor that influenced carrier air operations. During World War I, the Royal Navy was extraordinarily successful in intercepting and exploiting German radio signals.

Painfully aware of the vulnerability of radio communications, the postwar Royal Navy emphasized radio silence, which particularly limited air operations. For example, a carrier had to maneuver into the wind to launch and recover her aircraft. If she had to remain within visual signaling range of a battle fleet running on some other course, she could not turn into the wind to keep launching or landing aircraft for very long. This point was very forcefully made in "Progress in Tactics" for 1931, in an essay by an officer of HMS *Glorious*, explaining air operations. The introduction of arrester gear in British carriers in the mid-1930s was justified partly because it allowed a carrier to recover aircraft without leaving the fleet to run into the wind. Before that, British carriers had functioned without any arrester gear (World War I gear intended mainly to hold the airplane to the deck after it landed was abandoned in the early 1920s). The U.S. Navy, of course, had adopted its own arrester gear for a very different reason, to allow aircraft to land without crashing into others already parked forward.

Another drawback to radio silence was that it made aircraft navigation relatively difficult. For long-range operation, the Royal Navy therefore had always preferred multiseat aircraft, which could carry a navigator or trained observer in addition to the pilot. In 1930, the Fleet Air Arm was operating a mixture of long-endurance (five-hour) spotter/reconnaissance aircraft (S/R), single-seat torpedo bombers (TB), and short-endurance (two-hour) single-seat fighters. The TBs were single-seaters because existing engines lacked sufficient power to lift both a heavy torpedo and a second crewman. Because the pilot could not be expected to navigate, the S/Rs had to lead the torpedo bombers to their targets. They lacked performance because their spotting and reconnaissance roles both required long endurance, hence heavy fuel loads. The Fleet Air Arm hoped to shift to a new generation, to consist of two-seat fighter/reconnaissance (F/R) and torpedo bomber (TB) and a higher-performance short-range single-seat fighter. None would have quite the endurance (in hours) of the S/R, but all would be faster, so that the new F/R (three and a half hours, at 110 vs. 90 kn) could go almost as far (385 vs. 450 nm). The new fighter was the Hawker Nimrod, the last single-seat fighter to be designed specifically for the Royal Navy until well into World War II. (The later Gloster Gladiator was a stopgap bought while the two-seat Skua was being built.) The Hawker Nimrod therefore marks the end of the earlier carrier interceptor line of development. The 1930 carrier air plan included no spotters; presumably they would have been carried aboard battleships or cruisers.[12] The F/R was the Hawker Osprey; the TB was the relatively unsuccessful Seal. Two years later Fairey made the revolutionary proposal that the same airplane could conduct long-range reconnaissance and also spot and deliver torpedoes (it was called a TSR). It became the Swordfish.

At least until the advent of really powerful engines in the late 1930s, the effect of the second crewman was to limit performance drastically. Thus the World War II two-seat fighters, the Fairey Fulmar and Firefly, were easily outperformed by contemporary land-based aircraft. However, the demand for low takeoff (and therefore landing) speed was almost equally devastating. It demanded very large wings, and it limited maximum speed and, for that matter, rate of climb.

Airplanes operate in envelopes defined by maximums and minimums for stall and takeoff speeds. Envelope size is limited. Maximum speed, for example, is constrained by the shape of the aircraft (which affects drag), the configuration of the plane (whether it is carrying bombs externally or has its landing gear down), engine power, and the plane's gross weight (structure weight plus fuel and weapon load). In 1939 Director, Naval Air Division (DAD), stung by complaints that the Admiralty's demands for two-seaters were ruining performance, released a specification for a single-seater that would still have to meet standard requirements for range and takeoff speed. He suggested that it would differ very little from the unsatisfactory two-seaters. The Blackburn Firebrand, which met the specification, proved his point. It ended up as a torpedo bomber.

The prewar or early-war mix of British carrier aircraft seems odd compared to that of other navies, but it did have a clear inner logic, based upon the kind of fleet action that Royal Navy officers thought they would face in wartime. Their thoughts, however, were not subject to the kind of analysis and testing that the USN conducted during this same period. The primary roles of the Fleet Air Arm were to find the enemy battle fleet and to damage its battleships badly enough to slow it down. There also was an interest in air superiority over the gun battle (assuming that it took place in daytime). Helped by air spotting, battleships could make hits at greater ranges. Enemy spotters had to be neutralized, if only to prevent the enemy's battleships from doing decisive damage before the British ships could get into action. At one point the Admiralty wanted a three-seat spotter-fighter, which would both spot and destroy enemy spotters, but it was ruled out as impractical.

The only air weapon that could do a battleship much damage was the torpedo—a very heavy device that only a specialized airplane could lift. Torpedo attacks were difficult, partly because a torpedo was not much faster than its target. The prewar Royal Navy well understood the problem and developed a solution: a gyro-stabilized Monoplane Air Tail, which could guide a torpedo in a straight line over a considerable distance before it hit the water. In common with other navies, it also developed a magnetic exploder, which should have made single torpedo hits extremely lethal.[13] By the late 1930s, torpedo attack exercises were quite successful. Geoffrey Till describes a 1938 torpedo and dive-bomber attack on a battle line by twenty-seven Swordfish plus Skua dive-bombers: four of the seven ships were "hit," and all were forced out of line.[14] Of course it was impossible, on the basis of such exercises, to say how well attacks could be pressed home in the face of intense antiaircraft fire. Nor do the British seem to have realized just how vulnerable the slow Swordfish would be to well-directed fighters.[15]

Because the torpedo was by far the heaviest load a carrier airplane had to lift, the torpedo bomber was affected most dramatically by the speed and weight restrictions that the Royal Navy had imposed on itself. That is why the Swordfish seems the most egregious case of British naval aviation failure. Airplanes like the two-seat Fulmar fighter might be criticized as inadequate, but only the Swordfish seemed antediluvian.

By the early 1930s it was clear that the best way to hit a moving ship was by dive-bombing. The pilot literally aimed the airplane at a ship. As a side benefit, a dive-bomber was extremely difficult to hit on the way down, simply because it was changing altitude so rapidly. That the Admiralty was aware of dive-bombing is clear from the foreign section of "Progress in Tactics 1931" (e.g., the statement that the U.S. Navy considered it more important than torpedo bombing). Till (*Air Power and the Royal Navy*) reports that U.S. dive-bombers impressed a British naval visitor that same year. In 1933 the Royal Navy tried to compare the merits of level bombing and dive-bombing, using two-seat Osprey fighters to simulate high-performance bombers. The immediate conclusions seem to have been that high-altitude bombers could not be detected in time and that dive-bombers could be quite effective.

Before 1933, Fleet Air Arm tactical bombing trials had not been realistic. Pilots had been allowed to take their time approaching targets and sometimes even made practice runs before dropping their unarmed ordnance. In 1933, however, more realistic trials were conducted against the radio-controlled target ship *Centurion*. High-altitude level bombers hit *Centurion* with 22 percent of their practice bombs. This was a strong start; in 1934, the comparable figure was only 15 percent. So it appeared that a maneuvering ship might well be able to avoid bombs dropped from high altitude. The ship's antiaircraft fire might also break up attacks by high-level bombers because, as the aircraft approached the ship, they had to stay in regular and compact formation—just the sort of formation that heavier antiaircraft guns were designed to deal with. By 1937 the British were quite pessimistic, particularly given the limited numbers of aircraft aboard their carriers. According to "Progress in Tactics 1938," it would take eleven bombs dropped by dive-bombers or thirty bombs dropped by level bombers flying at ten thousand feet to score a single hit on a cruiser. By comparison, a torpedo bomber could be certain of hitting if it could get to within 1,000 to 1,250 yards of a target and launch its torpedo from an angle that was not too fine on the bow or stern. Attack by torpedo bombers was effective so long as the target ship did not steam at a speed greater than twenty-two knots. This apparent tactical superiority of the torpedo bomber accounts for both the investment in the Fairey Swordfish and the organization of Swordfish squadrons into subflights of three aircraft each.[16]

Unfortunately, dive-bombing heavily stressed the bomber, so that only very limited loads could be carried. And, in order to make hits, the bomber had to drop its load at fairly low altitude, so that the bomb reached only very limited velocity. The combination of the bomb's low velocity and limited weight made it most unlikely that a dive-bomber could destroy a heavily armored ship. Its bombs would lack the punch to crash through the stiff, thick armored decks of battleships. The Royal Navy tried to solve this particular problem with a novel weapon, the "B" (buoyant) bomb, which would be dropped near a ship, then rise to explode under it, rather like a mine. Such under-the-keel attacks can be extremely effective; they are probably the only way a small bomb could possibly sink a large ship. Effective attack required a sophisticated sight, because the bomb had to be offset from the target to rise under it. It seems likely that the Royal Navy's complaints that the Air Ministry would not develop an effective dive-bombing sight really refer to a sight suited to dive-bombing with "B" bombs. Though much was expected of the "B" bomb, it was never successful, and all stocks were destroyed at the end of World War II. However, the dive-bomber, even if it could not carry a heavy weapon, was and remained the ideal anticarrier weapon, so long as carrier flight decks were unarmored.

The dive-bomber, the Blackburn Skua, was much like its contemporaries; indeed, its characteristics would seem to show the Royal Navy was well up-to-date. The Skua was broadly comparable to the U.S. Northrop BT, the direct predecessor of the extremely successful Douglas Dauntless (SBD). Because carrier capacity was so limited, the Skua had to double as a fighter. In fact, it was actually called a fighter because it replaced the two-seat Osprey F/R airplane. Sadly, it became apparent that, against aircraft such as the Japanese A5M ("Claude") seen in combat over China after 1937, the Skua could not possibly perform well enough. Few Skuas were built, and they did not survive for long. The Admiralty therefore tried another combination. It asked that the torpedo- and dive-bombing roles be combined; the fighter was separated out. Again, the results were less than happy. The new universal bomber was another biplane, the Albacore. It was never particularly successful. The companion two-seat fighter was the Fulmar.[17]

The Fulmar fighter, too, seemed unimpressive. In 1940 it could barely outrun the modern twin-engine bombers the Germans and Italians sent against British units in the Mediterranean. The Fleet Air Arm hurriedly adapted the Hurricane (itself no sterling performer) as a carrier interceptor. However, the Admiralty could point out that the interceptor role itself was newer than the Fulmar. The two-seat fighter was conceived as a strike escort. Because the strike aircraft, particularly the Swordfish, were so slow, the fighters supporting them had to navigate independently to the target area. They needed that second-seat crewman.

The Fulmar seemed bizarre in comparison with higher-performance single-seat fighters, such as the U.S. Wildcat and the Japanese A6M Zero. However, the latter were also compromises, albeit tilted toward interception rather than strike support. The U.S. Navy, although it had experimented before WWII with aerial pickets like those tried by the Royal Navy, was fortunate in that, by the time it entered the war, it had radar. Given radar, interception was a very practical proposition. As a strike escort, the single-seat Wildcat performed badly at Midway. Pilots could not navigate well enough to join up with the strike they were expected to protect. The result was the massacre of the torpedo bombers. The U.S. dive-bombers—not the fighters—saved the day because all the Japanese fighters, having gone down to sea level to deal with the torpedo planes, could not rise to intercept them at high altitude, where the dive-bombers were vulnerable. It helped a great deal when a new generation of attack aircraft (Avengers and Helldivers) entered U.S.

service in 1942 and 1944, respectively, with speeds closer to the cruising speed of fighters, so that strikes could fly out together. The new two thousand horsepower–class engines made these aircraft possible.

Midway was a case of ineffective fighter control, probably due to a lack of radar (the Japanese apparently relied on lookouts). A radar-based fighter control system would have withheld fighters to deal with the dive-bombers. It can be argued that the Admiralty's prewar position—that fighter interception without radar might well be fatally flawed—was borne out by the Japanese experience. As for the fighters, the Fulmars might not have done brilliantly once they arrived, but Midway showed that something might be far better than nothing. The Admiralty knew that it would be difficult to build two-seat escort fighters to meet enemy single-seat carrier fighters on even terms, but that is just what it tried to do. It seems to have doubted that any other navy could produce satisfactory high-performance carrier aircraft.

In October 1938, British technical intelligence (as reflected in CB.1815, "World naval vessels and naval aircraft") credited the Japanese Navy with the following carrier types: Type 95 biplane fighter (600 hp, 190 mph at sea level: A4N), Type 96 monoplane fighter (900 hp, 260 mph at 7,000 ft: A5M [Claude]), Type 89 torpedo bomber (650 hp, 139.2 mph at sea level: B2M), Type 92 torpedo bomber (600/730 hp, 136 mph at sea level: B3Y), and Type 94 light bomber (460 hp, no performance data, 500 lb of bombs: D1A). Listed, but with no data available, were new Type 96 torpedo and dive-bombers, B4Y and D1A. Both were biplanes, and on the outbreak of war in 1941 the Royal Navy apparently believed that both were the main operational types. In fact, by 1938 the monoplane Type 97 torpedo bomber (B5N ["Kate"]) was in service; the early wartime monoplane dive-bomber was Type 99, D3A ("Val").

Of the others listed above, power output of the Type 95 fighter was somewhat underrated, but speed was accurate; this airplane was comparable with the British Hawker Fury. Data on B2M and B3Y were reasonably accurate. The Swordfish had a comparable rated performance. In the case of Type 94, the main (and significant) omission was that it was a dive-bomber. The only really impressive airplane of the lot was A5M (misidentified as a copy of the U.S. Northrop XFT fighter), and the British somewhat overrated its speed. Even so, it was clearly much faster than the Skua (which was about to enter service) and about as fast as the later Fulmar.

The tables in CB.1815 do not provide any indication of time to altitude, nor do any contemporary references, official or otherwise, give any indication of relative maneuverability, which might have more clearly revealed the superiority of the A5M over contemporary British aircraft. British technical air intelligence thus was very good at describing aircraft in current service (as seen in China, where the British had excellent contacts) but apparently could not penetrate the Japanese defense industry to obtain data on aircraft just entering service or to perceive trends in development. Although the Swordfish did not compare with the new U.S. monoplane torpedo bomber (the Douglas TBD Devastator), the British could reasonably have argued that they were working under very different conditions, and in any case they were unlikely to meet U.S. aircraft in combat. Japan was very clearly the main naval enemy.[18]

For its part, the prewar Royal Navy had become convinced that the fleet would never have enough warning of air attack, so there was little point in buying interceptors. Even warning might not suffice. Till, in his *Air Power and the Royal Navy,* cites a 10 April 1938 exercise in which *Hood* was successfully attacked despite having a screen of eleven fighters aloft at the time. There seems to have been a general expectation that fighters would be unable to intercept bombers. It took radar to change the situation. "Progress in Tactics 1939" still referred to defensive fighter patrols: on one occasion an air striking force successfully attacked a carrier because her defensive fighters were busy driving off shadowing aircraft. The Admiralty can be faulted for not having realized that it needed a carrier interceptor almost as soon as radar appeared aboard ships in 1938. Unfortunately, no surviving staff papers address this issue. Single-seat fighters (ex-RAF Gladiators) did appear in the Mediterranean in 1938, but only to fill a gap until Skuas entered service. The Royal Navy did try to buy Spitfires in 1939, but only to defend the shore base at Scapa Flow against air attack, not particularly to serve at sea.[19]

The next generation of British naval aircraft was so long delayed by World War II that it reached service after the Royal Navy had adopted very different U.S. aircraft. The next-generation two-seat fighter was the Griffon-powered Firefly. Its companion combination bomber (and reconnaissance aircraft) was the big Merlin-powered Barracuda, originally designed for the more powerful Exe engine. It suffered severe teething problems and did not enter service until 1943. Like the Albacore, it was less than successful. Because the wartime Royal Navy emphasized its most important weapon, the torpedo, it kept the Swordfish when Skuas disappeared. Later it depended heavily on the U.S. Avenger.

Both Albacore and Barracuda were widely condemned. It is only fair to point out, however, that no other navy was particularly successful in developing a combination dive-bomber and torpedo bomber. The U.S. Helldiver (SB2C) dive-bomber was credited with torpedo-bomber capacity (the Royal Navy badly wanted to adopt it), but it was extremely unsuccessful. The U.S. Navy was fortunate in learning early the advantage of having much more carrier capacity, so it could afford separate dive-bombers and torpedo bombers.

The way the prewar Royal Navy was organized and the way its staff officers conducted their analyses prevented the RN from seeing that it had painted itself into a corner by limiting both the number and performance of its aircraft. In 1931 an attempt was made to adopt U.S.-style deck operations, which required special arrester gear and barriers.[20] The Royal Navy bought the equipment, but it could not get the Air Ministry to recertify the ships for larger air complements. The 1931 edition of "Progress in Tactics" included a section on foreign tactics, including operating practices. The U.S. portion mentioned that "the number of aircraft in carriers is proportionately much higher than in our Navy, largely due to the practice of storing some aircraft permanently on deck." The U.S. Navy is credited with about 273 shipboard (including battleship and cruiser) aircraft, compared with 153 in the Fleet Air Arm. It appears that the British were not aware that the U.S. Navy had significantly more aircraft to back up each sea-based one, nor do they seem to have been aware of the magnitude of U.S. Navy pilot reserves.

"Progress in Tactics 1935" described massed U.S. air operations; *Saratoga* operated as many as 108, though this was considered excessive ("sixty aircraft are normally stowed on her deck when ready for action. It is not considered unsafe to carry this number on the flying deck as far as weather is concerned"). Moreover,

> The Americans express surprise that we do not stow some of our aircraft on the flight deck of the carrier and so increase the numbers carried. They remark that we carry aircraft exposed on our catapults and we could do the same on the flight deck where we have all the resources of the carrier to maintain them. One American opinion holds that the carrier will only be wanted to give her maximum effort once in a war, and at this time the greatest number of aircraft will be required.

This edition also mentioned the new Douglas TBD: "a new monoplane capable of carrying a torpedo up to 2,000 lb weight and stated to be very fast has been designed for use in carriers. The first few aircraft have been delivered and are very highly thought of." Like other victims of steeply improving aircraft technology, the TBD would be considered fatally obsolete by 1942 (by which time the Swordfish seemed comparatively primitive). But the Royal Navy had been hurt years earlier, at the onset of the Great Depression, when the British government, desperate to reduce defense spending, had chosen to gamble that an extension of the Washington Treaty would actually reduce carrier tonnage below the limit set in 1922. When this gamble failed to pay off, it was hard to catch up. To make matters worse, the RAF feared that an expanded Fleet Air Arm (on paper) might cut into its bomber force.

What is quite significant, though, is that no one in the Admiralty ever seems to have realized the connection between low performance, operating practice, and specifications. A partial explanation is that the Royal Navy had no technical department—like the Plans Division in the USN's Bureau of Aeronautics—that could evaluate the consequences of such choices. The larger explanation is the absence of interaction among a limited constellation of organizations with the necessary expertise and commitment to naval aviation. The Admiralty, for example, lacked an organization like the U.S. Navy's General Board, which could both ask the right questions and get answers. This failing was due partly to a traditional (and, alas, previously successful) practice in the RN of relying on outstanding and perceptive flag officers to force issues into established administrative processes.[21]

The RN's apparent inability to integrate technical data from different sources was also due, however, to organizational assumptions within the RN about how to deal with uncertainty. In particular, RN staff consulted with their Air Ministry counterparts regarding aircraft characteristics and the development of aircraft technology. But the Air Ministry staff could not grasp the operational imperatives of carrier operations because they were not part of a process that would compel them to face those imperatives. When the two staffs disagreed, they argued their respective points. They did not have an "impartial" method—such as special simulations—to bring them together in a shared analytic enterprise.

After 1918, technical aircraft expertise resided in the Air Ministry, the parent organization of the RAF. Surviving records show clearly that the Air Ministry technical departments were always glad to review proposed naval aircraft specifications for practicality. However, the experts knew little of naval operations. They could not, and were not expected to, comment on the larger consequences of particular naval choices. Only interaction among agencies, like that found in the USN, could have brought the necessary expertise to the process—alas, too often just the exchange of memoranda—of deciding what sort of aircraft the Royal Navy needed.

Instead, the Royal Navy had departments of naval construction, naval ordnance, and naval engineering. Although it might be argued that each made some poor technical decisions, at least each was available to advise the Board of Admiralty on the technical consequences of particular decisions. The Board of Admiralty, like the General Board of the U.S. Navy, was faced with great strategic and technological uncertainties. The difference was that, in aviation, the USN's General Board could (and did) always turn to a variety of experts—from the Bureau of Aeronautics, from the fleet, from the other technical bureaus, and even from the aviation industry. The need to open alternatives to the General Board was why Rear Admiral Moffett had worked so hard to create BuAer and then to make it part of a larger network of information exchange and discussion.[22]

Absent the proper institutional setting, could intelligence on foreign navies' carrier operations and aircraft have spurred a reexamination of RN carrier specifications? Each year, every Admiralty department issued a progress report. Examples include "Progress in Gunnery," "Progress in Torpedo/ASW," "Progress in the Fleet Air Arm" and "Progress in Tactics." "Progress in Tactics" seems to have been unique in including, from 1931 on, a section on foreign practices. Clearly it was intended for readers who might expect to face foreign navies in battle. The technical reports, such as "Progress in the Fleet Air Arm," contain no foreign data whatever; it seems likely that intelligence information was much too sensitive to place in the hands of ordinary staff officers. For example, the "Foreign Tactics" section generally carried a special notice, such as, "attention is called to the great importance of keeping secret the fact that this information is in our possession." Intelligence content may explain why, except for the 1939 edition, prewar issues of "Progress in Tactics" are not in the Public Record Office (PRO). The PRO run of "Progress in the Fleet Air Arm" seems incomplete, but the issues that have survived have no foreign intelligence content whatever. The 1937 edition of "Progress in Tactics" refers to further Intelligence Reports in the CB (Confidential Books) series, but no such materials have been released to the Public Record Office; nor have they surfaced at the Naval Historical Branch of the Ministry of Defence. It is therefore difficult to judge British naval views of foreign navies apart from the special sections of "Progress in Tactics."[23]

The intelligence sections of "Progress in Tactics" show a keen and, in many cases, an apparently accurate appreciation of other navies' ideas, particularly those developed by the U.S. Navy. Mirror imaging was generally avoided. It is tempting to ask why the Royal Navy, which knew that its air arm was so far behind, did not demand more. That begs a question: Just how widely was information diffused through the navy and particularly through its small and therefore hard-pressed air staff? That is, did they know what they needed to know when they could best use that information? It is a vital question but a difficult one to answer accurately. The same holds for the U.S. and Japanese navies, the RN's competitors. Intelligence gathered was not necessarily intelligence used—or used properly.

Intelligence publications and even the open technical literature often provide the interested operator with reasonably accurate information that, regrettably, has no apparent impact on decision making. Perhaps the impact of day-to-day experience on operators is so great that they automatically mirror-image unless distinctive foreign forms of reality are forced upon them. That was certainly true of the U.S. Navy in its night surface-ship battles with the Imperial Japanese Navy around Guadalcanal in 1942. In the ten years before World War II, the U.S. Navy's leaders had learned, through a series of major fleet exercises, that it was nearly impossible to protect large formations of surface ships from night attacks by "enemy" destroyers firing torpedoes. As the official 1934 *War Instructions* noted, "At night the superior or equal force risks forfeiture of the superiority or equality of its most valuable asset, its coordinated hitting power."[24] That was the problem.

Unfortunately, the U.S. Navy's doctrine assumed that the systems the Japanese could bring to bear on this problem—and so use it to their advantage—were basically the same as those in the hands of the USN. But the Japanese developed a torpedo, the infamous Type-93, which had the range and striking power of a battleship shell. With that weapon, Japanese destroyers could and did stay outside U.S. Navy defenses and, while undetected, bombard the American formations as soon as the latter, following doctrine, revealed their positions by using searchlights and firing their guns. It took about a year of combat experience for the U.S. Navy to grasp the solution to this tactical dilemma.

Our point is that military doctrine deliberately produces what students of bureaucracies call "programmed" behavior: action designed intentionally for use in *expected* situations. Flawed doctrine will produce the wrong kind of programming, and the months or years of practicing the wrong kind of programming will inhibit rapid change. One way of forestalling inappropriate programming is to hold realistic simulations and exercises. As we have noted, this is precisely what the U.S. Navy did at the Naval War College and in its fleet exercises, and what historian Jon Sumida has shown the Royal Navy did, as well, with its battleships. The question, then, remains: if the Royal Navy had a *systematic process* for evaluating fleet tactics, why couldn't that kind of process reveal the weaknesses of the Fleet Air Arm?

Part of a likely answer is that the Royal Navy was particularly unlucky in its timing. Its peculiar operating practices and ideas did not detract in a major way from its fighting power before the mid-1930s and the beginning of the steep improvement in aircraft engines that produced high-performance monoplanes. At just this time, finances contracted, denying the Royal Navy the chance to increase the rated capacities of its carriers (and thus to abandon multirole aircraft concepts such as those that condemned the Skua, a perfectly good dive-bomber). Then rearmament, oriented mainly against Germany, presented the RAF with ample reason to constrict purchases of naval aircraft.

At this time the Royal Navy still considered Japan the most likely enemy. Unfortunately, Japanese security improved, so that information on the airplanes the fleet would have to face in the Far East was limited to types in combat in China. That would have been fine (the Japanese put their best current aircraft into service there), except that technology was changing so fast that the best were but a shadow of what would enter service a few years later. Moreover, the rate of change increased drastically just as the small naval air staff was concentrating on supporting the Admiralty's attempt to split the Fleet Air Arm from the RAF. The fleet itself was badly strained, first by crushing financial depression (no 1933 edition of "Progress in Tactics" appeared) and then by the Ethiopian crisis, which began in the fall of 1935 (no 1936 edition of "Progress in Tactics" appeared). Under these circumstances, it was difficult to imagine anyone pausing to look at the larger picture, particularly when the RN was not organized to do so with the appropriate combination of technical and tactical insight. Indeed, the progress that *was* made in tactics and technology may have been rather miraculous under the circumstances.

Certain problems that arose in World War II seem to bear out the view that the Royal Navy could not get its operators and technical specialists to work together effectively *before* the war. Quite aside from inferior naval aircraft, the Royal Navy found itself with a very poor antiaircraft fire control system (the consequence of an early decision favoring what seemed a simple and robust approach) and with obsolete and inadequate machinery—the latter leaving the RN unable, among other things, to fuel at sea, with terrible consequences for fleet mobility. In each case, what seemed a simple and reasonable decision had unexpected technical consequences: negative "unknown unknowns."

The damage resulting from poor cooperation between the engineers and the operationally trained officers was apparently serious; this was the argument of Vice Adm. Sir Louis le Bailly in his memoir, *From Fisher to the Falklands.* Le Bailly described a failed prewar attempt to bring the engineers into the executive branch of the Royal Navy, blaming the failure particularly for the poor state of Royal Navy machinery technology in 1939. He strongly implied that the dominance of the technologically barely literate executive branch was to blame for the other failures cited. The author of the official British history of the Royal Navy in World War II, then Capt. Stephen Roskill, a gunnery officer, was particularly critical of the prewar antiaircraft fire control system. On the other hand, British radars and sonars (asdics) were quite good, as were the torpedoes, so clearly some technical branches performed quite well.[25] That is, the hypothesis put forward by le Bailly and others is too simple by far.

The inferiority of World War II Royal Navy carrier aircraft, despite the vigor of the British aircraft industry and the pioneering approach of the Royal Navy, can be traced to the organizational arrangements that generated a series of mistaken technical decisions, beginning with the assessment of carrier capability. This situation persisted because the Royal Navy lacked any effective organizational means of connecting technical choices to operational capabilities; it had to rely for most of its technical advice on an organization (the RAF) with little appreciation of how to go about understanding naval issues. Unlike the British army, however, the Royal Navy did not lose sight of the role of aviation in support. The reason is that the navy had already made a major investment in carriers and had also gained enough experience to show that it needed a naval air arm. There was too much "stuff" there for the RAF to ignore or eliminate.

Why did air-mindedness persist in the post-1918 Royal Navy despite so many obstacles? The navy was a functional organization dedicated to operations at sea, using whatever technology was available. Many senior officers realized just what aircraft could offer, and they fought hard to maintain and expand a naval air arm, whatever its ownership. After all, without this intense interest, the Royal Navy would never have fought, as it successfully did, to regain control of the Fleet Air Arm, which it obtained in 1939. British naval interest in aviation shows not only in continued support for carrier construction but also in intense work on naval air weapons, such as a very superior torpedo and the inventive (if ultimately failed) "B" bomb.

The RAF was a very different organization. Its unifying theme was the air, not the surface operations that aircraft might support. From the first, it had to fight for resources against the two senior services. Its argument had to be that it could operate independently, and that led it inevitably to concentrate on strategic or deep tactical bombing and, to a much lesser degree, on the air defense of the United Kingdom: the missions that it could carry out without the other services.

The RAF grew directly out of the former Royal Flying Corps and particularly out of its long-range bomber element. In this case, much more than in that of the Royal Navy, the elimination of a class of officers (specialists in ground support) could also kill off air-mindedness in a service (the British army) and could insure against further demands on the RAF from that direction. The effect was probably not altogether intended, but it had profound implications. It probably effectively eliminated any potential for British development of a blitzkrieg technique, whatever the advances in tank design the British might have achieved. Because it was British officers, particularly J. F. C. Fuller, who effectively invented the blitzkrieg idea, the sense of a failed military revolution is very strong. The question of what happened to the British army's efforts to put together what we now call a blitzkrieg force is worth careful study.

A military revolution involves much more than technology. It is a particular *application* of technology, through new or altered forms of organization, that radically changes the overall military situation. The key to the success of carrier aviation was that those responsible for gaining military objectives recognized that a new technology, the carrier-airplane combination, could help them do their job far more effectively. The story of the Fleet Air Arm shows that, once the idea had set in, those who might have been considered grossly un-air-minded—that is, far from the new technology—fought hard to retain it. That the Fleet Air Arm did not do as well technically as its competitor in the USN can be laid largely to the absence of interacting organizations that would have allowed the proper level of assessment of professional technical advice within the Royal Navy. The absence of such organizational arrangements permitted a chain of unfortunate technological errors to remain uncorrected until World War II. An analogue is the surface fleet of the USN, which was unprepared for its encounters with the Japanese. Even so, the Fleet Air Arm proved quite effective in 1939–40. It had been able to apply much of the carrier revolution.

The senior officers of the Royal Navy in 1914 grasped at the new airplane technology because it promised to solve problems that other naval technology could not solve. They focused more on the tactical problems than on the joys of riding battleships or submarines or, for that matter, airplanes. Fliers within the Royal Navy were, quite naturally, enthusiasts for their new technology; like their American counterparts, they loved to fly. Because they existed within a larger organization, however, they had to serve the tactical ends of that organization. In so doing, they convinced senior officers who had never flown at all of the value of aircraft. In the RAF, the air enthusiasts were freed from the constraints of playing particular, well-defined tactical roles. The result of these differing perspectives was a lack of realistic thinking across all the military arenas where aviation was to play a crucial role in the next war.

A very early photograph of *Langley*'s complicated arresting gear. There are fore-and-aft and cross-deck wires. Note how the fore-and-aft wires are held above the deck by thin blocks. Some of the blocks have been knocked down by the aircraft. *U.S. Naval Institute*

Langley with a deckload of aircraft. Under the leadership of Capt. Joseph M. Reeves (later Admiral Reeves), her aircraft complement was tripled—from twelve to thirty-six—and her status changed from that of an experimental carrier to an operational one. *U.S. Naval Institute*

Langley with her funnels lowered for flight operations and with a Pitcairn autogiro on deck, 1931. The autogiro was briefly a competitor with the small seaplanes carried by cruisers for the role of observation and antisubmarine patrol. But the autogiro was not a success because it could not carry bombs.
U.S. Naval Institute

The converted battle cruiser *Lexington,* shown here launching a strike of Martin T4M torpedo bombers. Unlike *Langley, Lexington* and her sister ship *Saratoga* had enclosed hangars below the flight deck. The lack of adequate ventilation for their hangars was remedied in later U.S. carrier designs. Note the size of *Lexington*'s funnel, marking her as a ship of great power (over two hundred thousand shaft horsepower) and speed (thirty-four knots). *U.S. Naval Institute*

A Martin T4M torpedo bomber with its wings folded, on *Lexington* in 1928. The hooks on the aircraft's axles are visible. The hooks were intended to engage the fore-and-aft wires of the ship's arresting gear. Just behind the T4M is a dolly used to aid in shifting this very large aircraft's position on the flight deck. *U.S. Naval Historical Center*

Ranger on her trials in May 1934. Her six smokestacks, which could be rotated to the horizontal, are here standing vertically. *Ranger*'s small size—compared to *Lexington* and *Saratoga*—was at first thought optimal. But the ship was too small and too slow to steam with the larger *Enterprise* and *Yorktown* during World War II. Note her three aircraft elevators—two amidships and one right astern. *Hone collection*

Aircraft being respotted in *Ranger,* 1938. Once all incoming aircraft had landed, they were moved aft—by hand—and refueled and rearmed in preparation for another strike. *Ranger*'s funnels have been rotated to the horizontal position. *Navy Department, National Archives*

Aircraft stowed forward of *Ranger*'s crash barrier during operations in 1938. These aircraft, about to be rolled aft to prepare for further flight operations, show the "deck park" in action. The aircraft closest to the camera are part of Scouting Squadron I. *Navy Department, National Archives*

Two Curtiss SOC scout-observation aircraft being prepared for launching from the catapults of a light cruiser during World War II. Catapult aircraft were initially more plentiful in the U.S. Navy than carrier aircraft. Some, like the two shown, could carry bombs or depth charges. Between the catapults is the cover to the ship's hangar, where an additional two aircraft were housed and maintained. *U.S. Naval Institute*

Douglas TBD Devastators in line for takeoff from *Saratoga* in 1938. The Devastator, which carried a torpedo under the fuselage, was the USN's first carrier-based monoplane. An advanced design when first deployed, it was obsolescent by December 1941. *Navy Department, National Archives*

Enterprise with her air group in 1939. Note her open hangar deck and the doors to the hangar amidships, which are partly closed. Just barely visible forward is the short extension of her cross-deck catapult at the hangar deck level. The purpose of the catapult was to allow the ship to fly off an armed scout-bomber on short notice, even if she were engaged in recovering aircraft. *U.S. Naval Institute, Miller Collection*

Attack aircraft from *Enterprise* fly over their carrier. The aircraft illustrate the "pulse" of striking power that a carrier's air group could deliver—usually against enemy carriers in the initial stage of any battle between fleets or task forces. This pulse could overwhelm enemy defenses and give the initial attacker a complete victory. *U.S. Naval Institute, Miller Collection*

A Douglas P2D-1 seaplane being armed in sheltered waters by sailors from seaplane tender *Wright*. The aircraft is from patrol squadron 3, based in the Panama Canal Zone. The first models of this aircraft were actually flown from *Langley* in 1927. Protests from the U.S. Army led to its being withdrawn from regular land-based and carrier service. With floats, later models remained in service until 1937. *Navy Department, National Archives*

A crash barrier on carrier *Wasp* in 1940. Just in front of it is a cross-deck arresting gear wire. Like the arresting gear wires, the barrier wires were designed to stretch when an aircraft flew into them. When not needed, the wires folded flat against the deck. Such barriers made the deck park possible, and the deck park, in turn, revolutionized carrier operations in the U.S. Navy. *Navy Department, National Archives*

Furious, showing her short flying-off deck forward, with the much longer deck for takeoffs and landings above it. The box-like object on her upper flight deck is a small, retractable chart house. *Furious* had neither an island nor raised funnels. Smoke from the ship's fire rooms was vented from openings beneath the flight deck aft. *Navy Department, National Archives*

Another view of *Wasp*'s flight deck. Note the barrier that is raised and the arresting gear wires forward of it. USN carriers could recover aircraft over the bow as well as the stern. The small platform for the ship's landing signal officer is right forward on the starboard side, and the letters WASP are visible at the leading edge of the flight deck. *Navy Department, National Archives*

A Fairey IIIF spotter-reconnaissance aircraft flying past *Furious* in 1936, at the end of the aircraft's effective service life. Because the Fleet Air Arm lacked the large patrol seaplanes fielded by both the U.S. and Japanese navies, it had to rely on its carrier aircraft for long-range reconnaissance. *Navy Department, National Archives*

A Hawker Nimrod fighter has caught an arresting gear wire on *Furious* in 1935. The Nimrod had a water-cooled in-line engine and was the first Fleet Air Arm fighter to carry a radio. Note the rigging designed to catch any aircraft in danger of rolling off the flight deck. *Navy Department, National Archives*

A Fairey IIIF returning to *Furious.* Note the standards that suspend the arresting gear wires above the deck. The Royal Navy developed arresting gear wires, then abandoned them for a time. But the development of heavier aircraft—the Fairey IIIF weighed fifty-three hundred pounds loaded—forced the RN to turn to them again. *Navy Department, National Archives*

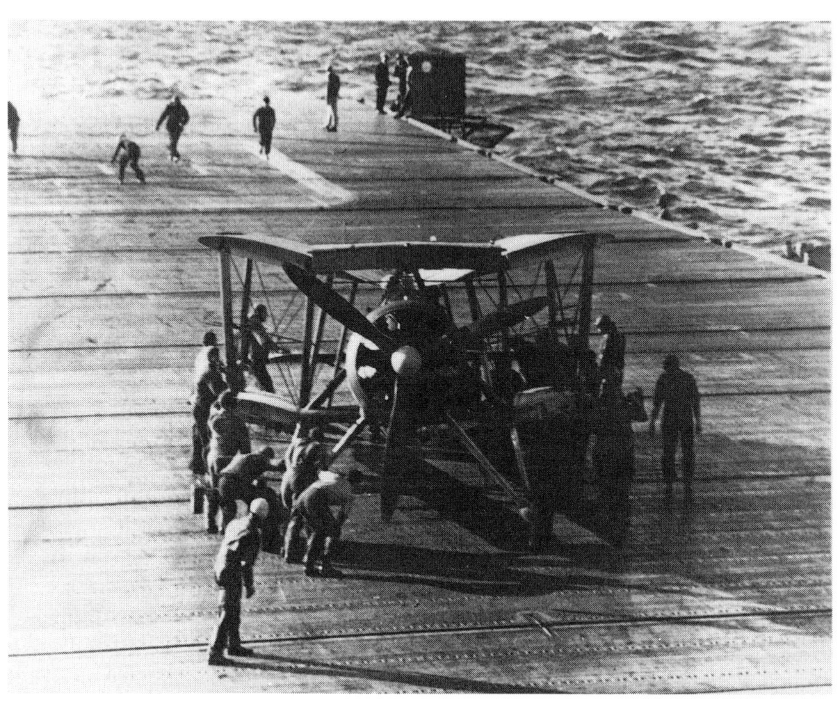

Wasp's flight-deck crew folds the wings of a Fleet Air Arm Swordfish torpedo bomber in April 1942. The U.S. carrier was ferrying Fleet Air Arm aircraft to Gibraltar. The Swordfish was a large, rugged, and maneuverable aircraft. Its nickname—"Stringbag"—belied its utility as a torpedo bomber, reconnaissance, and, in World War II, antisubmarine aircraft. *Navy Department, National Archives*

6 Two Navies on the Eve of War

AFTER TWO DECADES of uncertainties due to carrier vulnerability, treaty restrictions, and fiscal restraints, the U.S. Navy and the Royal Navy finally saw carrier aviation in the light of certain war. The relative positions of the two navies at that critical time are best reviewed in terms of those uncertainties.

The Royal Navy had jumped ahead of all its potential competitors in taking aviation to sea, but it then fell behind after its aviation arm was placed under the control of the Royal Air Force. The U.S. Navy had retraced the steps of the Royal Navy. Its first aircraft were not much more than powered kites, useful for observation but little else. The Americans were impressed and excited by what they saw in the Royal Navy once the two navies began cooperating in World War I, and U.S. Navy fliers and their seniors returned to the United States convinced that aviation had many important uses in campaigns at sea. Even as the Royal Navy was losing its aviators and aircraft to the Royal Air Force, the U.S. Navy's General Board was recommending that the secretary of the Navy support a major and sustained commitment to carrier aviation.

The 1919 General Board recommendations were a key development in U.S. carrier aviation. The utility of ship-carried aircraft as scouts and as spotters of long-range gunfire was clear to many U.S. Navy officers early on, certainly by the beginning of 1919. But ship-borne aircraft had not yet proven themselves in the attack role; any navy that committed itself to building carriers for that role in the interwar period was taking a risk. It was generally appreciated that carriers could launch fighters, which could sweep enemy scouts and spotters from the skies, conferring an advantage on the battleships of the side with carriers. However, advocates of carrier aviation in both the Royal Navy and the U.S. Navy argued that carrier aircraft and carriers were also justified as strike weapons, not just as specialized ships that supported existing battleships. Carrier advocates had to prove their point. In the U.S. Navy, they were given their chance by the recommendations of the General Board in 1919.

The Washington Treaty complicated matters, particularly for the Royal Navy. The latter had a number of other types of ships converted to aircraft carriers, such as *Eagle* and *Furious* and *Hermes,* and it lacked a standard carrier type. So the British, in the process of moving toward an optimal carrier design, were in essence frozen in place and forced to rely upon too many "carriers" that were in fact not well suited for that role; they were too slow or could not carry and launch enough aircraft to make them independent strike weapons.

The Washington Treaty was also a problem for the Americans. The U.S. Navy did get two converted battle cruisers (*Saratoga* and *Lexington*), but they were not an optimal type either. Though their great size enabled them to carry a large number of aircraft, converting them cost a great deal of money—Rear Admiral Moffett, chief of BuAer, spent some unpleasant hours explaining this to Congress—and took significantly longer than anticipated. Yet U.S. Navy aviation leaders, particularly Captain and later Rear Adm. J. M. Reeves, knew that the concept of the attack carrier had to be demonstrated even before *Lexington* and *Saratoga* were ready for service because opponents of the strike carrier concept—particularly the articulate Brig. Gen. William "Billy" Mitchell—were in full cry. The converted collier *Langley* would have to prove the concept.

Langley's flight-deck crew and air squadrons did prove it. Critical to their success in 1925 and 1926, however, was the concept of a crash barrier to protect those aircraft parked forward of the landing area, on the flight deck. The time saved by *not* sending each aircraft below as it landed was the breakthrough. Effective cross-deck arresting wires were important, too, but it was the combination of the deck park and the crash barrier that distinguished U.S. Navy carriers from their British counterparts. The Royal Navy did not develop these at that time, and so what the Americans called an "effective air effort"—the deployment of large numbers of strike aircraft—was limited by the slow recovery times of Royal Navy carriers.

It is important to remember, however, that the concept of "effective air effort" was tested first at the Naval War College and then in the fleet. The conceptually demonstrated need to fly off numbers of aircraft is what drove then Captain Reeves to change operations on *Langley.* But Reeves had no counterpart in the Royal Navy because former RN fliers were actually in the Royal Air Force by 1925, working on other problems. The difference in flight-deck practice between the two navies (based in turn on differences in the machinery of aircraft recovery) had implications for carrier tactics.

The U.S. Navy's carrier tacticians could prepare to fight and win a daytime battle between carriers such as the one they fought at Midway in 1942. By contrast, the Royal Navy's tacticians, because of their more limited numbers of aircraft, had to rely on stealth to avoid defending enemy fighters, as in the attack on the Italian fleet at Taranto in 1940.

The differences between the Royal Navy and the U.S. Navy in carrier aviation strength became obvious by the early 1930s. English-speaking moviegoers, for example, caught an interesting and exciting glimpse of U.S. Navy carrier operations in the 1932 MGM film *Hell Divers,* portions of which were filmed on *Saratoga* at Rear Admiral Moffett's insistence. Once that film hit the streets, the ability of the U.S. Navy's carriers to put large numbers of aircraft in the air all at once could not be denied. The Japanese were about to follow a similar path. The obvious difference between the RN and the USN in the numbers of carrier aircraft each had at sea added to the pressure from within the Royal Navy to reclaim control of the administration of the Fleet Air Arm.

Meanwhile, in fleet problems, the U.S. Navy was discovering, again and again, how vulnerable carriers were. In 1929 and 1930, the short range of carrier fighters and attack aircraft meant that carriers had to operate within one hundred nautical miles of an enemy force. In such a situation, a carrier steaming at high speed into the wind to recover her aircraft might well run into enemy surface forces. In the U.S. Navy fleet problems of 1933 and 1934, carriers were caught and "shelled" by "enemy" surface units because they had had to steam *toward* "enemy" forces while recovering aircraft.[1] Later, when the ranges of carrier aircraft improved, carriers remained the first targets of air attack; their vulnerability and their limited numbers made it possible for a first strike to destroy its opponent's effective air cover in one swift blow. In 1939, in Fleet Problem XX, communications intelligence personnel on carrier *Ranger* used high-frequency direction-finding equipment (HFDF) to locate the "opposing" carrier *Enterprise. Ranger*'s strike aircraft then staged a surprise "attack" on the latter, taking her out of the conflict that followed.[2]

This combination of vulnerability and indispensability marks carrier development in the interwar years. As we have shown, it drove the Royal Navy to embrace the concept of the armored deck carrier. But that decision limited drastically a carrier's air complement. The U.S. Navy (as well as the Imperial Japanese Navy) accepted carrier vulnerability as a given but went in the other direction, stressing high numbers of aircraft and the surprise, massed strike. The choice of these two different directions also had implications for other components of the two navies. The U.S. Navy, for example, developed long-range seaplanes for both scout and attack missions. Both the U.S. Navy and the Imperial Japanese Navy paid a premium for information, hoping thereby to gain a jump on the opposition. The Royal Navy was not allowed to develop such a seaplane force and had to rely instead on being able to survive attack.

In effect, both the U.S. Navy and the Royal Navy faced a severe decision problem under conditions of great constraint—"severe" because *not* solving it had grave implications. The constraints were many: fiscal, political (the Washington and London treaties), organizational (the relationship between the RAF and the Fleet Air Arm, for example), institutional (how the RN found and solved problems), and technological. Conceptually, the leaders of both navies can be thought of as gamblers facing one another over the dice table. They had to "play the game," but the cost of failure was terrible. Accordingly, they did what all prudent players would do: they tried to reduce the stakes of any given roll, so that one loss would not lead to total failure; they also tried to make sure that, if they did lose the initial roll, they could return to play again.

In this, the Washington Treaty helped them. On the one hand, it prohibited any given navy from building too many carriers while it was in effect. The London Treaty of 1930 also forced the signatories to count all carriers—even those under ten thousand tons standard displacement—as part of their carrier tonnage total. Because the number of carriers in peacetime was limited, all three major carrier navies (USN, RN, and IJN) found it difficult to practice actual multicarrier operations. On the other hand, the Washington Treaty allowed the signatories to replace old or "experimental" ships with new ones, as long as the addition of the new ones did not break through the overall tonnage ceiling for carriers set for each major navy. But the London Treaty also forbade the construction of "new" carriers of more than twenty-three thousand tons (23,368 metric tons) standard displacement. That restriction cramped designers, who were forced to choose between aircraft complement and armor for the carrier itself. The London Treaty also forced the signatories to inform one another of their ship construction programs.

In short, none of the "gamblers" (USN, RN, and IJN) had enough "chips" (carriers) to withstand severe losses and go on "betting against" the other two (assuming a high-scoring "toss"). There was just enough uncertainty to breed caution. Caution became reasonable. It was this caution that restrained Japanese Vice Admiral Nagumo at Pearl Harbor, when his aviators pressed him to attack the anchored U.S. fleet yet again. "Where were the carriers?" he wondered. There might be as many as four U.S. carriers just waiting for his forces to wear themselves out attacking Pearl Harbor before pouncing on him, wrecking Japan's premier naval strike force in one blow. Nagumo, like Admiral Jellicoe in World War I, was indeed a man who could "lose the war in an afternoon," and in fact he did just that, at Midway, but *not* because he was a poor commander. He was caught in a classical tactical dilemma, one that his experience as a professional officer had warned him was extremely dangerous.[3]

The "carrier revolution" was incomplete before World War II. Carriers were terribly vulnerable to one another and to well-trained land-based attack squadrons (as the Luftwaffe showed the Royal Navy in the Mediterranean in 1941). Only when carriers could protect themselves from air attack—which the U.S. carriers could not do until 1943—could they take the role of sustained combat presence away from surface forces. Carrier aircraft also could not attack other carriers at night. Attacks like that of the Royal Navy on Italian warships at Taranto were attacks on stationary targets, not on maneuvering carriers at sea. Furthermore, prewar exercises had demonstrated to the U.S. Navy that carriers needed to be withdrawn from zones of battle at night. The U.S. Navy's 1934 *War Instructions,* for example, argued, "Aircraft carriers should endeavor *to avoid night action* with all types of enemy vessels and should employ every means, speed, guns, and smoke, to assist them in this endeavor."[4] Is it any wonder that there were doubts among the officers of all the major navies regarding the carrier's potential?

Such doubts partly explain why, given the threats that faced them, both the U.S. Navy and the Royal Navy were slow to build up strong carrier arms, even after Japan pulled out of the Washington Treaty "system" of arms limitation in 1936. But another very important reason was the high cost of modern naval weapons. The U.S. Navy was still trying to round out a modern "treaty fleet" at the time of the Munich crisis in 1938, for example, and the U.S. Congress did not give the go-ahead to a "two-ocean fleet" until June and July 1940. The Royal Navy was constrained even more. As Britain's official history of World War II noted, "when in 1928 it had been laid down as the assumption on which the annual estimates of the Services should be based that there would be no major war for ten years from any particular agreed date, it was implied that the readiness of the fleet need be sufficient only to deal with a minor emergency."

The political leaders of Great Britain, a nation with world-girdling commitments, decided to plan strategically for the least militarily stressful *major* conflict—war with Japan. Between 1933 and 1935, however, the British government's official Defence Requirements Committee moved the leadership of the country away from the so-called one-power standard (strength enough to deal with Japan alone) and toward a policy of naval rearmament. Unfortunately, Britain lacked the material and human resources (and the time) to build a naval force adequate for her needs in 1940 and 1941, when she was hard pressed in the Pacific, Mediterranean, and Atlantic simultaneously.[5]

In an essay describing the Royal Navy's development of battle fleet tactics in the years between the wars, historian Jon Sumida argued that British efforts had been influenced primarily by three factors: technology, what other navies were doing, and finance. But these factors merely delineate the dilemma faced by the leaders of all three major navies. Technological advances and developments in other navies drove the British (and the Americans, and the Japanese) to modernize and enlarge, whenever possible, their naval forces. Financial restraints constrained and weakened those efforts. There was not enough money to pay for everything that needed to be bought or developed. As a result, every large navy (including the French and Italian) had to make some hard choices, *knowing that some would probably be wrong.*[6]

Complicating the process of making those choices was the rapid pace of technological change, especially in areas such as aeronautics and electronics, and the concomitant growth in the cost of weapons. The cost of constructing and outfitting the U.S. Navy's sixteen-inch-gunned battleship of 1923, *West Virginia,* was about $27 million. *North Carolina,* the first of the newer sixteen-inch-gunned ships built after the lapse of the Washington Treaty "system," cost about $48 million. Newer carriers in the 1930s, such as the U.S. Navy's *Enterprise,* cost about $24 million. *Ranger,* commissioned in 1934 and about three-fourths the displacement of *Enterprise,* cost $12.5 million, or about half what a battleship had cost eleven years earlier. Granted, the newer battleships, cruisers, and destroyers were far more capable, in terms of firepower, speed, and protection, than their predecessors. The newer carriers handled more aircraft, justifying increased costs. But the cost *per ship* (and even more so *per aircraft*) grew faster than every navy's overall budget. The result was a decline in numbers of expensive and powerful ships, which in itself increased the risk that tactical errors leading to losses could have grave strategic effects.

With aircraft, the problem was even worse, because it was not clear that marginal qualitative superiority could offset quantitative inferiority. Land-based aircraft performance steadily improved in the years between the wars, and that improvement generated a demand for more and even better (and hence more expensive) aircraft. But building a smaller number of superior aircraft was no guarantee that, in battle, they would defeat a mass of cheaper, marginally weaker planes. On the other hand, U.S. carriers carried so few fighters that they needed the best possible designs in order just to have some insurance against attack. (The Royal Navy "solved" this problem by armoring carrier flight decks, itself an expensive proposition.)

One expectation of the aviation zealots proved correct in World War II: the skies were often filled with aircraft. Aircraft battles became massed clashes, and attrition warfare moved from the ground to the air. The creation of "air armies," however, cost great sums, and so navies found themselves pressured on two sides: from within, by the rising costs of new technology, and from without, by the competing technology of land-based aviation. In 1933, for example, spending on the Royal Air Force was about a third of that for the Royal Navy. In 1935, it was about 42 percent; in 1937, it had grown to 80 percent. In 1939, because of the need to defend Great Britain from air attack, spending on the Royal Air Force was over 107 percent of that on the Royal Navy, even though the latter was being enlarged.[7] Nations building air armies were faced with a sobering quality-quantity tradeoff. If they failed to build a large enough force, they would lose the air war of attrition. On the other hand, a decision to standardize aircraft types too early would leave them with a host of less than adequate aircraft; the air forces of such nations would be qualitatively inferior and only quantitatively equal to those of their enemies.

As historian Jon Sumida has pointed out, matters were made even worse for navies by the fact that they could not hide their big ships or completely disguise advances in technology. A writer using a pseudonym pointed out in the 1935 edition of *Brassey's Naval Annual* that "during the last ten years . . . British naval air strength has fallen to a very low point. By comparison with that of foreign naval Powers, it is overwhelmingly out-numbered, and the unfavourable ratio is growing every year." Naval aviators could see the differences among American, Japanese, and British carriers and carrier aircraft, and the Royal Navy was clearly behind. On its part, the U.S. Navy's Bureau of Aeronautics was, for many years, very open with its annual reports. That for the fiscal year 1926, for example, mentioned the importance of air-cooled engines, explained in detail the "1,000-plane program," and also referred to the "remarkable record of landings made by the aircraft operating squadrons" on *Langley.* Through the interwar period, the missions of carriers and carrier aircraft were also widely and openly discussed. In the 1936 *Brassey's,* for example, Rear Adm. E. J. King wrote, "The mission of the fleet aircraft is to assist the battle line to the maximum in defeating the enemy," and "Carrier aircraft have a single function, the offensive; that is, to find and to strike the enemy, both on the surface and in the air."[8]

It was possible to hide the performance characteristics of particular aircraft. It was possible to conceal the methods by which aircraft were launched and recovered by carriers. It was also possible to limit the knowledge that other navies could gain about aircraft ordnance, such as bombs and torpedoes. But it was not possible to hide the shape of naval air forces. Both Japan and the United States, for example, invested heavily in long-range seaplanes; Great Britain did also, but her long-range flying boats were not under the control of the Royal Navy. These indicators of force size and institutional affiliation, coupled with the characteristics of the aircraft (inferred from photographs and direct observation), revealed that the Royal Navy and the U.S. Navy planned to use their naval air forces in different ways. The U.S. Navy, confronted by the distances of the Pacific, would rely on long-range seaplanes to find enemy formations and then attack and disable enemy carriers. U.S. carrier aircraft would then support battleships (by protecting battleship spotter planes) as the big ships pounded the enemy. The Royal Navy, lacking its own seaplanes, would rely on something else (code-breaking and HFDF) to find the enemy and something else again (night attacks by small formations of heavy surface ships) to defeat him.

Yet the pace of technological change, coupled with the lack of enough money to support all promising new technologies, kept carrier advocates (and even some of their more traditional, nonflying colleagues) edgy and hungry for improved technologies and tactics. In the Royal Navy, agitation by navy officers for full control of the Fleet Air Arm finally brought it back under formal Admiralty control at the very end of July 1937, though "the transfer of the administrative control of the Fleet Air Arm from the Air Ministry to the Admiralty did not take place until May *1939*." (Italics added.) Moreover, as we have shown, the performance of Royal Navy carrier aircraft left much to be desired. The Fleet Air Arm was saved once war began by its ability to purchase aircraft manufactured in the United States.[9]

In both the United States and Japan, aircraft designers during this period faced their own quandary. Should they continue the development of ever more powerful engines for carrier aircraft? If so, then the aircraft themselves would grow larger and heavier, forcing their navies to construct larger and more expensive carriers. If not, then carrier fighters would lack the ability to contest air superiority with land-based aircraft. On the other hand, reliance upon larger, more powerful, and heavier engines made naval aviation dependent upon a small group of engine manufacturers, and it was not clear in peacetime that such enterprises could produce enough such engines to meet wartime demand. The Japanese tried to stretch the concept of the lighter, more maneuverable fighter as far as they could. The result was the famous Mitsubishi A6M2 "Zero," an aircraft of great range and agility (wing loading of approximately 18 psf). The Americans went in a different direction, stressing engine power and aircraft weight for diving speed and strength; the result was the Grumman F4F, with a wing loading of approximately twenty-six pounds per square foot. Our point is that both navies were struggling to produce high-performance aircraft that met their perceived tactical needs in light of their respective industrial strengths.[10]

The Royal Navy was too starved of resources to "catch up," once naval limits were abandoned in 1936. Admiralty policy was to have, under the Washington Treaty, "five large aircraft carriers which would accommodate 360 aircraft," but in "November 1936 there were 4 carriers in commission accommodating just under 150 aircraft." To justify its planned post-treaty construction programs for 1936 and 1937, "the Admiralty estimated its requirements by 1942 as being 4 carriers for Home Waters, 4 for the Far East, and 5 for trade protection." Five hundred "first line" aircraft would serve as the flying contingent for this force of carriers—up from a strength just half that of the U.S. Navy's carrier squadrons (in 1936). Unfortunately for the Royal Navy, however, "there was no detailed programme of ways and means of reaching that strength," and, by 1939, "despite a steady carrier building programme, the aircraft and personnel position was, broadly speaking, as bad as ever."[11] Put baldly, there was no "catch-up" without help.

For the British, the lack of armaments had severe policy implications. It was the basis for British acquiescence in Germany's reoccupation of the Rhineland in 1936. As the Chiefs of Staff put it in their advice to the government, "if there is the smallest danger of being drawn into . . . war with Germany, we ought at once to disengage ourselves from . . . the Mediterranean."[12] The need to rearm also influenced British policy toward Italy's war with Ethiopia and the Munich crisis. And, after December 1941, the Royal Navy lost its dominance of the seas around and east of India, never to regain that dominance without the aid of the United States and the latter's naval forces.

Put another way, what might be called the "carrier revolution" did not come with a guarantee, as Japan discovered. A nation could invest heavily and still lose. Moreover, a nation that fell behind might never catch up without outside help, *because* the carrier revolution coincided with expensive revolutions in other military areas, especially in the fields of long-range aviation, air-to-ground cooperation, and armored forces. For fiscal reasons, the Royal Navy did not have enough modern carriers when it needed them most: in the prewar years when carrier and carrier aircraft tactics were being worked out and standardized. For organizational reasons, it lacked the right kinds of carrier aircraft. The problem was made worse because of what other navies were doing. The progress of the U.S. and Japanese navies in aviation, in gunnery, and in ship design and construction placed great pressure on Royal Navy tacticians. The result was a total reorientation of Royal Navy's battle tactics. In this sense, historian Jon Sumida is correct in saying, "The inferiority of the British naval air force, in comparison with the U.S. and Japanese, may have been unfortunate, given events as they unfolded after 1941, but was not unreasonable, given Great Britain's strategic requirements as they were perceived in the late 1930s."[13] But what would have happened if the Fleet Air Arm had been in the hands of the Admiralty ten years earlier? That is the sort of question we will address in our Conclusions.

We will also consider another factor—cooperation between the Royal Navy and the U.S. Navy. In a previous chapter, we showed that observations by U.S. Navy liaison officers of Royal Navy carrier operations under fire in 1940 and 1941 had led the USN's own carrier commanders to begin reassessing the vulnerability of carriers. In the summer of 1941, it began to look as though carriers could indeed protect themselves, using radar to direct combat air patrols. There was no time for the U.S. Navy to develop a full-fledged system of combat information centers, air search radars, and short-range radio communications for its carrier air patrols before it was plunged into war with Japan. Clark Reynolds was right: not until 1943 did the U.S. Navy's carrier *force* develop the equipment, the procedures, and the doctrine required to take a strategic air offensive against the Imperial Japanese Navy.

But the seeds of that offensive were planted in the summer of 1941, and one major source of those seeds was the experience of the Royal Navy. How interesting and ironic that the navy with the least powerful carrier force of the three navies served as the source of information for the most powerful—information critical to the success of the latter in 1944 and 1945.

7 Analysis

BECAUSE the story of the development of carrier forces is a complex one, our method in this chapter can be compared with that used by people assembling a complicated jigsaw puzzle. We will first put together the pieces of one corner, then the pieces of another corner. Gradually, we will link our assembled sections.

The Role of Individuals in Carrier Development

In 1919, for officers in naval aviation, it was the best of times and the worst of times. Governments were slashing military budgets, sending home the huge military forces that had engaged in World War I, and curtailing their acquisition of new technologies. The collapse of spending was coupled with claims—backed up by evidence from World War I—that navies were undergoing a technological revolution in three dimensions: aviation, the submarine, and radio. It seemed that the postwar lapse in funding would leave the victorious allied navies unable to take advantage of the great changes in technology that wartime spending had generated. Ambitious officers interested in these new technologies faced a difficult dilemma: stay with proven—and improving—areas of expertise, such as battleship gunnery, or jump into one of the new areas? With the future of these new technologies so uncertain, following one was bound to involve a great deal of professional risk. In the case of aviation and submarines, the risk was also to life and limb.

This dilemma was complicated, in the Royal Navy (RN), by the Royal Air Force's (RAF's) control of pilot and aircrew training and assignments. If you wanted to fly, you joined the RAF. If you chose to serve as a naval aviator, you were a "naval" officer only indirectly. You served in the Royal Navy, but you really were not on the ladder to senior naval command because your "home" was in the RAF. You did not share the professional duties of the regular Royal Navy line officer. You were evaluated in a different way through a different chain of command. This situation did not change until after 1938.

In the U.S. Navy (USN), by contrast, aviators did not have to pass through another service to fly naval aircraft, but they still had to go to sea in nonaviation commands to qualify for promotion. In theory, they could rise to the rank of admiral in the regular Navy line. In practice, the need to practice flying skills, coupled with the requirement that aviators abandon flying temporarily in order to hold "regular" commands, put U.S. Navy aviators behind in the race for flag rank. This "catch-22" pulled key aviators, such as Henry Mustin (the first deputy chief of the Bureau of Aeronautics) and John Rodgers (who led the San Francisco-to-Honolulu flight in 1925), out of aviation at crucial times for them and for the USN.

There was a great debate in the early 1920s about carrier aviation's proper military role, which raised a host of thorny issues for individual American military aviators. One issue was the professional standing of naval aviators. Should they be officers? If so, then how would they compete with other, nonflying officers for senior command positions? Another issue was who would exercise power over naval air forces—officers trained as pilots first or officers trained as sailors first?

The fact that Rear Adm. Moffett, the first chief of BuAer, spent much of his time and energy trying to resolve these issues is both a sign of their importance and evidence of his perceptiveness. It was not sufficient for him just to hold off those who wanted a separate air force. At the same time, he had to provide career paths for young, talented aviators such as John Towers and Marc Mitscher. Moffett had to placate his peers who had not selected to adopt aviation at an advanced stage in their careers. He simultaneously had to retain the allegiance of the young pilots. If they broke ranks with him and with the Navy, then Brig. Gen. Mitchell and his allies would win the larger institutional struggle.

The dispute over General Mitchell's claims concerning the bombing tests conducted in the summer of 1921 was so intense and bitter because it involved individuals with large, dynamic personalities—individuals who were convinced that their views were correct and did not like to lose any dispute in which they were engaged. The harshness of their attacks on one another showed that some of the most talented, articulate, and forceful officers in the Army and Navy were committed to what they thought was the proper future role of military aviation. The irony was that a contest that attracted so many of the best officers threatened to cost so many of them their careers precisely because they were men who did not duck a fight. The controversies generated in the early and mid-1920s affected so many individuals so deeply that the personal antagonisms that came out of them shaped U.S. military organization and policy for almost another two generations.

British aviators avoided the face-off that took place in the United States. What their American counterparts were wrestling with in 1921—bureaucratic and political struggles over an independent air service—had already been settled, but the solution, which was the creation of the RAF, had important implications for their professional futures. Aviators who wanted to work from carriers had less organizational status in their parent organization (the RAF) than those who opted for multiengine bombardment. In Britain, it was the bomber and land-based fighter pilots who would get the promotions and the best equipment. As a result, their image of "air power" would be the dominant one. For the Royal Navy, the problem throughout the 1920s and 1930s would be recruiting enough quality pilots and navigators for its carrier squadrons.

Because individuals matter, the fact that the U.S. Navy had its own Bureau of Aeronautics (BuAer) after 1921 affected the comparative development of the American and British carrier arms. As our chapters on the Royal Navy showed, British naval aviators at first thought of carriers as floating airfields. Several key USN aviators—especially Henry Mustin—rather quickly grasped that carriers were part of an offensive naval system, and not just platforms. The fact that the United States did not follow Britain's lead in establishing a separate air force for both land- and sea-based aviation allowed the U.S. Navy's aviators to explore and refine Mustin's sense that aircraft were part of an offensive system and so develop a concept of aviation at sea that emphasized the strike role of carriers and their air component.

But it was a near thing. The U.S. Navy came close to losing its aviation several times in the early 1920s, and young aviators consequently faced a decidedly uncertain organizational and professional future. How essential it was, then, for senior officers such as Rear Adm. Moffett and Captain Joseph M. Reeves to tie their stars to naval aviation's future, guiding and promoting younger officers. Moffett was especially good at surrounding himself with talent. A consummate bureaucrat, Moffett turned BuAer's Plans Division into an aviation "think tank" and schooled the future leaders of naval aviation (such as Marc A. Mitscher) in the tactics of influencing Congress and independent investigating committees. Many of Moffett's subordinates and peers did not like him or his methods; some, like Ernest J. King, openly quarreled with him. But his maneuverings protected naval aviation, and his need to create a staff to assist him in Washington's essentially political wars gave many aviator officers (another example is Arthur W. Radford) invaluable experience.[1]

Carrier aviation was a "near thing" from another perspective as well. It was very dangerous. It attracted adventuresome young men in droves, and then killed many of them (British, Japanese, and American) in the course of their careers. Clark Reynolds's superb biography of pioneer aviator John Towers is punctuated by riveting descriptions of Towers's own near brushes with death and by descriptions of his grief at the loss of many of his friends and associates. The open question for early USN aviators, "Will we be able to rise to major commands?" was matched by an unspoken concern: Would any of the really talented ones live long enough to exercise that command?

As exhilarating as it was to be a young aviator in the challenging, risky dawn of carrier aviation, a flying career also carried many professional costs. Nonflying officers resented the additional hazardous-duty pay and uniform insignia given to officer pilots in the U.S. Navy. The latter often found required nonflying duties dull and a distraction from their primary professional interest. The future was also uncertain. Recall that pilots such as John Towers thought in the early 1920s that carriers would be replaced within a generation by large, land-based aircraft. Despite the dangers and uncertainties, carrier aviation attracted both excellent pilots and talented officers, even in the Royal Navy.

Once the Bureau of Aeronautics was created within the USN, for example, aviation had an organizational "home," a separate budget for aircraft development, a "champion" in the chief of the bureau, and a potentially rewarding future for its members within the Navy. The RN lacked an organization like BuAer, yet, as our chapters on its carrier aviation show, the RN nevertheless put together a potent carrier force—one outmatched only by those of the United States and Japan. The evidence of carrier aviation's potential kept drawing personnel to it, even in a navy (like the RN) where resources and the chance for promotion were comparatively limited.

Clearly, more was involved in the success or failure of carrier aviation than organizational factors. That is why we considered personal factors—whether the love of flying or the eagerness of some young men to brave injury and death in the pursuit of adventure and achievement might have played an important role. We think these sorts of factors did. One cannot look through the memoirs, biographies, and newspaper accounts from this period in aviation's history without being struck by the excitement that flying created in the younger population of every nation where planes flew. Thousands of young men (and many women, too) jumped at the chance to fly. Many gave their lives in the effort. The losses, often highly publicized, did not dampen youthful enthusiasm. Flying was the exciting thing to do.

But what attracted senior officers who were not skilled aviators, or even pilots, to carrier aviation? That is where carrier aviation's story gets really interesting. The thrill of flying was not the draw. Some talented older officers, such as Moffett and Reeves and King (in the USN) and Rear Adm. R. G. H. Henderson (in the RN), were drawn to aviation by the belief that it would help them advance their careers while it also added another potent weapon to their navy's armory. Others, like Mustin and Rufus F. Zogbaum (an early captain of *Saratoga*), thought aviation would open a whole new horizon of attack and defense. Still others—Admiral Fullam is the prime example—were struck suddenly with a profound understanding of where naval aviation was heading. No matter what their motives, all were aided by their navies' commitment to professionalism, especially by the notion that professionals weighed and evaluated evidence as they made both operational and technical judgments.

This was an immensely important institutional rule, especially in the U.S. Navy. Admiral Sims put it very well in a letter to a colleague in 1908:

> If you can imagine a service in which all of the upper officers would carefully study and easily comprehend all criticism, and cheerfully and openly acknowledge all defects for which they were either actively or passively responsible, then there could be no such condition as that which we deplore.[2]

Sims wanted a navy whose tactics and doctrine were tentatively derived from simulations conducted at the Naval War College and then "tested" in exercises staged by a "permanent squadron of evolution."[3] This pragmatic, open-minded, experimentalist approach to tactics and doctrine had gained many adherents in the USN of the early twentieth century. The best senior officers, trained not to ignore evidence, would not turn their backs as the evidence of aviation's potential grew and its actual achievements increased. They responded by giving the new technology their support.

The officers, of course, weren't alone. They had the help of many civilians —engineers, pioneering manufacturers, and political leaders. Their many contributions can be summarized in an anecdote about Mason S. Chace, a naval architect who graduated from the Massachusetts Institute of Technology as a mechanical engineer in 1894. Chace went to France after graduating from M.I.T., and he was a distinguished student at the French navy's school for naval constructors. Upon his return to the United States, he served as a naval constructor for the U.S. Navy at Newport News, Virginia. Later, he left government service and eventually (after a distinguished professional career) became president of the United States Shipbuilding Company.

In 1921, an essay by Chace was printed in the *Transactions of the Society of Naval Architects and Marine Engineers.* The essay was entitled "Development of the Three-Plane Navy, with or without Battleships." By "three-plane," Chace meant the three domains of naval weapons—the surface of the sea, the depths, and the air above the sea. His point was clear: "[I]n the naval battles of the future, victory will go to the forces which control the air." Retiring in 1929, Chace "took up aviation and became a licensed pilot"—at age fifty-six.[4] His story is not that unusual. But that is precisely why it matters to us. It is a sign that aviation attracted not only adventurers, but also talented engineers, industrial managers, and thoughtful leaders.

Individuals and the Carrier Concept

When we began this study, we thought that the concept of the carrier as a strike weapon began with the Royal Navy. On the one hand, that service certainly pioneered the process of taking aircraft to sea (as well as the process of using land-based aircraft at sea) as a part of its battle fleet,[5] and the experience of the RN had a strong influence on the USN. On the other hand, the USN's earliest carrier concepts also date back to before World War I, and those nascent concepts fell into two categories. The first focused on taking airplanes to sea. The second, however, focused on increasing the range of the USN's striking power by using aircraft to do what battleships and other combatants already did: deliver ordnance.

This focus on delivering ordnance the way other combatants did, in salvoes or pulses, was Henry Mustin's. His approach was necessarily different from that of most of his contemporaries in either navy because most naval officers interested in developing aviation at sea had their hands full just getting aircraft on and off the water or on and off the first carriers. During World War I, Royal Navy officers quickly grew concerned about targets ashore (German aircraft and airship bases, for example) or about shooting down the reconnaissance airships that the German navy used in World War I to *avoid* battle with the superior British battle fleet.[6]

Captain Murray Sueter, the director of the Royal Navy's Air Service in World War I, dispatched torpedo-carrying floatplanes to the Dardanelles in 1915 "specifically to prove that an aircraft could torpedo a ship."[7] Though these planes successfully attacked shipping anchored in Turkish waters, their exploits were the exception and not the rule of the RN's experience with attack aircraft at sea during World War I. Mustin and his contemporaries who had served with the British knew all this, but not as novices.

The deeper we probed the origins of the carrier concept, the more we realized that there were multiple carrier concepts *from the first.*[8] One concept was to use carrier-based aircraft to attack land targets. Under this concept, the carrier was just a forward airfield. It did not work in concert with, or form an integral part of, a whole fleet. Another concept was that the carrier, though part of a larger fleet, was nonetheless an auxiliary to existing weapons such as the battleship. Under this concept, carrier aircraft scouted, drove off enemy scouts, and directed the gunfire of heavy ships. Yet another, different —and revolutionary—concept was that of the carrier and its aircraft as the centerpiece of a long-range striking force—the new battle line, so to speak.

These different concepts were present together in the minds of individual officers in both navies. Indeed, once the aircraft-carrying ship became something more than a transport for seaplanes, it was often hard to untangle these different concepts of the carrier's role. British experience was tantalizing for the USN's aviators because it showed how versatile carriers could be. Their wheeled aircraft and float seaplanes could and did scout, and shield friendly forces from enemy scouts, and spot gunfire, and launch torpedoes and drop bombs. Moreover, RN carrier aircraft had worked alongside seaplanes and land-based aircraft operating over water in World War I, demonstrating that aviation's strength was its great variety—seaplanes for patrolling, ship-borne aircraft for fighting off German scouts, and so forth. The cost of all this activity was not cheap, but the benefits were clear. The RN's World War I experience convinced USN aviators and some very influential non-aviator officers that aircraft at sea were worth the cost and the risks.

But it took two factors to turn wartime experience into a new concept for using aviation at sea. The first was the willingness of senior USN officers to use simulations conducted at the Naval War College to inform their decisions on naval aviation. The second factor was the simulations themselves, which, under Rear Admiral Sims's leadership, convinced then Captain Reeves that the carrier and her aircraft were a potent strike weapon.

We regard Reeves's insight as the essential element of the modern carrier concept. The concept would likely have been stillborn if *Langley*'s aviators, crew, and their supporters in BuAer had not been able to make *Langley* operational as a strike unit. It took a year to do it, and Reeves did not do it single-handedly. He built on a foundation already put in place by his predecessors and by the uniformed leaders of the Navy, and he depended completely on a cadre of adventuresome pilots and a flight deck crew willing to experiment. But under Reeves's leadership, *Langley* and her air group were turned from a testbed into an operational prototype. And, make no mistake, the function of *Langley* became the mission of attacking other naval units as an integral part of the USN's battle fleet.

In 1922, when the U.S. Navy's Bureau of Construction and Repair was planning the conversions of the large battle cruisers *Lexington* and *Saratoga,* it was assumed that it would take a very big ship to operate many aircraft. Though it was not clear at the time how their aircraft would be stowed, handled, and then arranged for takeoffs and landings, the two converted battle cruisers were assigned about seventy aircraft apiece. Bureau of Construction and Repair architects doubted that any converted merchant ship or naval auxiliary (like *Langley*) could carry enough aircraft in its smaller hangar to make conversion worthwhile. At the same time, the converted battle cruisers weren't ideal carrier designs either. The need to exhaust the gases from their large boilers, for example, required the construction of huge stacks and large smoke pipes from their fire rooms, thereby reducing hangar space and creating on the flight deck what amounted to a huge sail that pilots believed generated unpredictable air currents in the teeth of landing aircraft. The first post-*Lexington* carrier design therefore assumed that about the same size air group could be carried on a slightly smaller hull—twenty-seven thousand tons versus the thirty-six thousand tons for *Lexington.*

Reeves's work in *Langley* showed that this reasoning was dead wrong. Much smaller ships could carry air groups of twenty-four, thirty-six, or even (for emergencies) forty-two aircraft. This meant that the U.S. Navy could get a barely sufficient number of carriers within the tonnage ceiling imposed by the Washington Treaty. It also meant that the Navy could retain *Langley* as an operational carrier. As officially "experimental," she could have been replaced under the rules of the Washington Treaty. But Reeves showed that she could serve as an effective—if not ideal—carrier. More important was the evidence that smaller carriers could carry a strong air group, and so the Navy's first ship designed as a carrier from the start (*Ranger*) displaced less than half the tonnage of *Lexington* but carried, in peacetime, almost as many planes. Reeves's success with *Langley* also breathed life back into the Navy's plans for merchant ship conversions, which meant that naval mobilization for a Pacific war was a real possibility.[9]

The Royal Navy had its own carrier advocates, such as Capt. Murray Sueter, whom we have already mentioned. Sueter thought of carriers as "an independent Offensive force" as early as 1914.[10] Later, when control over the Fleet Air Arm was shared between the RAF and the RN, the latter produced some outstanding carrier leaders. The most notable was Rear Adm. R. G. H. Henderson, appointed to serve as the first seagoing flag-level commander of the RN's carriers in 1931. Yet Britain also had its share of doubters. Historian Geoffrey Till, in his *Air Power and the Royal Navy,* cited Sir Warren Fisher, who served years as the permanent undersecretary of the treasury. According to Till, Fisher effectively opposed allowing the Fleet Air Arm to be pulled back out of the RAF. In the 1920s, Fisher apparently exercised influence over then Chancellor of the Exchequer Winston Churchill, and the latter ruthlessly slashed carrier funding in the RN.[11] Corresponding funding for the USN's carrier development efforts, while also limited in the 1920s, was comparatively stronger because of support from influential members of Congress.[12]

Another factor deserves mention: the way in which certain technologies became identified, within the Royal Navy, with certain individuals, to the detriment of those technologies. Historian Jon Sumida discovered that such an identification of one individual with a kind of technology hindered the adoption of effective fire control for the RN's heavy guns.[13] Captain (later Admiral) Murray Sueter may well have had an unintended hand, because of his acerbic personality, in driving aviation out of the RN and into the RAF. Put another way, USN "champions" of aviation did not own it the way at least one of their RN counterparts claimed to.

It is clear that certain individuals played critical roles in the development of carriers in the Royal Navy and the U.S. Navy. At the same time, what individuals could do was constrained by the positions open to them in the organizations that existed at the time. British historians, such as Geoffrey Till and Stephen Roskill, have made much of this point. Both have argued that the U.S. Navy's comparatively great progress in carrier aviation in the 1920s was due in large measure to the fact that the U.S. Navy had a special *bureau* for naval aviation. Their argument rests on the time it takes for a military service to learn how best to use a new technology. Where that technology is changing rapidly—as it certainly was in the field of carrier aviation —it is important for operating forces to receive the latest, most modern equipment in time for them to find the best means of using it.

The Royal Navy's Fleet Air Arm, for example, paid heavily during World War II for prewar decisions that, though they appeared sensible enough, underestimated what carrier aircraft would soon be able to accomplish. The improvements in what carrier aircraft could do in the 1930s were dramatic. Aircraft got faster, carried more ordnance, and performed better; they also got heavier. The Royal Navy, according to historians Till and Roskill, was less able to anticipate these trends than the U.S. Navy because the latter, through its Bureau of Aeronautics, was linked closely with both aircraft and aircraft engine developers. A classic example of the fruits of this Navy-industry interaction was the series of events that led the Bureau of Aeronautics to support Pratt & Whitney's design of the innovative "Wasp" and "Hornet" radial engines in the late 1920s.[14] With the creation of Britain's Air Ministry, by contrast, the Royal Navy lost its direct link with industry and therefore its chance to promote technology that would have strengthened the performance of Fleet Air Arm aircraft.

An innovation is more likely to succeed to the degree that it attracts and holds the interest and commitment of individuals with talent and energy. At the same time, however, these individuals must be committed to developing something *that will work.* As we have argued, this is what makes the contribution of American naval officer Joseph M. Reeves pivotal—his focus on evidence and practice, on what today are termed "operational effectiveness" and "operational suitability."

The Organizational Level of Analysis

When we had finished our initial research, Andrew Marshall asked us to identify briefly the factors that most affected the maturing of the carrier concept. The first factor was the existence of a consciously designed means (war-gaming and exercises) within the USN for testing new naval concepts before whole new systems were built. The second factor was the general economic situation. Money for aviation's development was easy to get during World War I, but the available equipment and pilots could only rarely be set aside for experimentation. After the war, the RN was in the position of having already made its initial investment—its "first move" in the competition to develop the new technology. The USN lacked carriers and carrier aircraft in 1919 but had not sunk scarce funds into inferior equipment. Moreover, the USN could and did evaluate the RN's successes and failures and learn from them.

The third factor was the availability of good equipment. The USN's BuAer got the funds to do what the RN could not: facilitate the development of engines, engine starters, arresting gear, and aircraft recovery gear that would lead to faster launch and recovery times, thereby making possible the large strikes that turned carriers into serious weapons. BuAer's support and encouragement of the development of air-cooled aircraft radial engines is a classic example of how important it was for the USN to have an organization dedicated to improving naval aircraft technology and able to spend the funds to do so.

The fourth factor concerns the openness of American political institutions, such as the Congress. In the United States, aviation issues were given a thorough and public airing before final decisions were made. The comparative quickness with which the British government created the Royal Air Force was not matched on the other side of the Atlantic, despite pressure to do so from many aviators, political leaders, and aviation enthusiasts. Because the government of the United States was "open," multiple streams of advocacy first converged to support military aviation, then diverged, as the advocates of an American "air ministry" debated those opposed to the creation of such an agency. Sometimes these "streams" of support simply did not interact. It depended on the specific situation. Overall, however, the process of deciding how to develop carrier aviation was far more public in the United States than in Great Britain, and we believe that this "openness" worked to the advantage of the Americans, because it allowed more effective error identification and correction.

The fifth factor was the most important. It was the communication and cooperation among the Naval War College, the fleet, and BuAer. Each institution took a complementary role. BuAer projected technology. The Naval War College integrated those projections into its war games. The more interesting results of the games were "tried out" in the annual fleet problems. This cycle of projecting, simulating, and experimenting (in the fleet problems) did not happen just once. It was an ongoing cycle, lasting from the early 1920s until at least the early 1930s.

(Then) Commodore Joseph Reeves, for example, took command of the U.S. fleet's aircraft squadrons just before the court-martial of Army Brigadier General William Mitchell in 1925. He was quite aware of the controversy that had raged over Mitchell's claims since 1921, and he knew that Mitchell had charged in September 1925 that the Army and Navy had criminally neglected aviation. It was time to produce—time to refute Mitchell's charges with hard evidence. Moffett, BuAer's chief, had held off Mitchell and his allies in Congress mainly with arguments. By the time of Mitchell's trial, however, the Navy's leadership felt under heavy pressure to make aviation at sea operational.

Mitchell himself tried to portray his struggle with both the Army and the Navy as that of a perceptive visionary opposed to die-hard obstructionists—as that of the individual martyr opposing the faceless bureaucracies of the Army and Navy. But Rear Adm. Moffett was anything but a "faceless" bureaucrat, though bureaucrat he certainly was; he knew the value of an organization such as BuAer in the campaign to put naval aviation to sea. Moffett used BuAer's talented staff as his tool, but BuAer could not perform the essential task of demonstrating that the experimental carrier *Langley* could be made operational. It took Reeves, leading *Langley*'s crew and her aviators, to do that, and he did it on his own, without specific instructions from Moffett. No one—not Moffett, not Reeves, not John Towers—knew just what to do. Individuals had to use the organizations under their control to turn aviation, a promising innovation, into an operational tool for fleet use. Fortunately, the American naval innovators had the resources that their organizations gave them—the resources to deal with industry, to contest the claims of the partisans of a unified air service, and to turn their experimental carrier into a real weapon.

Compare the organizational setting of the American case with that of the British. The Royal Navy had no analogue to the U.S. Navy's Bureau of Aeronautics. The RN also lacked an organizational counterpart to the USN's Naval War College. While the organizations central to the maturation of the carrier concept in the USN turned an innovation into a striking arm in the 1920s, the RN had to appeal at the highest level of Great Britain's national defense establishment for control of carrier aviation—for the right to create an organization analogous to the USN's BuAer. For the RN, it was a matter of persuading the Committee of Imperial Defence (CID) to allow the fleet to have an air arm under its own control. Because the RN had lost its own aviation arm to the Royal Air Force, there was no body analogous to the U.S. Navy's General Board to make the trade-offs necessary if scarce resources were to be used efficiently. Instead, the RN's leaders had to appeal to the CID.

However, for most of the years between 1919 and 1939, the Committee of Imperial Defence had only five members, most of whom during this time were drawn from Britain's aristocracy—not from that part of British society most likely to understand the technology of aviation. The committee felt compelled to accept the argument of the RAF that the foundation of empire defense could rest on the strength of Britain's air units, yet the committee—even with the support of its staff—lacked the means to evaluate this position from a technical or operational point of view. Think of the CID during the interwar years as a kind of court, charged with evaluating competing claims. On the one side, there was the RN, asking for control over its own fleet aviation arm. On the other side were the Air Ministry and the RAF, claiming that only through the centralized control of aviation assets and technology could the powerful weapon of military aviation be used successfully to defend Britain and attack her enemies. What reason was there for the CID to depart from established policy and side with the RN?

There was a reason, if the CID had only known of it and understood what it implied. In the 1920s and 1930s, the RAF had nothing equivalent to the famous Norden bombsight for its high-level bombers, yet the provision of such a bombsight was essential if the limited numbers of bombers, carrying limited numbers of bombs, were to have the necessary effect on any enemy equipped with modern interceptors or antiaircraft guns. Of course the assumption was that the RAF's equipment would do well enough "policing" the empire, where the likely enemies of the Crown would have neither interceptors nor effective antiaircraft guns. But even after the notorious "ten-year rule"—which specified, as government policy, that Britain would not face an enemy for another ten years—was abandoned in 1933, the RAF still could not develop an effective high-altitude bombsight. Here was a service saying it could effectively carry the war to a continental enemy when, in fact, it could not.

Our point is that the Committee of Imperial Defence, which possessed great influence, did not also possess the expertise to know what questions to ask of the staff officers who supported it. Moreover, because so much of the committee's work was not open to public scrutiny or even to scrutiny from within diverse segments of the executive organization of government, the members of the CID did not even know what it was they should have been asking questions about.[15] The situation with regard to the U.S. Navy's General Board was quite different. Though testimony at the board's hearings was given in strict confidence, the members of the board knew where the relevant expertise was. No one with a contribution to make was left out, and so potential errors of judgment were more easily identified.

To understand the maturing of the concept of the aircraft carrier and its air group as a strike weapon, it was essential to consider individuals, technology, organizations (such as BuAer and the Naval War College), the availability of funding, and the larger institutional setting within which individuals and organizations acted. Though we separate the individual, organizational, and institutional "levels of analysis," we are also aware that, *in practice,* they are so closely linked as to be inseparable.

In the U.S. Navy's case, for example, the influence and prestige of BuAer were dependent to a great degree on Rear Adm. Moffett's personality and abilities. But where had such a "bureaucratic entrepreneur" come from? The simple answer is that Moffett was the product of a navy whose leaders had stressed performance over social status, and evidence over speculation. But why had the Navy's leaders at the end of the nineteenth century done that? Why were Moffett and Reeves not visionaries but instead true innovators? Our final chapter will address some of the reasons.

Organizations and the Maturing of the Carrier Concept

The carrier concept had several components, and these matured at different rates. In the U.S. Navy, the organizational model—that of the aviation bureau

—essential to the development of effective carrier aviation was adopted even by nonaviators as early as 1921. The USN concept of the carrier as a strike weapon goes back farther, to at least Mustin's tenure in 1916 as commander of the aviation training station at Pensacola, Florida. But the concept began to mature only in 1926, when *Langley* ceased being an experiment and became an operational carrier. It only matured completely when carrier aircraft could carry enough ordnance in a single strike to wipe out whole enemy forces. Maturity depended heavily on technology, but the U.S. Navy needed organizations to call for and then incorporate new, improved technology.

In the Royal Navy in World War I, certain officers were quick to embrace the airplane as a means of performing functions (scouting, screening, and attack) once done only by surface ships. Though the benefits of naval aviation were appreciated by a number of senior nonaviators, control over the aviation side of carrier operations was lost to the RAF at the end of World War I before the RN had an "organizational home" for its carrier aviation forces. The Royal Navy's conceptual "model" of the airplane at sea was therefore stillborn. It began as something around which a larger system (carriers and aircraft operating together with surface escorts) could be built. Over time, the conceptual model became much more limited. Carriers and their aircraft were to coordinate with the surface fleet to bring enemy forces to battle on terms advantageous to the RN.

In organizational terms, the RN engaged in "premature programming." The RN's leaders assumed that the relationship between evolving technology and operations was predictable and would not entail significant surprises. Our point is that concepts can expand and contract, sometimes relatively quickly, and whether they expand or contract depends on whether organizations exist to protect and foster them. The British military treated both the airplane at sea and the combined tank-infantry-aircraft force ashore as routine developmental problems that would not require extensive investment and expensive experimentation. Once the Royal Navy regained control of the Fleet Air Arm, however, its aviation officers—freed at last from responsibility to the Air Ministry—had resources and access to senior decision-makers, and they used their *organizational* resources to compile an extraordinary record of innovations (including the angled deck) in carrier equipment design and use. The record of accomplished innovations in the RN's carrier forces after 1942 is very much like that of the USN's carrier units in the mid and late 1920s. This parallelism is no accident.

The two decisive factors in learning how best to employ carrier-based aviation were experience and simulations coupled with exercises. As we have argued, exercises, even if artificial, were another form of experience. Experience, whether at war or in peacetime, was essential for innovation. In peacetime, however, something needed to guide experience because exercises were expensive. In the USN, simulations conducted at the Naval War College guided experience—particularly those done while Rear Admiral Sims was president in the early 1920s. There was a simulation-exercise (and fleet problem)-simulation cycle in the USN. Rear Admiral Pratt certainly sought to encourage it during his tenure as president at Newport.[16]

Simulations based on data provided by BuAer suggested how carriers and carrier aircraft could be used tactically. Then the alternatives explored at the Naval War College were tested at sea in the fleet exercises. What gave the whole process an orientation toward the future were the projections supplied by the Bureau of Aeronautics—projections drawn from close contact with industry, from its own studies, and from the emerging field of aeronautical engineering, which was strengthened by studies funded by the National Advisory Committee for Aeronautics. What made intimate contact with industry possible, in turn, was the small size of both the aviation industry and the science and engineering base on which it drew.[17] The USN, therefore, had a process for refining and testing operational concepts. The Royal Navy did not have a similar process, and senior RN leaders were not allowed to create one.

The success of this testing process depended on the relationships among individuals in their particular organizational settings. In the USN, in the early 1920s, what mattered was cooperation among Sims, Moffett, and—later—Reeves. Mattering just as much was the confidence the early USN aviators won from senior officers who lacked aviation backgrounds. The 1919 General Board hearings, though often acrimonious, were nonetheless a place where younger officers could gain the support of their seniors. They gained that support by adhering to an important institutional and organizational rule—providing evidence. When the admirals sitting as the General Board asked their aviator colleagues for evidence of aviation's performance and promise, the latter never answered back that the demand for evidence was unfair. Their enterprise—the search for valid evidence—was shared by senior and junior officers alike. Another example of this shared professional perspective was the support, after World War I, for an aviation bureau on the part of Rear Adm. David Taylor, the highly respected chief of the Bureau of Construction and Repair. Taylor's support was based on his professional analysis of the role of aviation, and his analysis was supported by his strong scientific and engineering ability.

Our focus here is on professional relationships among officers in different organizations within a navy. There is no evidence, for example, that Sims and Moffett were friends, or that Moffett and Reeves were friends. In fact, the available evidence suggested to us that their personalities were not only different but in many ways incompatible. Yet the emphasis on evidence, coupled with the creation of positions that gave officers the authority to run trials and gather evidence, brought these very different individuals together in a shared endeavor.

The existence of the War College presidency, the bureau chief's position at BuAer, and the commodore's post as head of aviation squadrons in the fleet gave officers such as Sims, Moffett, and Reeves places from which they could interact professionally. Each had authority and prestige; each could command the respect of the others; all could work together toward a common goal. They were not locked into a competition for leadership that kept them from working together. There is no question that they were ambitious and competitive. Moffett, for example, stayed in his post as BuAer chief until he was killed in the crash of airship *Akron* in 1933—a tenure of nearly twelve years. To stay there, he had to defeat several attempts to have him removed and replaced by younger officers.[18] Reeves used his record as commander of the aviation squadrons to lever himself eventually into the post of commander in chief, U.S. Fleet. In the mid-1920s, however, Sims, Reeves, and Moffett could cooperate without directly competing.

By contrast, the removal of the aircraft component of naval aviation from direct Royal Navy control after World War I not only robbed the RN of its most experienced aviators, it also left officers who were also pilots with no place to go within the Royal Navy as aviators. And they were needed there. Debates about the proper role of the carrier could not be conducted within the RAF, or between the RN and the RAF. They needed to be carried on within the RN, in an experimental setting. The existence of an "air ministry" and a special force for air warfare (the RAF) kept the RN from building an organization that could hold enough senior people to carry on the planning and design the experiments and exercises essential to fleshing out the carrier concept.

Still another significant organizational factor was that the "rules of evidence" in the two navies were different in the field of aviation. In the USN, the emphasis was, especially in the senior ranks, on evidence gained through experience. Officers focused on how much ordnance carrier aircraft could drop and whether they could drop it accurately. Senior officers, such as the members of the U.S. Navy's General Board, also studied the effect of that ordnance. Exercises were staged to determine whether carriers could use their fighters to defend themselves, or whether they had to send every available aircraft to strike at the enemy. Reeves, first a champion of aviation as a striking force, later also took a direct interest in using exercises to study the tactical implications of communications and communications warfare. It was through his efforts, for example, that the fleet began using great caution after the mid-1930s in its radio communications. His approach to tactical and operational uncertainty was to gain reliable evidence from tests and exercises. It was an approach understood and accepted by the leaders of the USN.

For the Royal Navy's carrier advocates, by contrast, there was a special, suspicious audience to be dealt with—the RAF. The senior aviation positions were in the RAF, and they were mostly held by officers with experience in land-based air forces. It was these officers who were responsible for making decisions about resources and for evaluating the evidence of aviation's military potential. The fact that, in the USN, the naval air force was still an integral part of the Navy, coupled with the role of the Navy's General Board as a high-level integrator of new technologies, operational concepts, and tactics, meant that the "voting" on the future of aviation was done within one community of professionals with a shared sense of what mattered. In England, there were two communities, and very little brought them together professionally. Indeed, the RN's carrier program before World War II looks impressive in light of the organizational split between the RN's Fleet Air Arm and the RAF.

There were also tactical problems that had organizational-level effects on the development of carrier forces. The inability of carrier aircraft to find and then strike moving targets at night is an example. Night landings were attempted—successfully—on both USN and RN carriers in the 1920s. However, recovering night strikes was less a problem than attacking at night.

In the 1920s, carrier aircraft, especially torpedo planes, did not have great range. The danger of a night attack for the attacking force was that its torpedo planes would not find the enemy, but that the enemy's surface forces would instead find the torpedo planes' carrier, which had to stay relatively close to the enemy's suspected position in order to gather up its brood of torpedo planes as they returned from their mission. Moreover, as its own aircraft landed, the carrier that had launched a strike would be visible because it would turn on marker lights to help guide its own aircraft home. That would render it vulnerable to enemy aircraft and to enemy submarines.

The RN's night attack on the Italian battle fleet in Taranto in 1940 was successful because the targets of the RN's torpedo planes were stationary and because the British Swordfish aircraft had much greater range than their predecessors. By contrast, the U.S. Navy withdrew its carriers during the night after their initial daytime success against Japanese carriers at Midway. It was well that the American commander, Rear Adm. Spruance, did. As they had so often practiced in peacetime exercises, strong Japanese surface forces pursued his carriers through much of the night.

Even the nature of aircraft ordnance had *institutional* effects. The torpedo launched from aircraft was perceived as a ship killer early in naval aviation's history, and torpedo planes equipped the first carrier squadrons. But torpedo planes were limited in their tactics by the nature of their weapon. In their final approach, torpedo planes were very vulnerable, both to defending fighters and to antiaircraft guns.[19] The USN and the Imperial Japanese Navy developed concerted tactics, where level bombers and dive-bombers coordinated their strikes with the attacks of the torpedo planes. The RN developed escort fighters, designed to shield the torpedo planes from serious attack until the last moment. But all these approaches had flaws. Coordination could simply fail, as it did for the Americans at Midway, or the escort fighters could —as they did for the RN—turn out to be inferior to the aircraft they were meant to fight.

The real barrier to success in this instance was the torpedo itself—its short range, and its tendency to fail once released from the airplane. Early torpedoes demanded too much of the aircraft that carried them: the planes had to fly very low and at slow speeds when launching a torpedo, and aim the torpedo by flying the aircraft at the target. Bombs were better. They could be dropped from altitudes above effective antiaircraft fire, and larger bombs (one thousand and two thousand pounds) were deadly against unarmored ships. Unfortunately, the success rate for high-flying level bombers in the late 1920s was about 5 to 7 percent hits against maneuvering targets. Lower down, at five thousand feet, level bombers of the U.S. Navy hit the stationary obsolete armored cruiser *Pittsburgh* 50 percent of the time in tests conducted in 1931.[20] But the target was anchored and lacked defenses. Consequently, the tests showed only that air-dropped ordnance was growing more destructive. In a war, defending fighters would have shot down attacking level bombers faster than the bombers could have scored hits on the carriers which had launched the fighters.

Dive-bombing was both more accurate than high-altitude level bombing (70 percent hits versus 7 percent) and safer for the pilot. When the technique of dive-bombing was combined with large (500 kg or 1,000 lb) bombs in the late 1930s, the dive-bomber became a great threat to all warships. In 1930, bombing trials against maneuvering obsolete destroyers had shown the USN's aviators the potential of dive-bombing,[21] but they needed a plane that could control its dive speed (and hence its accuracy), still carry at least a one-thousand-pound bomb, and have the range to attack enemy ships at a great distance from its home carrier.

It took years to get such a plane. The Curtiss O2C-1 of 1931 normally carried only two 116-pound bombs; the SBC-4 of 1938 could carry a one thousand-pounder over a short range but usually flew with one five-hundred-pound bomb; the famous SBD "Dauntless" of World War II fame carried a one-thousand-pound bomb over its full fighting range but only a five-hundred-pound bomb when scouting.[22] In the meantime, surface officers refused to accept the idea that a few such bombs could knock a battleship out of commission. The vulnerability of carriers was another matter. A few large bombs could turn unarmored carriers into floating volcanoes. Armored carriers, however, couldn't carry many aircraft—perhaps two-fifths of an unarmored carrier's complement.

Carrier aircraft needed weapons that could be launched at ships from long range or tactics that thwarted antiaircraft guns. Dive-bombing, as we have noted, provided the latter in the early years of World War II.[23] However, in 1943 USN task forces developed an effective means of vectoring their combat air patrols onto attacking enemy aircraft, thus subjecting enemy dive-bombers to often severe attack from Navy fighters even before the enemy planes had to run the gauntlet of heavy antiaircraft fire from surface ships. To penetrate this form of layered defense, the German Luftwaffe developed radio guided bombs, but the signals controlling such bombs could be—and were—jammed. The Japanese resorted to the suicide aircraft, or piloted cruise missile, which had to be shot down because it could not be jammed.

The destructive power and accuracy of aircraft ordnance influenced the decisions of the major navies as they experimented with carriers. Unfortunately for carrier advocates, uncertainty about the effectiveness of ships' defenses in the face of bomb and torpedo tactics was very high in the 1930s, and senior officers in both the USN and the RN had too much confidence in existing antiaircraft guns. Not until October 1939 did the USN have a radio-controlled drone aircraft target that could simulate a dive-bombing attack. Tests with the drone revealed that existing antiaircraft fire control systems and five-inch antiaircraft shells in the USN were quite inadequate against dive-bombing.[24] The test results revealed the vulnerability of all ships to attack from the air but also added to the perceived vulnerability of carriers. So while the ordnance loads of carrier aircraft increased dramatically in the years just before World War II, carriers themselves remained particularly vulnerable to attack by aircraft.

The Institutional Level of Analysis: Politics and the Carrier Concept

The "politics" of military aviation's development in the United States in the 1920s had both positive and negative effects for the carrier concept. The primary negative effect of the controversies waged in the press, in Congress, and over the June 1921 bombing trials was that all tended to oversimplify the basic issue, turning a complex problem of technology and tactics into a face-off between the airplane and the battleship. The primary positive effect was to drive USN aviators and nonaviators together.

Navy aviators had toyed with the idea of forming a separate organization within the service, along the lines of the Marine Corps. They had also considered the utility of allying with their Army counterparts to form a separate air force. Mitchell's campaign, and the great controversy generated by his claims, led to a discussion among naval aviators that, contrary to Mitchell's intentions, increased their loyalty to the Navy and their conviction that aircraft had to be fully integrated with the fleet. This would not have happened had major decisions about military aviation been taken quickly and behind closed doors.

Put another way, the "battleship vs. airplane" controversy stimulated meaningful, as well as oversimplified, debate and discussion. It also highlighted, for the Navy's nonflying officers, a question: What was the proper role of aviation in the Navy? Fortunately, reformers such as Sims, building on the insights of Rear Adm. Stephen B. Luce, founder of the Naval War College, and assisted by subordinates such as Harris Laning, had a means for answering that question.

Sims understood how to use simulations to explore concepts that could not be tested with existing equipment and tactics. His leadership of the War College in the early 1920s laid the intellectual foundations of the Navy that won World War II. Under Sims, the classes of the War College studied the effects of new technologies such as the submarine and the airplane. To those in the Navy who objected to his methods and challenged what was being learned at the Naval War College, Sims could always answer by pointing to the public debate, as well as to the consensus within the U.S. Navy that the service needed to take advantage of the innovations applied to naval warfare during World War I.

Sims had no need to raise the specter of an independent air force robbing the Navy of aviation because Rear Adm. Moffett did it for him. Moffett was the "bridge" between the aviators and senior officers in the Navy who weren't aviators. In 1922, for example, at the urging of then Chief of Naval Operations Robert E. Coontz, Moffett had argued to the secretary of the Navy that "Any normal individual can become a good flyer in a few months, but it takes years of other kinds of training in addition to flying to make that individual competent to perform aviation duty with the fleet."[25] Moffett's point was that pilots should be officers, trained to take the initiative after assessing the tactical situation. Moreover, they needed to be naval officers, with experience in the fleet. Moffett wanted to stop dead any effort to create a separate Navy flying corps. He also wanted to use General Mitchell's advocacy of a separate air force to pressure the secretary of the Navy to adopt his (Moffett's) personnel policy. In this effort, Moffett was supported by seagoing officers like Rear Adm. William V. Pratt.[26]

We suggest, then, a paradox: a key (not *the* key, but *a* key) element in the maturing of the carrier concept in the USN was the existence of the public debate over the airplane vs. the battleship. Without that debate, the navy's aviators and nonaviators would not have explored their differences and common interests so intensely. Without it, there would have been less (or no) pressure on Sims at the War College and, later, on Reeves in *Langley.*

But of course the public debate was not everything. The Navy did not ask Congress for a Bureau of Aeronautics primarily in order to put off the advocates of a unified air force. Instead, members of the General Board and the chief of naval operations, responding to their own evaluations and the arguments of technical experts such as Rear Adm. David Taylor (chief of the Bureau of Construction and Repair), decided that the conceptual organizational model of aviation they had been working with was no longer suitable. They abandoned the notion that airplanes were just another form of equipment (like ship's boats and cranes) and accepted Taylor's position that aviation was a coherent but different field of technology equal in scientific and engineering status to the established fields of steam engineering, ordnance, and naval architecture.[27]

Rear Adm. Moffett, however, understood how and where to present this professionally developed perspective so as to gain the most political benefit. As he wrote to the influential and knowledgeable Congressman Carl Vinson in 1931, "Upon my return from the flight of the [airship] Akron over your district . . . the thought occurred to me . . . that the people were all your friends and how fortunate they are to have you represent them in Congress. . . . I have had the honor and pleasure of knowing you a great many years, and feel that they are to be congratulated."[28] Moffett's ability to pen such a personal note to an influential member of the national legislature was simply not open to his counterparts in the Royal Navy. One of Moffett's assistants called him "an accomplished public relations man."[29] Though not necessarily meant to be a compliment, the comment reveals how much access Moffett had to political figures and how Moffett's political skill was essential to carrier aviation's early years.

Barriers to Innovation

We have discussed individuals who opposed carrier development, and we have pointed to tactical uncertainties and organizational obstacles. There were also many institutional barriers to change and institutional arrangements that channeled or shaped change. The first was the unwillingness of both the American and British governments to invest heavily in carrier forces. Though aviation in the USN got more than its "fair" share of funding in the 1920s, that still was not enough from the perspective of Moffett and his colleagues, who were promoting both lighter-than-air and fixed-wing technology.

Aviation was a "greedy" technology. It needed R&D facilities, such as wind tunnels. Pilots and engineers needed training. Aircraft were easily damaged during operations and training, so the RN and the USN needed lots of aircraft. The planes themselves needed hangars and airfields. Airships, such as the giant *Akron* and *Macon,* needed even more space, and even the smaller nonrigid airships, or blimps, required storage out of the weather. Aircraft needed lightweight radios and instruments, and special kinds of ordnance. Pilots encountered extremes of cold, g-forces, and a lack of oxygen. Their needs gave rise to a whole new field: aviation medicine. This continuing expansion of aviation technology made it the "enemy" of fiscally conservative governments.

A second institutional-level barrier was the "treaty system." The Washington Treaty, which imposed major restraints on warship construction by those party to it, was based on the notion that holding down spending on new naval technology and warship construction was essential to guaranteeing international stability. The treaties of 1922 and 1930 had concrete effects on carrier development plus a more subtle but nevertheless influential impact on public opinion in England and America. *Life* magazine went so far as to say in October 1940 that "during most of the past 20 years Americans had all but forgotten that they had a Navy. It was little more than a newsreel."[30] Though exaggerated, *Life*'s assessment showed that the treaty crafters had at least partly achieved one of their goals—to reduce the visibility of navies.

We believe that these constraints hurt the RN more, for several reasons. First, the RN's carrier force, because it was the first to be built, had too many marginal units—ships turned into carriers before enough was known about designing a carrier for the continuous operation of aircraft. Second, the RN fell behind both the USN and the Imperial Japanese Navy in the 1930s in terms of aircraft performance. Because the RAF understandably focused first on bombers and then on fighters to defend the British islands against attack from Germany once the German regime began to rearm, RN and Coastal Command aircraft development got less attention and money. But this, as we have shown, was a critical time for aircraft development, when agencies like the USN's BuAer were beginning to plan the shift from the one-thousand-horsepower engines to those with two thousand horsepower.

By the end of U.S. participation in the "treaty system" in 1938, the USN was nearly ready with its *Essex* carrier design, and the Bureau of Aeronautics was preparing to shift from biplanes to heavier wing-loading monoplanes. When war came, the USN would have the ships, the aircraft, and the training process required to field a massive sea-borne air force, but it still took nearly five years to move from the "treaty system" to the post-treaty world. The RN was readying its armored carrier design when Japan withdrew from the treaty system in 1936, but it was still hamstrung by the requirement that its aircraft have a slow landing speed. Given the demands of rearmament and war on Britain's aircraft and shipbuilding industries, the RN carrier forces did not grow (and could not have grown) and advance like their USN counterparts, though British land-based aircraft designs were good and the RAF did nourish a strong aircraft industry.[31]

The Washington Treaty was designed to limit both qualitative and quantitative naval arms competition. It succeeded. By restricting the numbers of carriers which the principal navies could build, it made the development of multicarrier tactics difficult. The USN, for example, was not sure how best to organize a formation of carriers because, until 1938, it only had three "fast" carriers (*Lexington, Saratoga,* and *Ranger*) to work with, and *Ranger* was already seen as not fast enough. The value of clustering carriers' strike squadrons was demonstrated in exercises. So, too, was the vulnerability of carriers to air attack. The Japanese demonstrated the value of concentration at Pearl Harbor; they were victims of its dangers at Midway. The Washington Treaty deliberately hindered carrier tactical development. Not one of the three navies with major carrier forces overcame this hindrance.

A third institutional-level barrier to carrier development was promotion and personnel policies. Every naval flying force needed lots of pilots. It also helped to train numbers of those pilots as officers because exercises showed that they would often have to take independent decisions once in the air. But what did you do with an officer once he passed his prime as a pilot? Put him in a training unit? No. You actually wanted your best pilots there. Older, experienced pilots could (and did) organize and command training units, but other places had to be made for these veterans if the service did not intend just to discard them once they had flown for ten years or so.

There were several conceptual solutions to this problem. One was to create a separate "flying corps," so that pilot officers competed with one another for command positions and not with nonflying officers. Another "solution" was to rotate pilots back into the larger service, making them gain the same kinds of experience as nonpilots, and then evaluating the pilots and nonpilots together. A third solution was to draw the bulk of pilots from the enlisted ranks, so that they would not, as they aged, constitute a "bulge" in the ranks of the officer corps. A fourth approach was to set aside commands for older pilots—carriers, shore stations, seaplane tenders, and pilot training facilities.

All these solutions were tried. Each had advantages and disadvantages. In the USN, for example, the effort to solve the problem of what to do with older officer pilots, and how to evaluate their performance as officers when they spent most of their early years flying, produced bitter, lasting enmity between line officers and their aviator colleagues. The former were often jealous of the latter's hazardous duty bonus pay, special insignia and uniforms, and glamorous image. The pilots, on their part, developed early in their careers a sense of themselves as special and of their duty as especially hazardous and daring.

Because of the very real differences between the two groups, which was amplified by the pugnacity of the younger regular and aviation officers, the administrative leaders of each (the chiefs of the bureaus of Aeronautics and Navigation) fought a series of "paper wars" in the 1920s.[32] As chief of BuAer, Rear Admiral Moffett wanted his organization to set training schedules, assignments, and evaluation criteria for aviators. His argument was that only aviators could have the experience and knowledge required to create and administer a sensible personnel policy for other aviators. Nonaviators did not have it and could not acquire it except by becoming aviators themselves. Moffett's counterparts in the Bureau of Navigation consistently opposed him. They argued that all regular (vs. reserve) officers were basically the same, and that aviators were not a special class of officers deserving special attention.

Though Moffett was successful in his campaign against those senior USN officers who suspected that naval aviators simply wanted to form a separate clique within the Navy, the bitterness of the long dispute survived into World War II.[33] This lasting enmity is a sign that the issue was a real one.[34] For example, if aviators were eventually to gain task force and fleet commands, how were they to gain the experience necessary to direct battleship formations? The command of carriers and seaplane tenders would not give them that experience unless carriers were the capital ships of the future, in which case it would be the regular surface officers who would be at a disadvantage.

As it happened, carriers were (for the USN) the capital ships of the future, but no one knew that in the 1920s or even by 1940.

Moffett also faced a variation of his struggle with the surface navy within the naval aviation community itself. By 1930, for example, USN aviation had great variety: carrier strike aircraft (torpedo planes, level bombers, light bombers and fighters), catapult floatplanes from battleships and cruisers, large seaplanes, and lighter-than-air, which included the large aircraft-carrying airships *Akron* and *Macon.* This "community" was itself very diverse. To hold it together, BuAer required aviators to train with every type of aviation except lighter-than-air. Pilots who wanted to fly from carriers also had to serve six months or more with seaplanes and with a floatplane detachment.[35] The idea behind this policy was to give them an understanding of the variety and uses of naval aviation and the special problems facing each subcommunity within naval aviation. Not coincidentally, this policy also muted some of the criticism of naval aviators as overspecialized, pampered opportunists.

In the development of a new military technology, the mundane activities of personnel training, promotion, and evaluation can be ignored in the rush to field new weapons. This omission, when it occurs, can have major consequences once a nation goes to war. An example is Rear Adm. Moffett's decision to accept a high rate of damage, during peacetime operations, to naval aircraft, especially carrier aircraft.[36] Moffett knew the pilots would take risks; risks were inherent in aviation, especially carrier aviation. His intent was not to punish them for doing what they had no choice but to do.

Contrast his willingness to accept accidents with the decision by senior submarine officers to deliberately avoid peacetime operational risks. During Fleet Problem XV (May 1934), for example, a Navy submarine taking the "enemy" role slipped into the cluster of darkened supply ships and tankers supporting "friendly" forces. When challenged by one of the support ships, the surfaced submarine responded in Morse code with a flashlight that it was a private yacht. To avoid ramming the "yacht," the support ships showed their lights, which the surfaced submarine then used as aim points. After "torpedoing" one "friendly" ship, the submarine escaped, and escorts of the support ships "fired" wildly on one another in their efforts to ward off further submarine "attacks."[37]

This clever ruse did not win its creator praise, nor did it inspire a reconsideration of existing submarine attack tactics. Instead, the commander in chief's report of the incident noted that the effectiveness of such nighttime attacks on the surface was "very doubtful."[38] The USN had already lost submarines in highly publicized peacetime accidents, and the Navy did not want to exaggerate the danger of submarine service. If a carrier airplane crashed, at most only the pilot and perhaps one or two aircrew were lost. Whole crews were usually lost when submarines sank. The difference in the potential toll is only one explanation, however, for the difference in policy. Submarine doctrine was very conservative in the 1930s: subs concentrated on attacking enemy combatants instead of merchant ships, submerged approaches to enemy targets were slow, cautious affairs, and operations on the surface in daytime were avoided. The constraints placed on submarine operations, especially in exercises, limited the ability of submarine officers to sense how and when submarines would be most effective

The Costs of Change

The major navies were faced with a dilemma after World War I. Technology had presented them with more opportunities (aircraft and submarines, for example); politics had reduced the money available to develop those alternatives. Opportunity costs were high, and key technologies were in flux. The problem was one of mitigating the effects of errors because, in a time of such rapid technological change, errors were inevitable.

Carrier air forces were expensive because they could not supplant the battleship and battle cruiser altogether and so had to be added on to existing fleets. Carriers did indeed cost less than a battleship to build. Carrier *Enterprise,* for example, cost about half as much as battleship *North Carolina,* its contemporary. But carriers were much more expensive to operate over their expected lifetimes because of the costs associated with operating an air group.[39]

The Washington Treaty imposed both established technology (the battleship) and tentative technology (the carrier) on the major navies, but it did not give the USN, the RN, or the Imperial Japanese Navy enough carriers to show that the battleship was about to be superseded. No navy had enough battleships *or* enough carriers, so all three major navies had to invest in both. None of the three gambled on just one technology. All three spread the limited available funds as judiciously as possible. In short, the "treaty system" imposed a conservative (i.e., risk averse) approach to building up naval strength on the major navies. The only way to progress beyond this approach was to have an organization that could formulate the right questions (identify the problems), conduct tests of likely answers (or solutions), and then evaluate the results honestly.

The question, then, is "What kind of opportunity cost did the introduction of carrier aviation impose?" Put another way, what was given up to get carrier aviation? For the USN, the answer was "not much"; the fast battleships, cruisers, auxiliaries, and destroyers the USN wanted in the years before World War II were denied by treaty or because Congress would not spend the money. It was somewhat different for the RN, which had to rely on a smaller industrial base to supply ships and weapons to a navy with wider responsibilities than those of the USN. The lost opportunity was, perhaps, most frustrating for the aviation component of the U.S. Army, which wanted to build bombers with intercontinental range but was not permitted to as long as the Navy's seaplanes and carrier planes could provide aerial support for the U.S. Fleet. In the spring of 1938, for example, the Joint Board of the Army and Navy recommended that the Army not procure any bomber "having a greater practical ferrying range, greater tactical operating radius, and greater carrying capacity than those of the B-17."[40]

In the USN and RN, the real "cost" of carrier aviation was not so much financial as doctrinal and tactical—figuring out how to use surface forces and carriers together. Because of their speed, it made sense to turn carriers loose in independent striking forces. Because there were few carriers, it made sense to shield them from attack, but it was not clear how best to do that. Armor them? Release them from the battleships so they could strike and then retreat? Or shelter them under the umbrella of battleship antiaircraft weapons? All these approaches were debated and tested in exercises, but there were not enough carriers to risk safely an incorrect "solution" to the problem of operating carriers and battleships together.

Unfortunately, exercises didn't solve the tactical issue, so carriers were—inevitably—placed at risk once war came. The "cost" of wartime operations was high. Of the seven fleet carriers (*Lexington, Saratoga, Ranger, Yorktown, Enterprise, Wasp,* and *Hornet*) with which the U.S. Navy began the war in December 1941, only one (*Ranger*) had not been sunk or seriously damaged by the end of 1942. The RN suffered similar losses. By the end of 1942, it had lost five of its seven prewar carriers. Only *Furious* and the experimental *Argus* remained. It should not surprise any reader that the advocates of land-based aviation regarded these initial losses as a sign that valuable resources had been wasted.

Related to the concept of cost is that of risk. Even a very high opportunity cost may be acceptable if it reduces risk. As we have shown in preceding chapters, the USN developed carriers for independent strike operations, while the RN combined its carriers with its battleships in order to provide reconnaissance for the latter. The tactical risks facing the two navies were accordingly different. In the U.S. case, the risk was that carriers operating at the heart of independent strike forces would be lost through poor tactics or by surprise, leaving the fleet's battleships open to enemy air attack. For the RN, the tactical risk was that its carriers would not field enough high-performance aircraft to support the battleships they accompanied, opening both battleships and carriers to attack by enemy surface and air forces. The Japanese, who went down the same road as the USN, accordingly found it relatively easy to sweep the Royal Navy from the Pacific. Yet the real tactical risk for the RN lay much closer to home, and indeed was borne by the RAF—the danger that Britain's air defenses would be overwhelmed, opening up the country itself to air bombardment and to a combined air and naval blockade by German forces.

Uncertainty about the future, and the high risk of costly error associated with that uncertainty, could be accepted far more easily by the USN because of its organizational ability to identify and solve problems, especially in the field of aviation. This capability, added to the productive power of U.S. industry, gave the USN a decided advantage. If more carriers were needed once war began, they could be built. If the attrition of carrier aircraft from operations and accidents in wartime was high, then more aircraft could be produced. So long as success in naval warfare hinged on both productive power *and* organizational capability, the USN was in a strong position. It could—and did—produce sound aircraft requirements, an optimal carrier design, a training program that produced large numbers of well-schooled pilots, aircrew, and maintenance personnel in short order, and senior officers who knew how to apply the ships and aircraft which U.S. industry could produce.

It would be wrong to assume, however, that the carrier "revolution" was inevitable in the U.S. Navy because it played to American economic, industrial, and political strengths. The Navy could still have made the "wrong" technical and tactical choices. Industrial capacity was not a sure guarantee against American naval failure, as defeats at the hands of the Japanese in the struggle for Guadalcanal in 1942 showed. What made aviation in the USN a success was the combination of the right people, a set of organizations that could learn, the institutional relationships among those organizations, and a potentially huge aviation industrial base, which included the automotive industry.

The RN could not fall back on the unique strengths of the USN, especially the latter's organizations and industrial base, unless the U.S. were its ally. In this sense, large "fleet" carriers and their aircraft complements were more and more like battleships—complex, expensive, and hard to replace. Expansion to meet wartime ship and aircraft production requirements would falter (as it had during World War I for U.S. military aviation) unless there were existing organizational templates, or models, that would allow for rapid increases in production and training.[41] In the United States, the aircraft production template was the assembly-line model provided by the automobile manufacturers. In Great Britain, on the other hand, the aircraft production template took advantage of the diverse nature of British industry. The very effective Mosquito bomber and reconnaissance plane, for example, was composed of wood as well as metal, and was manufactured on the basis of the wood-glue expertise developed by the firm of de Havilland.[42]

By 1941, the U.S. Navy knew what types of carriers and carrier aircraft to build, how to train qualified pilots in large numbers, and how to use its carriers against Japan's fleet. The problem of financing and then building a large carrier fleet could be taken as solved. A related issue, as Clark Reynolds's biography of John Towers reveals, was whether the USN would have, when war came, naval leaders capable of wielding the awesome forces that American industry and society could provide. USN aviators were not sure. In 1941, many of the leaders of U.S. carrier aviation—admirals King and Halsey, for example—were latecomers to aviation. Prominent leaders of the Navy, such as admirals Chester Nimitz, Husband Kimmel, and William Leahy, were not aviators at all. The prewar suspicion of aviators toward nonaviators remained. The question was whether the USN's wartime leadership had learned the lessons of the prewar games and exercises, and whether, once in the war, they could continue to learn.

We believe that the capacity to learn operational and organizational lessons in the course of daily operations was and is a major means of reducing risk. We believe that this is the sort of argument that Rear Adm. Sims made when he was president of the Naval War College after World War I—that the "opportunity cost" associated with losing an officer to the War College course for a year was more than compensated for by the insights that the officer gained. We also believe that the experience of the U.S. Navy with carrier aviation in the years before World War II substantiated the view of Rear Admiral Sims.

The Importance of a Threat or a Rival as a Spur to Innovation

Potential threats are a standard by which to gauge the strength of one's own forces. For example, on the one hand, if the USN had not been forced to consider fighting Japan in the waters of the far Pacific, it would not have needed to worry so much about the need to take aviation to sea. On the other hand, if the RN had not moved ahead with carrier aviation so rapidly during World War I, the aviators in the USN would never have had so persuasive a case to put before the General Board in 1919. If U.S.-British naval rivalry had not replaced cooperation after World War I, the USN would not have had the RN as a competing standard—in carrier operations and in battleship gunnery.

But rivalry is not the same as having an enemy. An enemy generates an incentive that rivalry may not. In the first three-fourths of the nineteenth century, for example, the RN regarded the French navy as its most likely enemy. The French returned the suspicion. As a result, the two navies competed in terms of doctrine and warship designs, each looking for technical and tactical means to gain clear mastery over the other. Once France and Britain allied against Germany, however, the French navy was simply a friendly rival, and the pressure came from the German navy. The Royal Navy's leaders focused then on what German ships could do, how many of them there were, and so forth.

The Washington Treaty was designed to turn potential enemies into mere rivals by denying each signatory the power, while the treaty lasted, to overwhelm his most likely opponent in his opponent's waters. But the existence of the treaty did not eliminate pressure on the USN to at least plan for a Pacific campaign. Treaty or no treaty, Navy leaders had to plan to send the U.S. Fleet from California, through hostile waters, westward to a besieged Manila Bay, there to fight the Japanese fleet.

At the engineering and immediate operational levels, however, the competition was with the British—the rivals. So little was known about the specifics of Japanese carrier aviation within the USN's aviation community that first the British and then the "ORANGE Fleet" of the war-gamers became the standard for competition. In war games at the Naval War College, ORANGE (for Japan) was usually given a strategically defensive role, and ORANGE carrier aviation was usually given the same general characteristics as USN carrier aviation—an example of "mirror-imaging." The "threat" was not well understood.

U.S. Navy planners, however, were affected by the widely held assumption that Japanese carrier aviation was less capable than their own. Though carriers and other classes of large warships were impossible to hide, it was much harder to discover what Japanese naval aircraft could do and how quickly they could be prepared for a strike. Even the Japanese were uncertain about the military potential of their carrier forces. USN intelligence knew that the Japanese used their carriers and naval aircraft in combat against Chinese air units, and were building more carriers—as well as a land-based bomber force and a large force of long-range seaplanes.[43] Yet what drove the development of USN carrier aviation was not the specifics of the Japanese "threat," but what the war games at Newport had revealed for years—that the USN faced a great challenge in moving across the Pacific against determined Japanese resistance. The USN's push for carrier aviation depended more on anticipating serious resistance to its trans-Pacific campaign than on having knowledge of specific enemy systems.

Was competition between navies an incentive to innovate? "Competition" means more in the development of carrier-based aviation than just reacting to the actions of a potential enemy. "Competition" covers, as well, the contest within and among nations such as the United States and England to develop profitable commercial aviation. "Competition" includes the desire to win air races and establish air records in order to gain publicity. Indeed, the military competition among the USN, the RN, and the Japanese navy was overshadowed in the public's eye by the race to be first across the Atlantic, or the first to circle the globe by air, or the first to fly over the North Pole. U.S. and British military aviators tried to "cash in" on this friendly competition, and the accepted wisdom was that it actually did some good (it spurred research on higher powered engines, for example). But the inauguration of operational carrier aviation by the USN in the years 1925–29 owed little to any "spillover" from air racing or civilian aircraft developments.

Over time, however, there was a valuable exchange of technology and information between the civil and military wings of aviation. Facilitating this exchange in the United States was the National Advisory Committee for Aeronautics (NACA), which promoted what today would be called "dual use" technology.[44] Innovations such as aerodynamic streamlining, supercharged piston engines for use at higher altitudes, and internally pressurized aircraft cabins were developed under NACA auspices with the financial and engineering support of both the Army and Navy.

Moreover, it was still possible, even into the 1930s, for relatively small enterprises to produce aeronautical innovations. As a result, the field of aviation stayed "open" to newcomers with unorthodox views. In fact, because of restrictions imposed on the services' freedom to contract in the USA, commercial industry often led the Army and Navy in adopting new technology.[45] The NACA then served as the forum where such new technology was exchanged and its implications discussed.

This link between the civilian and military aviation worlds was not the final answer to promoting innovation in military innovation. As historian I. B. Holley has shown, the process and institutional relationships among firms and military organizations that kept advancing piston engine technology in the United States also failed to move industry into turbojet propulsion.[46] One reason for this was that NACA and the Army's Materiel Division engineers adopted complementary roles. Until 1925–26, NACA focused on fundamental aerodynamic research; thereafter it began to emphasize applied research. Throughout the 1920s and 1930s, the Army and Navy concentrated on advancing the performance of existing (i.e., piston engine) technology. So long as existing technology kept advancing at a pace that was at least equal to that from any competing air service, there was no demand from the services for a fundamental redirection of research.

That tendency was not challenged by developments overseas—by a new "threat." Nor was it challenged by developments fueled by the infant airline industry. Yet, as Holley has shown, theoretical papers on reaction—jet—propulsion were presented at a technical conference held in Italy in 1935, and by then NACA investigators knew that propeller-driven aircraft would soon hit a speed ceiling.[47] To break into the field of jet engine technology, someone needed to invest in a concerted program of research and development. The services could not fund industry to do the necessary R&D because, in peacetime, the only means of reimbursing industry for its R&D efforts was through production contracts. No private firm would take the risk of doing the R&D on its own because it would have taken so long to move from the research required to mature turbojet technology to the manufacturing of operational jet aircraft.[48]

This situation shows not only the need for competition, which serves as a source of pressure on decision makers who control scarce resources, but also the problems of sustaining it in a cost-constrained environment. A lack of funds is a two-edged sword. On the one hand, the inability to procure large amounts of existing technology, such as battleships, can open the way for innovators to press for a competing technology, like aircraft carriers. On the other hand, the lack of funds can throttle the implementation of those innovations that require, *before* they get into production, large sums for which no commensurate military benefit can be gained. This is why the pace of aeronautical innovation—strong before World War II—ballooned during the war itself. There was enough money to support all the "marginal" projects that had not been affordable before the war. Once war began, aeronautical commands, especially in the United States, were like rich gamblers in a casino. They could afford to take more risks than their poorer prewar counterparts.

How important were expectations to the development of new combinations of technology and tactics? Optimistic expectations about the future role and capability of carrier-based aviation were essential to inventing new technologies, tactics, and the organizations to foster them. However, different people reached expectations about carrier aviation's potential in different ways. Rear Admiral Fullam of the USN, for example, had a sudden insight. John Towers, the Navy's dashing champion of its community of aviators, both enjoyed the thrill of flying and perceived the military and civil potential of long-range aircraft. Henry Mustin was perhaps the first U.S. Navy officer to propose that the striking power of aircraft at sea could and would equal that of the battleship. The growth of carrier aviation in the USN benefited initially from the fact that its supporters could reach their shared commitment to it by following separate developmental paths. What mattered in the long run, however, is that they also shared a commitment to deciding rationally, on the basis of evidence gathered from simulations and experiments, how to judge among their different proposals.

Air-minded officers in the RN, by contrast, found themselves—once all British military aviation was consolidated under the control of the RAF—either out of military aviation altogether or part of the RAF, and there was no effective aviation staff within the Royal Navy. There was a formal link between the RAF's technical specialists and Royal Navy officers charged with setting future aircraft requirements. But what was missing was a naval staff led by a senior naval aviator and composed of naval aviators and naval aeronautical engineers. In comparing the USN and the RN in the 1920s, what is striking is the difference in the level of senior officer involvement in carrier aviation's development. Admirals or future admirals in the USN, such as Moffett, Reeves, and Towers, were central, influential figures. Their leadership was essential, we believe, to implementing the innovation of carrier aviation in the USN. Carrier aviation in the RN, however, lacked that kind of skilled senior leadership. As a result, RN aviation reached a kind of plateau and stayed there until just before World War II.

Unlike the USN, the RN did not embrace in time the more advanced aeronautical technology (based on more powerful engines) which came along in the 1930s.[49] In 1930, for example, a typical carrier-based fighter was powered by an engine that developed four hundred to six hundred horsepower. In about 1936, much better fighter engines, such as the British Merlin, which produced one thousand horsepower, began to appear. About three years later, the best new engines for fighters produced about two thousand horsepower. These engines were small enough and light enough to power fighters, and they made possible the transition from low-wing-loading biplanes to high-wing-loading monoplanes.

After 1935, aircraft engine development changed at a pace that was almost too rapid for nations and navies to keep up. Hard decisions had to be made. When might war come? If sooner rather than later, then the correct policy was to order lots of aircraft. But if war came later, then the air force that bought lots of aircraft now would be saddled with obsolete types once war did begin. To prepare its aircraft industrial base for wartime rates of production, the RAF placed large orders in 1938, before the two-thousand-horsepower engines were suited for fighters. This policy, though it won the Battle of Britain in 1940, nevertheless delayed the movement of the British engine manufacturers into the next cycle. Because the Royal Navy's aircraft requirements had a lower priority than those of the RAF, the former's two-thousand-horsepower-engined aircraft did not appear until over a year after the U.S. Navy began deploying its own fighters with two-thousand-horsepower engines.

There was, in short, a trade-off that had to be made between present danger and future potential. Complicating this trade-off was a quirk of aerodynamics. More powerful engines meant faster aircraft, but only to a point. The biplane aircraft's drag held down its speed. Increased engine power at the same engine weight brought heavier loads and greater ranges but not necessarily greater speeds. This is one reason why both the Royal Navy and the U.S. Navy invested in two-seat fighters in the later 1920s. The second seat, for a radioman and gunner, did not cost much in performance given the increased power of newer engines. But when the more powerful engines were combined with streamlined aircraft fuselages, retractable landing gear, and single (vs. double) wings, aircraft speeds jumped. In the early 1930s, it was difficult to see how this would all play out, especially for carrier aircraft. Assuming carrier fighters got faster, for example, how could they be brought back aboard their carriers at speeds that would not wreck so many aircraft that a carrier would lose her aircraft strength just through accidents?

The analysis necessary to anticipate and then make these trade-offs is done by a navy's staff. Senior officers provide guidance, and make sure that the proper questions are put to the staff. But then it's up to staff officers to list the options and the trade-offs, and, as well, the consequences of making one trade-off as against another. The U.S. Navy's Bureau of Aeronautics had a staff suited to identifying and then making these trade-off analyses. Moreover, they could request the Naval War College to anticipate the operational consequences of their choices, and they were always getting "feedback" from the fleet about the operational performance of deployed aircraft. The Royal Navy's staff did not have all these advantages, though its officers compensated a bit by openly and repeatedly comparing their own carrier aircraft (in numbers and quality) with those of both Japan and the USA, especially the latter.

We are making a subtle point here. The Royal Navy got the carrier aircraft it asked for. But these were not necessarily the aircraft it should have had. One reason for this mismatch between wants and needs is that the RAF's requirements were given priority during a time when aeronautical engineering was rapidly advancing. A second reason is that the Royal Navy did not have an organization like the U.S. Navy's BuAer (or the Imperial Japanese Navy's similar Naval Aviation Department). But a third reason is that there were so few aviation staff officers in the Royal Navy at all—not enough to generate the kinds of expectations that kept American (and Japanese) naval aviators straining for innovative concepts and weapons.

As historian Stephen Roskill showed in his second volume on naval developments between the wars, the Royal Navy had to create a "new Air Division of the Naval Staff" once it regained control of the Fleet Air Arm in

1938. Manning that new division was difficult because the Royal Navy lacked "aviation officers of middle seniority" and "technical officers."[50] Put another way, the Royal Navy had for years lacked an adequate naval aviation staff to which its leaders could turn for the study and analysis that is the essence of good military staff work. So the RN's carrier aircraft requirements were not based on the same kind of analytically based expectations that the USN's Bureau of Aeronautics created.

Our more general point is that the existence of a threat, a rival, or a competitor is not sufficient to generate an adequate, innovative response on the part of a complex bureaucratic organization. Indeed, the arguments usually offered against a bureaucracy are in this case turned on their head. A smaller organization may indeed act faster than a larger one, but only the larger organization may have the expert staff required to process the available information and produce alternatives for senior leaders to choose from. A smaller organization may also have very loose routines, and so be able to accommodate changing circumstances. But the larger may still have the advantage that regular processes and practiced routines bring. Make no mistake about it—the carrier revolution was not brought about in an ad hoc way. It was, instead, a revolution brought about through bureaucratic organizations acting according to regulations. Without the spur of competition, however, those very organizations might never have been created.

The Phenomenon of the "Bureaucratic Entrepreneur"

A "bureaucratic entrepreneur" is an official who uses the authority and influence granted him as the leader of an organization to enlarge the scope of that organization's authority beyond its formal boundaries. The literature on military innovation contains many examples of bureaucratic entrepreneurs, including Rear Adm. William Moffett, first chief of BuAer. New military technologies may need such aggressive leaders because the payoff from innovations is often remote and therefore dependent upon an initial allowance of funds from patient and sympathetic leaders and politicians. Such bureaucratic entrepreneurs buy time for innovations by making sure, as did Rear Adm. Moffett, that initial failures do not kill the innovation.

In the case of USN carrier aviation, the innovation was also threatened by its potential to alter the fundamental distribution of influence and resources within the Navy. Thus, aviation needed more than its share of clever leaders, because those military officers who were its primary advocates in its infancy were mostly young and therefore junior in rank. The RN's experience with carrier aviation during World War I was therefore crucial to the success of carrier aviation in the USN because, by providing the evidence that won support for aviation among senior USN officers, it substituted for the lack of a "bureaucratic entrepreneur."

By generating further evidence in carrier aviation's favor, the war games sponsored by Rear Admiral Sims at the Naval War College added to aviation's allies within the USN. The games persuaded senior officers like Reeves and Pratt of carrier aviation's potential. So did the fleet problems, even before there were many carriers that could participate in them. Once *Lexington* and *Saratoga* joined the fleet, officers such as Reeves and Pratt made every effort to learn how best to use them. They needed to. Rear Adm. Moffett had staked his reputation among members of Congress and in the Coolidge administration on the performance of those two ships. When they were judged successful, Moffett's ability to function as a bureaucratic entrepreneur was strengthened.

Embracing aviation was professionally risky for naval officers right after World War I. The RN's experience was very promising, and USN aviators witnessed—and at times participated in—the RN's achievements. They knew what they wanted—aviation with the fleet. Their contemporaries in the Imperial Japanese Navy (IJN) were in a similar situation. In both nations, young officers pressed for an air arm. In both nations, the younger aviation-minded officers were led by older "champions." In the U.S. case, the "champion" was Rear Adm. Moffett. In Japan, he was Rear Adm. Isoroku Yamamoto.[51]

In Moffett's case, however, there was another "bureaucratic entrepreneur" with whom he had to compete—Brigadier General Mitchell. Mitchell had witnessed the maturing of large-scale air operations in Europe in 1918, and he came away with "lessons" that set him on a collision course with Moffett. The competition between them actually hindered the development of the new technology both supported. Moffett's criticism of Mitchell was that Mitchell's operational concept of military aviation was flawed and that Mitchell's effort to force that flawed concept on all U.S. military aviation was a serious error.

To combat Mitchell, Moffett used the openings that the political and military institutions of the United States provided him. A model bureaucratic entrepreneur, Moffett wrote to prominent figures in the Republican Party to persuade them to support naval aviation in their discussions with the president. He also spoke with and wrote to members of Congress, taking advantage of the access that his position as bureau chief offered. He also appealed to the public through the press and addressed veterans and citizens groups whenever the opportunity arose. He patiently and skillfully built a base of power within the Navy, using his record and the achievements of naval aviation to gain support among his peers in the service.

Most of these potential "tools" were also available to General Mitchell, and he used them. Unfortunately for Mitchell, he lost the official support of the Army just when he needed it the most. But he very nearly carried the day in his quest for a unified air service separate from the Army and Navy. American political leaders were accessible, and Mitchell courted them. Many newspapers and magazines, hungry for stories and eager to present drama to their readers, became Mitchell's partisans in his campaign to copy the RAF in the United States. So the audience for his 1925 court-martial was huge and often intensely partisan. Mitchell gambled on using his public image, allied with support from within Congress, to gain his goal. As we have shown, Moffett's ability to gain political support was given an important boost by the work that year and the next on *Langley.*

The situation in England was different. First, the most effective bureaucratic entrepreneur was Air Marshal Hugh Trenchard, first head of the RAF. Second, only selected members of the RAF and the RN had the right to approach senior elected officials the way the relatively junior Moffett could in the U.S. The Royal Navy's leaders had less opportunity to present their case to the public or to elected leaders than Moffett and his supporters. The RN's struggle with the new Air Ministry and RAF was waged more through confidential memos and letters than in public confrontations. There was no chance for a Royal Navy "champion" of carrier aviation to come to the fore.

However, the Air Ministry staff and the RAF could not deny the strike potential of carrier aviation because the USN's carrier aviation was highly publicized. As early as 1932, for example, movie audiences in Great Britain could watch "Helldivers," an exciting and highly accurate film on USN carrier aviation, and other adventure films and newsreels kept USN carriers in the public eye as the decade progressed. Rear Adm. Moffett had used his authority to facilitate the making of "Helldivers." His goal was to spread an appreciation of naval aviation's potential through the American public, and, through the public, to Congress. In consequence, by the late 1930s, any American with enough money for movies and an interest in naval aviation knew what carriers were, how planes were launched and recovered, and even how naval aviators were trained. This method of reaching the public was simply not available to the RN officers struggling to gain control of the Fleet Air Arm. Indeed, it was the RAF that benefited from publicity about military aviation.

Moffett, however, was far more than an effective publicist. As we have noted, he shaped BuAer's structure and personally composed many of the initial regulations that governed U.S. Navy aviation. Though eager for positive publicity, Moffett understood that achieving military objectives mattered more to the progress of carrier aviation than any clamor about visions of war in the air. This is why Moffett accepted Reeves and supported Reeves's efforts to make *Langley* an effective unit of the fleet. What's striking about Moffett as a bureaucratic entrepreneur is that his politically shrewd, influence-conscious Washington personality was complemented by his understanding that naval aircraft needed to cope with immediate and clear operational problems. Unlike General Mitchell, Moffett was not a visionary. Though personally confident—even arrogant—Moffett was a careful strategist.

Evidence of his cleverness is the way he gained the loyalty of the younger naval aviators. Unlike Mitchell, he did not stand as a gallant symbol and as a defiant martyr. Instead, he kept his aviators in the spotlight, and he championed their cause effectively within the Navy. He won support from successive secretaries of the Navy and from influential members of Congress. The products of his efforts were resources and personnel for aviation at a time when the overall Navy budget was in sharp decline. This pragmatic approach bound naval aviators to the Navy as a whole, and they stayed bound. The experience of the RN's aviators appeared, in the eyes of their USN counterparts, to confirm Moffett's judgments and his methods.

In his *Winning the Next War: Innovation and the Modern Military,* historian Stephen Rosen has argued that military organizations tend to be "political" in peacetime and "pragmatic" in wartime.[52] That is, there is no way in peacetime to know just what will win the next war, and this uncertainty forces advocates of different tactics and weapons to argue with one another about the virtues of their ideas and their preferred weapons. When others refuse to accept their arguments, the proponents of a given force or weapon turn to politics. They try to gain the approval of the government in order to "win" the contest of ideas. In wartime, by contrast, the experience of battle serves as a ruthless test of what works. Arguments among advocates are replaced by a pragmatic assessment of the available evidence.

Assume for the moment that Rosen's argument is correct. Then the reason why a bureaucratic entrepreneur like Rear Adm. Moffett plays such an important role becomes clear—disputes about what type of force to build are resolved by argument and by political maneuvering, and "entrepreneurs" like Moffett are masters of both. However, Moffett needed the support provided by Reeves's work on *Langley.* It was Reeves's success that sustained naval aviation by adding hard evidence to the persuasive arguments of Moffett and his staff. In effect, carrier aviation in the USN was sustained in its early years by both "political" and "pragmatic" factors.

Summary: The Case against "Vision"

There was an interaction between the development of carriers in the RN and the USN. The experience of the RN in World War I convinced the USN's carrier advocates that carrier aviation was feasible. Later, the publicity surrounding the USN's carriers spurred carrier aviators in Britain. Once the RN used seaplanes and land-based aircraft for naval missions in World War I, the proposals for naval aviation in the USN became more focused. The true "dreamers" were the advocates of long-range strategic bombing. They maintained a "vision." Naval aviators developed specific programs that were then tested at sea and made a part of naval tactics—in both the USN and the RN.

Early proponents of carrier aviation employed effective means—simulations, experiments, and exercises—to explore existing and anticipated technology, its uses, and its limitations. They worked to turn concepts into practice, especially in the USN. For example, Henry Mustin, Moffett's deputy in BuAer, was not a "battleship man," though he had begun his naval career as a gunner. He apparently held the view that battleships were only platforms for carrying weapons that directed ordnance at the enemy. Things such as battleships and airplanes were, for sailors like Mustin, only a means to an end. They weren't ends in themselves.

Reeves and Mustin were similar in this regard. John Towers thought Reeves lacked enough concern for the safety of *Langley*'s aviators when the two served together in 1926. We believe Reeves's supposed callousness was due to a conception of pilots, as well as their aircraft, as means to an end—

gaining and then using air superiority to achieve victory through whatever means of delivering ordnance was at hand.

Yet military aviation in the 1920s held a symbolic position similar to that once held by cavalry. Aviators, like cavalrymen, were dashing and adventuresome, with special pay and uniforms. Their achievements were visible; their exploits celebrated. Reeves seems to have been quite unaffected by this image. Something similar happened in the RN because it was the RAF that held the dashing image.

We believe that the image—the symbol—can obstruct clear thinking about the system and its technology. This leads to a paradox: image can bring status, which in turn attracts talent and justifies funding; but image can also cloud judgment. The symbolic status of a system can obscure sensible decision-making about its use by placing in positions of authority those who see the system as an end rather than as a means. Elevated symbolic status can weight the "voting" or decision rules and procedures in an organization in favor of those officials best able to appeal to symbolism—that is, to the nonrational. The battleship has often been accused of serving as such a powerful, expressive, and emotive symbol. Surely the manned aircraft—particularly the strategic bomber—has been used the same way by its adherents.

This argument suggests that officers favoring the same basic technology may sort themselves out into two camps. The first group contains what might be called the "unconstrained" visionaries—those less willing to change their ideas given the available evidence. The second group contains the more realistic officers—those intent on developing a novel technique for fulfilling an existing mission. Brig. Gen. William Mitchell was a visionary—the first sort; Rear Adm. Reeves represents the second type of what's now often called a "change agent." His perspective was practical.

We wonder what might have happened if World War I at sea had taken the course of war on the Western Front: siege warfare of the most brutal sort, whose outcome was dictated often by an appalling process of industrialized human slaughter. After all, Brig. Gen. Mitchell pressed so fervently for his vision of strategic air bombardment for good reason: conventional ground combat had become untenable. Conventional war at sea had not, and so the naval proponents of aviation were not motivated by a nightmare image. They were motivated by their beliefs and hypotheses of the potential of aviation at sea. General Mitchell was absolutely—and understandably—driven. Military professionals can and do choose their beliefs about the future advantages of new technologies. Experience may thrust a vision on them that they embrace with a religious passion, but that passion may rob them of the ability to consider their vision critically. Put another way, innovation is dependent less upon "vision" than upon having means (organizations and procedures) for turning ideas into programs and then realistically testing the products of those programs.

Conclusion

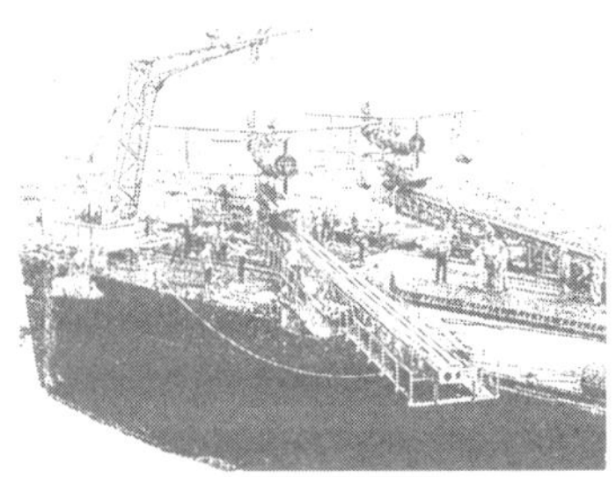

THE HISTORY OF innovation in carrier aviation says something of great importance about military innovation generally: it is not a process that usually proceeds in a linear way. But hindsight tends to make us think that it does. Because we try to compose coherent histories of innovation, we may actually overlook the uncertainty and chance that inevitably exist.

Soviet military analysts fell into this trap because they had grown accustomed to looking for patterns and causes in history—to see history as the purposeful unfolding of a dialectical process. The idea that changes in warfare were random clashed with their view of history. But the dialectic, on the one hand, and randomness, on the other, are not the only alternatives. The world is usually a lot more complicated than we want to admit, and we think that our case studies back up our view. We also believe that the evidence shows individuals matter a great deal. But they play their roles in organizational and institutional settings that shape alternatives, constraining them in some cases and opening up opportunities in others.

We do not believe that anyone placed in the same position as a Moffett or a Reeves would necessarily have acted the same way. But the organization of the Navy and of the U.S. government created opportunities for Moffett and Reeves to exploit. Other officers might have acted differently, but the institutional and organizational settings would still have affected them.

The technology of aviation did not dictate one clear path to the future. It was up to each individual to decide what path he would support. We want to stress that there was a lot of uncertainty and ambiguity attached to that decision, and there was no one way the individuals involved in developing carrier aviation were drawn to gambling their professional careers (and even their lives) on it. Indeed, what is so striking about the maturing of carrier aviation between World Wars I and II are the parallels between navies—similarities reached without the kind of intense analysis of the potential enemy's carrier forces that characterized naval developments and competition during the Cold War.

We have argued that the inferiority of British carrier aviation was partly the result of a series of unfortunate, but almost inevitable, technical decisions made within particular organizations and institutions. For example, the fact that RN carrier aircraft had to warm up their engines on their carriers' flight decks, coupled with the small size of most of those flight decks, meant that RN carriers could not launch the large air strikes that even small USN carriers like *Ranger* could. As a result, the RN could not get enough experience with the "pulse" of ordnance that a carrier could deliver—a pulse which Rear Admiral Reeves of the USN perceived when he participated in the Naval War College games and which he made happen when he took command of the fleet's air squadrons.

But the negative consequences of the way the Royal Navy operated its carriers did not stop there. Because the RN's carriers could not launch large strikes, the British navy relied heavily on catapulted aircraft from cruisers and battleships to deliver ordnance (recall that battleship *Warspite*'s floatplane sank a German submarine at the second battle of Narvik in 1940, for example). Because these aircraft had to be capable of becoming airborne at relatively low speeds, they had to be biplanes. The stress on low landing and takeoff speeds, combined with small carrier aircraft complements, kept the RN from having the high wing-loading, high-speed monoplanes that became available just as World War II threatened. The retention of biplanes also meant that the RN's carriers were not forced to refine measures, such as the crash barrier and the deck park, whose purpose was to increase aircraft cycle times. In his fascinating memoir, for example, former FAA pilot John Wellham noted that carrier Eagle had no crash barrier as late as 1939.[1] In consequence, the USN, decidedly inferior to the RN in carriers and carrier operations and aircraft in 1919, was ahead of its former ally by 1929.

Why did this happen? Not because the Royal Navy did not appreciate the value of carriers. Not because the British aircraft industry could not design quality aircraft. Not just because the RAF supplied the RN with its aircraft and dominated aviation policy in Great Britain. The RN did not have high levels of informal access to decision makers. Its debate with the Air Ministry stayed within Britain's executive. The RN did not have anything like the U.S.

Bureau of Aeronautics or its Japanese counterpart, nor did it have an analogue to the General Board or to the organizational relationships within the USN that generated empirical evidence from simulations, experiments, and exercises. Finally, the RN did not have senior officers like Moffett and Reeves when it most needed them (in the mid-1920s) because they had already been transferred to the RAF.

An aviation bureau was important for several reasons. First, it represented the interests and needs of naval aviation at the highest levels of the military and civilian bureaucracy. Second, it provided an alternative to the land-based aviation establishment—even a form of competition. BuAer, for example, financed the development of the radial air-cooled engine, which was an innovation that the Army accepted but had not planned to support. Third, the bureau's Plans Division fed data on the progress and potential of aviation to the Naval War College, so that the college could simulate future (as well as existing) aerial operations.

Fourth, BuAer—because it was a technical establishment—gave naval aviation technology special status. As a weapon, the carrier and its aircraft may have been auxiliary to the battle line. As a technology, however, naval aviation had the same formal and organizational standing as naval ordnance, naval engineering, and naval architecture. Like them, it could claim resources; like them, it was rooted in science; like them, its practice was professional, with specialized schools, training programs, and tests for entry and advancement. Even before the creation of the Bureau of Aeronautics, the U.S. Navy had extended to aviation the professional standing accorded to ordnance and mechanical engineering. The brightest graduates of the Naval Academy had the opportunity to enter graduate programs in aeronautics and then circulate during their careers with the finest technical professionals in industry. BuAer became the home and sponsor for these professional engineers.

The Bureau of Aeronautics was not what the younger leaders of U.S. naval aviation wanted. What they really wanted was a deputy chief of naval operations for air, with aviators holding high positions on the Navy staff and in the operational chain of command. What they got in the first chief of BuAer, however, may have been even better. Rear Adm. W. A. Moffett was a superb bureaucrat. He won—and then kept—extraordinary authority for his bureau; he fought off the challenge from General Mitchell of the Army; he gained funds for aviation at the expense of other parts of the Navy. He expanded the influence of his bureau at a time of highly constrained funding, and he pushed to completion projects such as the huge airships *Akron* and *Macon.*

Moffett grasped that the creation of the Bureau of Aeronautics meant the Navy had accepted a new model of aircraft employment in the Navy. He also shielded aviation in the fleet while the political battles over the control of aviation raged in Washington. But Moffett did not make carrier aviation effective operationally. The credit for that belongs to Reeves and to Reeves's subordinates such as Towers. Credit is also due the USN's General Board, which endorsed the potential of carrier aviation despite aviation's relatively high cost and the uncertainties associated with it.

Much maligned during its lifetime, the General Board was perceived by many USN officers in the 1920s and 1930s as a kind of Star Chamber. Its deliberations were secret, and, as the senior advisory board to the secretary of the Navy, it had the last word on ship design, and its recommendations were always influential in the areas of arms control policy and naval strategy. Because it worked secretly (and secrets were kept in those days), its recommendations were often seen as the result of an arbitrary process. Once the stenographic record of its deliberations was opened to researchers, however, they gained a more sophisticated and accurate understanding of the board's methods and role—an understanding which the board's contemporaries could not have had.[2]

Analysis of what the historical record reveals to us about the actions of individuals and organizations within an institutional setting provides several points to consider. First, the institutional setting provides opportunities and obstacles to organizations and organizational arrangements. The institutional setting may not tolerate a great deal of interaction among people assigned to different organizations. In consequence, coordination within a navy may be relatively easy, but there will be fewer opportunities to identify and correct far-reaching errors that transcend the organizational jurisdiction of that navy. This was the situation that the Royal Navy had to live with before it got the Fleet Air Arm back from the RAF. The U.S. Navy held a less organizationally isolated position. Its aviation organizations—in its aviation bureau and in the fleet—cooperated and debated with their army counterparts, and both naval and Army aviation interacted regularly with political, industrial and technical leaders outside the executive branch of government. That is, the institutional setting in the United States tolerated or encouraged a great deal of interaction within and between organizations, and therefore it was easier to identify and mitigate errors.

Second, there is no guarantee that a deliberate effort to alter a country's institutional setting in a way that will enhance the adoption of a "revolution in military affairs" will succeed. Political institutions and military organizations may retain processes and procedures that fail to confront and solve the difficult task of coordinating large numbers of people, complex military technologies, and associated combat organizations into an effective fighting force. Military organizations don't necessarily "evolve." They may or they may not have leaders able to create organizational processes and institutional rules that are essential to that military's ability to increase its combat potential.

Our conclusions drawn from the British and American case histories bear on the present. Modern navies are multidimensional forces that rely on the expertise of many disciplines. In the years between World War I and World War II, the term "the fleet" actually masked growing technological and tactical differences among the components of the major navies—the USN, the RN, and the IJN. For a long time, fleet doctrine in all three navies rested on the assumption that the elements of the three fleets—battleships, cruisers, aircraft carriers, and submarines, for example—would work together in coherent formations in wartime. As it happened, that was a mistaken assumption. Submarines could not work well with surface ships and aircraft and so were operated independently. Major fleet-against-fleet battles were rare. Even at Midway, in 1942, when the IJN hoped to lure the major USN forces in the Pacific out for a fleet-vs.-fleet confrontation, carriers fought carriers, and the IJN battle line withdrew after learning that its carrier losses were severe.

Had the doctrine developers created more problems than they had solved? No. They had no choice. But what every senior officer in every major fleet should have assumed was that things could go very wrong and therefore individuals and organizations should have been prepared to learn quickly and learn well.

In each major navy, some organization or process had to connect the technical branches with their operational counterparts. Furthermore, some organization or process had to combine the various operational communities of each navy together. In the years after World War I, there were not enough resources to develop every promising naval technology to a high level, especially in an environment constrained by the Washington Naval

Treaty. This meant that the leaders of the USN, RN, and IJN had to make hard choices about priorities. The General Board, assisted (sometimes even countered) by the CNO, performed this function in the USN.

A classic and well-documented case where the existence of the board saved the USN from making an unfortunate decision was when the board deferred judgment on whether to build cruisers with flight decks. The flight deck cruiser was Rear Admiral Moffett's pet idea. He believed that securing permission from the other signatories of the Washington Treaty to construct cruisers that also carried flight decks would solve the USN's problem—highlighted in simulations and fleet problems—of not having enough carriers.[3] Because Moffett was a member of the American delegation to the London Conference of 1930 (called to renew the Washington agreements), he was able to insert a clause into the treaty negotiated there which allowed the USN to equip 25 percent of its total cruiser tonnage with flight decks.

That done, he approached the General Board in December 1930 and requested that the members recommend to the secretary of the Navy that such flight-deck cruisers be built. The CNO, who then sat as a member of the board, promptly asked the Naval War College to conduct simulations comparing the military utility of a conventional cruiser with nine eight-inch guns with that of a cruiser with nine six-inch guns and a flight deck holding twenty-four aircraft, each of which could carry one five-hundred-pound bomb.[4] At the same time, the General Board began a lengthy series of hearings on the flight-deck cruiser concept. In the hearings, representatives of the bureaus and the fleet told the members of the board what offensive and defensive characteristics their organizations required and favored in a flight-deck cruiser. The witnesses also answered questions put to them by the members of the board.

From the first, the basic issue was whether the development of the ship's characteristics should begin with a carrier concept or that of a cruiser. The representatives of fleet aviation and of BuAer (including Rear Adm. Moffett himself) favored beginning with a carrier concept and modifying it with the addition of a cruiser's armament. The representatives of the Bureau of Ordnance favored exactly the opposite approach: starting with a cruiser concept and then adding a flat deck and aircraft.

Both sides presented strong arguments in favor of their positions. Capt. John Towers, representing BuAer, said, "I see nothing in this aviation feature attached to the cruiser that hurts it as a cruiser. . . . I see a great increase in offensive power."[5] Towers's contemporaries from the other bureaus, however, did perceive problems: a fire hazard from high-octane aviation gasoline, the weight of the flight deck and hangar high in the ship which reduced the vessel's stability, and the problem of building smokestacks that could fold down while planes were launched and recovered. The thorough consideration of such factors led one of the members of the board to observe, "We are up against a proposition of compromise all the way around."[6]

As it happened, no satisfactory compromise could be found. The board considered the matter in a series of hearings that began in December 1930 and picked up again in mid-July 1931, after the War College had had time to examine the flight-deck cruiser concept in tactical simulations.[7] The hearings were frustrating for all involved. The aviators argued that such flight-deck cruisers could operate singly or with the battleships, freeing up the large carriers for independent operations. Fleet spokesmen wanted the cruiser tonnage allowed by treaty devoted to the functions normally fulfilled by cruisers: scouting, convoy escort, and defense against destroyer attacks.

The Bureau of Ordnance claimed that the ships would be too vulnerable to attack by other aircraft. If their flight decks were damaged, they would be unable to recover their aircraft and only half-suited to serve as cruisers. As Rear Adm. M. M. Taylor, chief of the War Plans Division in the Office of the Chief of Naval Operations, cautioned, "The effort seems to be to get all the aviation facilities on a 10,000-ton cruiser that you have on the *Saratoga* and *Lexington* and I think it is absolutely out of the question."[8] He was right. As the members of the board found themselves unable to agree on a design for the flight-deck cruiser in 1931, 1932, and 1933, BuAer began to accept the fact that bombing and scouting aircraft would soon grow too large and heavy for a combination cruiser-carrier of ten thousand tons. The idea of the flight-deck cruiser was overtaken by the advance of aviation technology combined with the long treaty lifetimes of cruisers. It made no sense to build an aviation ship that would not be able to carry up-to-date aircraft. The board hesitated because it could not find a technically and tactically satisfactory compromise, and the matter eventually became moot.[9]

The case illustrates the role played by the General Board in linking technology to operations—in integrating different technologies (such as aircraft, ship design, ordnance, safety, and communications) with the desires of fleet representatives to solve their basic tactical problems in a fiscally constrained environment. The British[10] and Japanese navies went through similar processes of making trade-offs and reaching design compromises, but neither the British nor the Japanese had one senior board whose members elicited and evaluated technical and tactical arguments and counterarguments for and against proposed characteristics of all their navies' systems. The IJN's "substitute" for such an organization was actual combat experience in China. The RN's battleship tacticians had the experience of Jutland to analyze and overcome. The RN's carrier officers watched with envy the peacetime exercises of the U.S. Navy's carriers, and carried on a long campaign (eventually successful) to get their air arm back.

The case of the flight-deck cruiser also illustrates the great uncertainty involved in developing new technology. On its face, the concept was very appealing. The USN was short of flight decks; the fleet problems had shown the need for more. War College simulations showed that a flight-deck cruiser could hold its own tactically, in one-against-one engagements, with conventional cruisers. The London agreement on naval arms limitation of 1930 allowed the USN to build such ships. So USN officers kept coming back to the idea because it promised to solve some of their most pressing immediate tactical problems. In November 1938, for example, the director of the War Plans Division in the Office of the Chief of Naval Operations suggested to the CNO that the concept be revisited because "[f]or scouting we need numbers of carriers in order to spread them out; we need to reduce their vulnerability (as regards the number of planes put out of action by a damaged flight deck or by underwater damage); we need some increased gun power in order to reduce their dependence on close and constant cruiser protection."[11]

But the flight-deck cruiser concept could not stand close scrutiny. The smaller fleet carriers such as *Ranger* (CV-4) and *Wasp* (CV-7) were actually too small to combine all the characteristics which a carrier needed in order to be successful: a large aircraft complement, high speed, great steaming range (or endurance), adequate stores of gasoline and ordnance, and passive protection (armor and compartmentation). Carrier size was driven by aircraft size and by the need to work with the fleet. The latter requirement could be dispensed with and was, during World War II, when the slower escort carriers were built. The former could not. The flight-deck cruiser, an attractive concept, had to be turned into a set of specific characteristics through the process of hearings before the General Board. In the give-and-take of the hearings, the board could not overcome the obstacles to a satisfactory peacetime compromise.

For innovation to occur, a military force must have a set of organizational relationships and a process which examine critically and fairly all new concepts with the potential for exploitation. No such process or set of relationships can be foolproof. No such process or relationships, no matter how faithfully and intelligently executed, will always succeed. Moreover, no such process and organizational relationships will be, or should be immune from larger questions taken up by organizations, such as the American Congress, that are outside the military.

The USN and RN cases that we have explored present a picture of organizations in which multiple strands of decision making overlapped and intertwined. Carrier development in the USN and the RN did not proceed in a straight line. It did not always move logically from step to step. As the case of the flight-deck cruiser suggests, there were blind alleys. Moreover, the process of military innovation was not immune to political intervention, and that intervention was not always harmful. Rear Adm. Moffett, for example, coupled his bureaucratic skills to his sense of how to generate positive publicity and won budgetary and institutional conflicts to the advantage of USN carrier aviation. So, too, did reformers such as rear admirals Sims and Fullam. In these cases, as when the issues of carrier and aircraft development came before the General Board, the basic question was the same: how should we evaluate the evidence? When a military technology is new and its future uncertain, the judgments of "outside" organizations such as Congress may be just as sound as those of professionals. The pressure of outside scrutiny may even provoke military professionals to act when they would prefer not to. That action, like Reeves's pressure on *Langley*'s aviators in 1925 and 1926, may be risky, but it may also be essential if the new technology is to survive.

USN carrier aviation survived three major crises in the 1920s. The first was the struggle to keep Navy aviation from being absorbed in a separate air force. The second was the challenge, within the Navy, to set aside sufficient resources for aviation's development. The third was to show that aviation was an important element of fleet operations. Rear Admiral Moffett and his supporters (including members of Congress) fought the first struggle—mainly in the press, in Congress, and before special commissions such as the Morrow Board—in the years 1921–26. At the same time, Moffett used the threat that a separate air force would strangle naval aviation to persuade senior Navy officers to provide funds for his bureau's aviation programs. Finally, it cannot be just a coincidence that Reeves's leadership of fleet aviation in 1925 and 1926 so closely coincided with the Navy's attempts to refute General Mitchell's claims that it had neglected aviation.

All the political, organizational, technical, operational, and bureaucratic activity involved in waging and winning these three "campaigns" shows how important it is to consider (1) individual behavior and perceptions, (2) the organizational setting, and (3) the larger institutional context. Carrier aviation in the USN, the RN, and the IJN developed in the ways it did for understandable reasons, but getting at those reasons requires simultaneous analysis at three levels (individual, organizational, and institutional).

This analysis reveals a mix of critical factors. The USN, for example, gained an advantage by having both a Bureau of Aeronautics and a General Board. The USN also gained an advantage from what might be called a "spillover" effect produced by a wave of innovation that began in the years before World War I. The foundations of this spillover were laid when the Navy's best technical minds became intimately involved in major organizational decisions, such as that committing the Navy to the all-big-gun dreadnought battleship. Some of the same names (Capt. H. I. Cone is an example; Rear Adm. David Taylor is another) crop up in multiple areas of innovation. They would not have played such strong roles if the U.S. Navy had been hostile to innovation or if the larger society had not encouraged invention and change.

The USN also developed, because of the efforts of officers such as Sims, Moffett, and Reeves, a cycle of simulations, fleet exercises, and more simulations (leavened with accurate projections of aircraft performance) that both drove the development of carrier aviation and won support for carrier forces in the unrestricted line officer community. This cycle seems to have been less successful, from the perspective of the USN's aviators, in the 1930s than it was in the 1920s because the rules of the fleet problems were slow to account for the rapidly growing destructive power of the ordnance delivered by carrier aircraft.

USN (and Japanese) carrier aircraft dramatically increased their combat ranges and ordnance loads in the late 1930s, giving carriers the ability to deliver great pulses of power against surface forces while remaining beyond the reach of the guns carried by even the largest and fastest surface warships.

The Japanese navy showed what could be done with this combination of the carrier and long-range, powerful aircraft in 1941–42. The USN responded with successful campaigns of its own in 1944 that destroyed the Japanese fleet because the Americans were able to solve the problem of carrier vulnerability. The Royal Navy, swept out of the Pacific by Japanese carrier air power in 1942, was able to get back in 1945 only as subordinate part of a much larger USN force (while also using American-made aircraft). The Americans capped off their progress by developing a system of underway replenishment that gave their carrier forces the military initiative.

The real carrier revolution came to fruition during World War II. The Japanese and Americans were prepared for it by 1941. The British were not prepared in 1939. U.S. Navy historian Jeffrey Barlow once made the difference very clear in a little talk. He compared British and American carrier task groups in the Pacific in the spring of 1945. Task Group 58.1, composed of two U.S. Navy *Essex*-class carriers (each of 27,000 tons standard displacement) and two *Independence*-class light carriers (each of 10,600 tons standard displacement) carried about 280 aircraft. Of that total, about half were strike aircraft (dive-bombers and torpedo bombers). Task Group 57.2, composed of three of the Royal Navy's *Illustrious*-class carriers (each of 23,000 tons standard displacement) and one *Implacable*-class carrier (which was about one thousand tons larger than *Illustrious*), carried about 235 aircraft. Of that total, approximately sixty-five were strike aircraft.

The total standard displacement of the U.S. task group was 75,200 tons; for the four Royal Navy carriers, the figure was about 93,000 tons. The ratio of attack aircraft per total group standard displacement for the U.S. Navy force was 140/75,200, or 537 tons (standard displacement) per attack aircraft. The comparable figure for the four Royal Navy carriers was 65/93,000, or 1,430 tons (standard displacement) per attack aircraft. This is just an indication of the superior ability of U.S. Navy carriers to mount attacks—an ability that was a function of how aircraft were stowed on and operated from U.S. carriers.

This ability gave the USN's carriers an advantage. The more aircraft you can throw at an enemy, the more mass you have in your attack, and hence the more likely that your forces will gain air superiority and not have to return to the target for a second strike. The U.S. Navy's carriers could put up a larger strike, and therefore the pilots and aircrew flying that strike were under less risk. On average, more of them would return safely than pilots and crews from a smaller strike against the same target. In a campaign of attrition, where aircraft fly strikes again and again, this initial advantage of numbers becomes more important day after day. In the Pacific in 1944 and 1945, victory went to the U.S. Navy because it had numbers of aircraft flown by skilled crews.

We have tried to explain why the U.S. Navy had this advantage. Our explanation rejects the hypothesis that military revolutions such as the strike carrier develop linearly. We argue, instead, that such revolutions are not easily predictable. In fact, there is always plausible data against what later turns out to have been the right choice. There is no crystal ball solution—no straightforward, rational means of predicting the future of military revolutions because the process by which they are achieved is clear only when we look backward. As historian Jon Sumida has observed in a review of another study, the goal of research such as ours is to depict "real people and their relationships within a large and complex organization and social milieu over a quarter century."[12] We have tried to do that as part of a more general effort to improve our understanding of how military organizations field tactical and operational innovations. We believe that the famous American carrier leader, Adm. Marc A. Mitscher, had it right when he observed, in an introduction to an official history of carrier operations in World War II, "aviation was a relatively new weapon and we learned as we went."[13]

Appendix. The Japanese Experience, 1918–1941

The Imperial Japanese Navy (IJN) is both a very important case of the aircraft carrier revolution in war and, unfortunately, a poorly documented one—at least in English. The dramatic Japanese successes in 1941–42, beginning with Pearl Harbor and the sinking of the British capital ships *Prince of Wales* and *Repulse,* were generally taken at the time as demonstrations that the two primary Western navies had failed to adapt air power to operations at sea—and that the Japanese had succeeded, brilliantly. This was less evident by mid-1942, when the Japanese were defeated at Midway, but even there initial reports credited U.S. Army B-17s with a role equal to that of the U.S. Navy's carriers. It took the U.S. Navy successes of 1944, especially in the great air battle of the Philippine Sea, to convince the advocates of land-based strategic bombing that American aircraft carriers were both powerful and superior to any similar force that the IJN could field.

The Japanese case does not figure in detail in the main section of this book because the kind of information that we had for the U.S. Navy and the Royal Navy was not available for the IJN. With the other two navies, we could actually compare reliable information about the influence of individuals, organizations, and institutions on technical and tactical innovations in the field of carrier aviation. We could not—and still cannot—do that with confidence in the Japanese case. However, the recent publication of the excellent *Kaigun: Strategy, Tactics, and Technology in the Imperial Japanese Navy, 1887–1941,* by David C. Evans and Mark R. Peattie, allows at least the beginning of a systematic comparison. Were the Japanese really that much more successful than the British and the Americans?

There were certainly many parallels. The Japanese, like their American counterparts, were strongly influenced by the experience of the Royal Navy in World War I. Though the IJN had begun using aircraft for reconnaissance as early as 1912, it was only in 1918 that the Japanese Diet approved construction of the IJN's first carrier, *Hosho.* Just over two years later, in August 1920, the Diet allowed the IJN to begin planning for two somewhat larger carriers. In November 1921, a British mission led by aviation pioneer Sir William F. Forbes-Sempill shared considerable aviation expertise with the IJN and the Japanese army. Nearly thirty British officers with aviation experience spent two years in Japan, and one group helped Japanese pilots prepare for the first landings on *Hosho* in February 1923.

The IJN also adopted the British practice of lowering a just-recovered aircraft to a carrier's hangar before allowing the next aircraft to land on the flight deck. Like the contemporary British conversions of the cruisers *Glorious* and *Courageous,* the first two IJN carriers—*Akagi* and *Kaga,* converted from two partially completed capital ships—had hangars opening out onto short forward auxiliary flight decks. This allowed the lighter fighter aircraft of the 1920s to take off quickly while larger attack aircraft were assembled on the main flight deck one level higher. The influence of Royal Navy thinking declined in the 1920s, however. By the 1930s, the IJN was branching off in directions that the Royal Navy did not pursue—especially in the construction and use of long-range land-based bombers and large, long-range seaplanes.

Like the U.S. Navy and the Royal Navy, the IJN was affected strongly by the Washington Treaty. The treaty limited the tonnage of Japanese carriers by the same ratio that it applied to battleships—a ratio of 5 to 3. That gave the IJN eighty-one thousand total tons of carriers. *Hosho,* like the USN's *Langley,* was not counted, but *Akagi* and *Kaga* together took up 53,800 tons of the total. The treaty limited any new carrier to a maximum of twenty-seven thousand tons, and so Japan could legally build one of that size, but the Diet turned down the IJN's request for such a ship in 1924 on the grounds that it was too expensive. Like the USN, the IJN then looked to a smaller, cheaper carrier design as the next step in building its carrier forces. The result was the seventy-one-hundred-ton *Ryujo,* authorized in 1929.

Ryujo did not count as a carrier under the terms of the Washington Treaty and hence seemed to be the answer to the IJN's quest for numbers of carriers. But the London Treaty, which came into effect while *Ryujo* was being built, *did* count her as a carrier. The new treaty also counted hybrid cruiser-carrier designs as carriers if their "specific and exclusive purpose" was "carrying aircraft." Hybrid carrier designs were consequently scrapped, and *Ryujo* herself was modified to carry more aircraft. Though the modifications raised her displacement by approximately one thousand tons, *Ryujo* officially displaced only seventy-one hundred tons, which meant that the IJN had just over twenty thousand tons left for any new carrier. Like the American and British navies, however, the IJN was hurt by the worldwide economic depression, and so the last of the "treaty" carriers—*Soryu* and *Hiryu,* authorized in 1934—officially displaced only 10,500 tons each (though both, when launched, were significantly larger than that).

The Japanese were different from both the British and the Americans in developing a powerful, long-range land-based air striking arm. In this development we see the hand of Adm. Yamamoto Isoroku, head (as rear admiral) of the technical section of the IJN's Naval Aviation Department in the years 1930 through 1933 (and later director of the whole department in 1935–36). According to Evans and Peattie, Yamamoto's section issued a specification in 1932 for a bomber that could fly more than two thousand nautical miles and carry more than two tons of bombs. The following year, the admiral asked Mitsubishi to design a special reconnaissance aircraft capable of flying from Japan to U.S. fleet bases in the Philippines and at Pearl Harbor. Although the prototype aircraft was not a success, the design and testing of it led directly to the development of a very long range bomber/reconnaissance aircraft, the Type 96 medium bomber (G3M1, code-named "Nell" by the allies during World War II). These were the aircraft that sank the *Prince of Wales* and *Repulse* off Malaya. The British and Americans were taken by surprise again and again early in 1942 because of the great range of this airplane.

Starting in 1931, the Imperial Japanese Navy also pursued dive-bombing, though at first with modified fighter planes. Initial experiments were so encouraging that the technical section procured the first biplane dive-bombers in 1933. A second design competition authorized in 1936 led to the D3A monoplane (nicknamed "Val") in 1939. Through a series of design competitions and experimental prototypes, the IJN's Naval Aviation Department shifted from a reliance on biplanes to an emphasis on long-range, high-performance monoplanes. The A5M fighter from Mitsubishi (with the code name "Claude" during World War II) entered service in 1936. Combat experience in China in 1937 showed that the A5M's performance was not adequate, and work on a successor produced the famous Mitsubishi A6M, or "Zero," in 1940. The B5N, or "Kate," long-range torpedo and horizontal bomber entered service in 1937. The B5N was lighter than its American counterpart (the Devastator), faster, with a slightly longer range, and had a higher cruising speed.

The differences highlight the different design philosophies of the two Pacific navies. The Japanese, with a more limited industrial base, squeezed the maximum performance (especially range) from engines of one thousand horsepower. The Americans put their faith in the larger, two-thousand-horsepower engine and its advantages in terms of lift and performance. So the so-called Val dive-bomber was roughly comparable to the U.S. Navy's contemporary, the Dauntless, and the Kate was comparable (though superior in terms of range and speed) to the Devastator. But the next-generation torpedo plane built for the U.S. Navy, the famous Avenger, outclassed the Kate, just as the powerful F4U Corsair fighter outmatched the Zero. Our point is that the IJN, like the Royal Navy, had to accept the production limitations of its society's industrial base.

While framing their 1934 building program, the leaders of the IJN pressured the Japanese Cabinet to withdraw from the Washington and London treaties. Japan had to announce its withdrawal by 31 December 1934 or accept a renewal of the naval arms limitation agreements. The decision to pull out of the treaty "system" was prompted by the IJN's demand that it be given "parity" with the

Royal Navy and the U.S. Navy. Though the British government tried one last time to forestall the collapse of the treaty limits, Japan would not go along. One reason was that the Japanese were unable, through diplomatic means, to reduce the number of carriers that Britain and the United States were allowed to possess.

The result was a carrier arms race, at least for the Japanese. In 1934, the naval staff estimated that the Imperial Navy needed, within the next ten years, at least five new carriers. One would replace the aging *Hosho*; the other four would be additions to existing strength. But building more than two new carriers from the keel up was not practical, so a series of conversions was planned. Some of the converted ships were seaplane carriers or submarine tenders. Others were merchant ships; another was a heavy cruiser. The result of this expanded construction program was significant. By mid-1941, the IJN had more carriers and better aircraft than any other navy in the world. The Japanese also had a program in place that was producing new (if converted) carriers steadily. That is why the IJN's loss of four carriers at Midway in 1942 did not lead to its defeat. It had more carriers coming along, and they were the backbone of the force that took on the U.S. Navy in the Philippine Sea in June 1944.

Finally, we need to say something about the relationship between the Japanese navy and army. The Japanese army did not press for or build a force of four-engine, strategic, land-based bombers. There was no separate air force in Japan, and not, apparently, even a strong group of advocates—no Billy Mitchell or Sir Hugh Trenchard. Instead, the Japanese army and navy pursued separate *tactical* aircraft development programs. Indeed, these efforts were so compartmentalized that it took several years for the army and navy to coordinate their air campaigns once war with the United States and Great Britain began at the end of 1941. We do not know why this was so. We *do* know from available sources that the IJN was free to pursue its own aviation programs without severe competition or criticism from the Japanese army. This was an extraordinary situation for a society as resource-constrained as Japan. It makes the Japanese case both incredibly frustrating for the analyst and extremely fascinating. It reminds us again of the need to examine all the evidence—at the individual, organizational, and institutional levels of analysis. But this, unfortunately, is just not possible in the Japanese case.

Sources

We have relied heavily on three sources for information about the Imperial Japanese Navy's carrier programs. The first is a series of articles written by Eric Lacroix for the *Belgian Shiplover.* The articles appeared in the following issues:

2/1971, 2/1972, 3/1972, 4/1972, 4/1973, 1/1974, 3/1974, 4/1974, 2/1975, and 4/1975. Eric Lacroix also provides data on Japanese naval policy in his *Japanese Cruisers of the Pacific War* (Annapolis, Md.: Naval Institute Press, 1997). Our second major source is the set of studies prepared by the Military History Section of the Headquarters, Army Forces Far East, after World War II. The monographs in this series, *Outline of Naval Armament and Preparations for War,* that we found most useful were prepared by anonymous Japanese historians for the U.S. occupation forces. We have used Part I (Monograph 145); Part II (Monograph 149); and Part III (Monograph 160) from the series. Our third major source is David C. Evans and Mark R. Peattie, *Kaigun: Strategy, Tactics, and Technology in the Imperial Japanese Navy, 1887–1941* (Annapolis, Md.: Naval Institute Press, 1997), especially chapters 8, 9, 10, and 13. We also drew on Robert C. Mikesh and S. Abe, *Japanese Aircraft, 1910–1941* (Annapolis, Md.: Naval Institute Press, 1990). On the design philosophy of the "Zero" fighter, see Jiro Horikoshi, *Eagles of Mitsubishi: The Story of the Zero Fighter,* translated by Shojiro Shindo and Harold Wantiez (Seattle: University of Washington Press, 1981). Robert C. Mikesh, "The Rise of Japanese Naval Air Power," in *Warship 1991* (London: Conway Maritime Press, 1991), pp. 102–20, contains interesting information as well as some striking photographs of Japanese naval aircraft.

Notes

Introduction

1. Heinrich's argument is in his "The Role of the United States Navy," in *Pearl Harbor as History* (New York: Columbia University Press, 1973), ed. Dorothy Berg and Shumpei Okamoto, 197–223. The long quotations from the essay are from pp. 197–98 and 206. A response is T. Hone and M. Mandeles, "Managerial Style in the Interwar Navy: A Reappraisal," *Naval War College Review* 32 (September–October 1980): 88–101.

2. See Arthur L. Stinchcombe, *Constructing Social Theories* (New York: Harcourt, Brace & World, 1968), 47–53. There is also physics Nobel laureate Philip W. Anderson's statement, "More Is Different," *Science* 177 (4 August 1972): 393.

3. Douglass C. North, *Institutions, Institutional Change, and Economic Performance* (New York: Cambridge University Press, 1993), 3–5.

4. On the development of armor plate for the navy, see B. F. Cooling, *Gray Steel and Blue Water Navy: The Formative Years of America's Military-Industrial Complex, 1881–1917* (Hamden, Conn.: Archon Books, 1979). The machine gun case is discussed in P. D. Jamieson, *Crossing the Deadly Ground: United States Army Tactics, 1865–1899* (Tuscaloosa: University of Alabama Press, 1994), and M. D. Mandeles, "Review Essay—*Crossing the Deadly Ground,*" *Journal of America's Military Past* 24 (Spring 1997): 67–76.

Chapter 1. *The Early Years*

1. The literature on the development of modern naval gunnery is extensive. We have drawn on John T. Sumida, *In Defense of Naval Supremacy: Finance, Technology, and British Naval Policy, 1889–1914* (London: Routledge, 1993), and Norman Friedman, *U.S. Battleships: An Illustrated Design History* (Annapolis, Md.: Naval Institute Press, 1985).

2. The debate over the shape of the fleet was not confidential. Much of volume 14 (1906) of the openly published *Transactions of the Society of Naval Architects and Marine Engineers* was devoted to it. Our quote of Rear Adm. David Taylor in 1910 is from *Transactions* 18 (1910): 26. Our quote of Captain Rodgers is from *Transactions* 21 (1913): 72.

3. Most of our dates for important events in naval aviation are from Clark Van Fleet and William J. Armstrong, *United States Naval Aviation, 1910–1980* (Washington, D.C.: Government Printing Office, 1981), as are dates for the Navy generally that are not otherwise sourced.

4. Our most important sources for the early years of Navy aviation are, first, Rear Adm. George van Deurs, USN (Ret.), *Wings for the Fleet* (Annapolis, Md.: Naval Institute Press, 1966), and, second, Clark G. Reynolds, *Admiral John H. Towers: The Struggle for Naval Air Supremacy* (Annapolis, Md.: Naval Institute Press, 1991). The quotations describing flying at North Island are from *Wings for the Fleet.* The citations are, in order in our text, pp. 63, 64, 81, 71, and 83. Another source is van Deurs, *Anchors in the Sky: Spuds Ellyson, The First Naval Aviator* (San Rafael, Calif.: Presidio Press, 1978).

5. Maurice Holland, with T. M. Smith, *Architects of Aviation* (New York: Duell, Sloan & Pearce, 1951), chap. 1.

6. See Reynolds, *Admiral John H. Towers,* 69. Also see William R. Braisted, "Mark Lambert Bristol: Naval Diplomat Extraordinary of the Battleship Age," in *Admirals of the New Steel Navy,* ed. J. C. Bradford (Annapolis, Md.: Naval Institute Press, 1990), 334.

7. Van Fleet and Armstrong, *United States Naval Aviation, 1910–1980,* 9.

8. This division between carrier and noncarrier aviation is discussed in Charles M. Melhorn, *Two-Block Fox: The Rise of the Aircraft Carrier, 1911–1929* (Annapolis, Md.: Naval Institute Press, 1974.

9. The letter from Mustin to Bristol, dated 24 August 1914, is in the files of the historian of the Naval Aviation Systems Command. The quote is from p. 2. Mustin's lecture, "The Naval Airplane," is undated but was prepared while Mustin was in command at Pensacola, 1915–17. The lecture is in the file entitled "The Naval Aeroplane," Container 6, Mustin Papers, Library of Congress. Sims refers to the contact with Mustin in a letter to Mustin dated 21 October 1912, Mustin Papers, Library of Congress.

10. Another source for this period and the specific source for Whiting's concept is A. D. Turnbull and C. L. Lord, *History of United States Naval Aviation* (New Haven, Conn.: Yale University Press, 1949), 132.

11. Wayne Biddle, *Barons of the Sky* (New York: Simon and Schuster, 1991), describes the business side of the early years of military and civilian aviation. The quote is from p. 89. The U.S. Army's problems and programs are presented and analyzed in I. B. Holley Jr., *Ideas and Weapons* (New Haven, Conn.: Yale University Press, 1953).

12. Mustin's ideas are contained in a memo from him to the chief of naval operations, "subject: Plans for Air Operations against German Naval Bases and Fleet, including a Plan for Air Attack on Essen," 19 August 1917, File No. 28754-3: 132/69, from the collection of Capt. A. L. Raithel Jr., USN (Ret.). Turnbull and Lord, in *His-*

tory of United States Naval Aviation, discuss the "sea sleds" and other ideas, at pp. 132–35. Photographs of the sleds can be seen in Raithel, "Sea Sleds," *Naval Aviation News,* September1980, 34–37. The notion of transporting large aircraft close to German targets was first put forward by aviation pioneer Cdr. J. C. Porte of the Royal Navy in 1916. See H. A. Jones, *The War in the Air,* vol. 6 (Oxford: Oxford University Press, 1937), 352.

13. Memo, M-00266, "from: W. F. Nicholson, to: The Chief of Naval Operations," subject: "Operations with Large Americas and Towing Lighters," 18 December 1917, in the collection of Capt. A. L. Raithel Jr., USN (Ret.). The Naval Planning Section's memo is from *The American Naval Planning Section—London,* Office of Naval Intelligence, Historical Section, Pub. No. 7 (Washington, D.C.: Government Printing Office, 1923), Navy Department, 91 and 98–99. See also pp. 107 and 112. This reference is also in the collection of Captain Raithel. For the operations of *Furious,* see Jones, *The War in the Air,* vol. 6, chap. 10.

14. W. F. Trimble, *Wings for the Navy: A History of the Naval Aircraft Factory, 1917–1956* (Annapolis, Md.: Naval Institute Press, 1990), 7–8, 13.

15. This exchange is covered in Norman Friedman, *U.S. Aircraft Carriers: An Illustrated Design History* (Annapolis, Md.: Naval Institute Press, 1983), 33–35.

16. "Hearings before the General Board of the U.S. Navy." These records are in the National Archives, Record Group 80, Microfilm Roll 4. We cite the following hearings from 1919: 27 March (p. 370 and 371), 10 March (p. 234), and 18 January (p. 1). See also 12 May (pp. 18–19) and 17 April (p. 14). The quotation about Kenneth Whiting is from van Deurs, *Wings for the Fleet,* 157.

17. Memo, from the General Board to the Secretary of the Navy, "Future Policy Governing Development of Air Service for the United States Navy," General Board No. 449, Serial No. 887, 23 June 1919. This memo is with the records of the General Board in the National Archives, Record Group 80.

Chapter 2. Great Risk, Great Achievement

1. Much of the early part of this chapter is drawn from an excellent paper by Ashbrook Lincoln, "The United States Navy and the Rise of the Doctrine of Air Power," *Military Affairs* (Fall 1951), especially pp. 146–48. The views of then Congressman Fiorello La Guardia are taken from his *The Making of an Insurgent* (Philadelphia: Lippincott, 1948). Rear Admiral Fullam's views were expressed in "Battleships and Air Power," *Sea Power* 7 (December 1919). Also see "End of Sims Inquiry, Charges by the Admiral Sustained in Every Important Detail," *Sea Power* 9 (July 1920): 39–41. Finally, we rely on Melhorn, *Two-Block Fox,* 52–59.

2. The congressional hearings are documented in U.S. Congress, House of Representatives, *Hearings Before the Committee on Naval Affairs,* 66th Cong., 3rd sess.,

1921, pp. 660–61, and in *Proceedings and Debates of the Third Session of the 66th Congress,* vol. 60, pt. 3 (29 January–17 February 1921), pp. 2987–96. The General Board's support for a navy "second to none" is well documented in George W. Baer, *One Hundred Years of Sea Power* (Stanford, Calif.: Stanford University Press, 1994). The quotation is from p. 83. The *New York Times* covered the congressional hearings and the debate between Mitchell and the Navy. Admiral Fullam's testimony in the Senate, for example, is discussed in the 20 February 1921 *Times,* p. 19. Fullam's argument about carriers as movable landing fields is from an undated speech in a file labeled "Speech, Article, Books," Container 7, Naval Historical Foundation Collection, Library of Congress. Other *New York Times* references are from 13 February 1921 (p. 9), 1 March 1921 (p. 17), and 13 March 1921 (p. 16). Another valuable source was Lincoln, "Rise of the Doctrine of Air Power," 147–49. Finally, there is the General Board's memo to then Secretary Daniels, "The Battleship Is Still Paramount," p. 187.

3. The impact of Rear Admiral Sims on the War College is described in Ronald Spector, *Professors of War* (Newport, R.I.: Naval War College Press, 1977) and in G. J. Kennedy, "The United States Naval War College, 1919–1941: An Institutional Response to Naval Preparedness" (Ph.D. diss., University of Minnesota, 1975). Captain Craven's letter is in File UNAO, Folder 1-1A, Naval War College Archives. The archives also contain fleet organization and force structure charts for the tactical and campaign simulations, as well as charts of aircraft characteristics (see UAN-1920 File). An 11 August 1921 letter from aviator John H. Towers, then with seaplane tender *Aroostook,* to J. H. Tomb, of the Naval War College faculty, is in File UA 1921-151 (ltr 02-WLM). The letter from Rear Admiral Sims to the CNO is "subj: United Air Service," File UA, ltr. No. 1-7-2, P1(0).

4. The senator's comments are from *Proceedings and Debates of the Third Session of the 66th Congress,* vol. 60, pt. 3 (29 January–17 February 1921), p. 2992. For evidence supporting the four generalizations, see T. Hone and M. Mandeles, "Interwar Innovation in Three Navies: U.S. Navy, Royal Navy, Imperial Japanese Navy," *Naval War College Review* 40 (Spring 1987), and Melhorn, *Two-Block Fox,* 66–68.

5. The roles of Lt. Pride and Lt. Cdr. Chevalier in developing arresting gear for *Langley* are described in Melhorn, *Two-Block Fox,* 79. Melhorn discusses the decision of the Joint Board at p. 73. Photographs of the work at Hampton Roads are in Capt. A. L. Raithel Jr., USN (Ret.), "Trap 'Em," *The Hook* 10 (Fall 1982): 14–20. The early carrier designs are described in Friedman, *U.S. Aircraft Carriers,* 41.

6. The standard discussion of the Washington Treaty is Harold and Margaret Sprout, *Toward a New Order of Sea Power* (Princeton, N.J.: Princeton University Press, 1940). There is also R. G. Kaufman, *Arms Control during the Pre-Nuclear Era: The United States and Naval Limitation between the Two World Wars* (New York: Columbia University Press, 1990). That Sims welcomed close cooperation with the new Bureau of Aeronautics is clear from a letter he wrote to retired Rear Admiral Fullam on 15 February 1922. See Melhorn, *Two-Block Fox,* 152, n.11. For Benson's

interest in links between the fleet and the Naval War College, see "Relations of War College with Department and Fleet," from CNO to president, Naval War College, 16 August 1919. Also "Memorandum for Chief of Staff," subject: "Relations of War College with naval and military service [*sic*]," p. 2. Both are in File UNT 1919–1923, Naval War College Archives. Also in the archives are the fleet war instructions (File UNI). The citation from the section entitled "Mission of the Aircraft Squadrons" is from p. 22. Read's lecture, "Aviation in the Fleet," was presented on 14 July 1922 and is No. 649, Record Group 4 (Publications), pp. 1–2. The tactical manual, entitled *Tactics,* is dated June 1922 and is No. 336, Record Group 4 (Publications), Naval War College Archives; the citation is from p. 12 of Section VI, "Aircraft in Battle." Moffett's lecture, dated 6 April 1923, is entitled "Aircraft in the Navy—Their Use and Limitations," and is in File UA, 1924-104, Document No. 1204/4-23. The citations are, respectively, from pp. 18, 6, and 14.

7. The letter from the president of the War College to Commander Aircraft Squadrons, Battle Fleet, dated 24 July 1923, is in File UNOpM, Naval War College Archives. The letter is "subj: Battle Problem maneuvered by Aircraft Squadrons, Battle Fleet," and the citation is par. 4. The second letter is from the president of Naval War College to Commander, Aircraft Squadrons, Battle Fleet, "subj: Requesting information on aircraft operations needed in connection with War College work," par. 2, 22 August 1923, File UNOpM. The board games are described in M. A. Campbell, "The Influence of Air Power upon the Evolution of Battle Doctrine in the U.S. Navy, 1922–1941" (master's thesis, History Department, University of Massachusetts–Boston, 1992), chap. 5. See also Michael Vlahos, *The Blue Sword: The Naval War College and the American Mission, 1919–1941* (Newport, R.I.: Naval War College, 1980), 138 and 119, and T. B. Buell, *The Quiet Warrior: A Biography of Admiral Raymond Spruance* (Boston: Little, Brown, 1974), 58. The "Estimate of the Situation" citation is from the 1932 edition (published by the Dept. of Operations, Naval War College), chap. 1, par. 1. The contribution of Chester Nimitz is noted in E. B. Potter, *Nimitz* (Annapolis, Md.: Naval Institute Press, 1976), 138–40. The tactics manual is *Tactics,* Section I, "The Naval Battle," Naval War College, June 1923, p. 17, in Naval War College Archives, Record Group 4, File 33 I. Commander Whiting's interest in the games is noted in Henry Woodhouse, "U.S. Naval Aeronautic Policies, 1904–1942," U.S. Naval Institute *Proceedings* 68 (February1942): 49–50. The "n-square" law is discussed in Capt. Wayne P. Hughes Jr., USN (Ret.), *Fleet Tactics: Theory and Practice* (Annapolis, Md.: Naval Institute Press, 1986). See also Peter Perla, *The Art of Wargaming* (Annapolis, Md.: Naval Institute Press, 1990), 71. The "Maneuver Rules," Naval War College, June 1922, pp. 81 and 84, are in Record Group 4, File 32 J, Naval War College Archives. Material from Laning's memoirs, "An Admiral's Yarn," is from chap. 36, pp. 455–62, Manuscript Collection 115, Box 3, Naval War College Archives. Laning used both words—"untried" and "untested"—in his memoirs, at p. 459.

8. Eugene E. Wilson, who was Rear Admiral Reeves's chief of staff in 1929, noted

in his memoirs that the unit commanders submitted their own proposals for fleet problems. See E. E. Wilson, *Slipstream: The Autobiography of an Air Craftsman* (New York: McGraw-Hill, 1950), 121. By "unit commander," Wilson meant someone like Reeves, not the commanders of particular ships, though the latter could suggest scenarios. The case of Fleet Problem IX is taken from Appendix III, "Chronological Running Historical Record of Problem IX from 23 January to Its End," by Fleet Observer Black, p. 52, and from a memo, "from: Chief Observer, Black, U.S. Fleet Problem IX; to: All Observers, Black; subj: Procedure," listed as "Enclosure A," Microfilm Roll 12, Fleet Problem IX, Record Group 80, National Archives. The quote regarding damage assessments during Problem IX is from the same source.

The questions of how to do damage assessments and how to apply them during an exercise are raised in a letter from the commander in chief, U.S. Fleet, to the president of the Naval War College, "subj: System for Damage Penalties in Fleet Problems," 17 July 1930, Record Group 8, Box 54, Folder UNT 1930-110, Naval War College File, Naval Historical Center, Washington, D.C. See also Campbell, "The Influence of Air Power," 121 and 130. The dismay about the umpire's decision is from a letter written by Adm. A. K. Doyle to Vice Adm. G. C. Dyer and cited in the latter's *The Amphibians Came to Conquer: The Story of Admiral Richmond Kelly Turner*, vol. 1 (Washington, D.C.: Government Printing Office, 1969), 124.

Admiral Pratt's views are in "The Naval War College: An Outline of the Past and Description of the Present," 20 May 1927, File UNT, Naval War College Archives, p. 32. We have also used a letter from W. V. Pratt to H. A. Wiley (CINC, U.S. Fleet), 20 September 1928, pp. 4 and 9, Pratt Correspondence File, Naval War College Archives. The Pratt Correspondence File also holds another letter on the same topic from Pratt to Wiley for 17 October 1928; see pp. 4–5.

9. The question of combining cruiser and carrier is from a letter from the secretary of the Navy to the General Board, "subj: Use of 10,000 ton cruisers for carrying aircraft," 31 March 1925 (Serial No. 1270), Record Group 8 (UNC), Naval War College Archives. The response is a letter from Rear Adm. C. S. Williams, president of the Naval War College, to the General Board, "subj: Use of 10,000 ton cruisers for carrying aircraft," 23 April 1925, p. 3, Record Group 8 (UNC). There is an article about the 1924 study: W. M. McBride, "Challenging a Strategic Paradigm: Aviation and the U.S. Navy Special Policy Board of 1924," *Journal of Strategic Studies* 14 (1991): 72–89. The data on battleship gunnery is from "Annual Report of the Commander-in-Chief, U.S. Fleet, 1 July, 1926 to 30 June, 1927," p. 30, par. 93, 97, and 98, Microfilm M971, Roll 6, National Archives.

10. The court-martial of Brigadier General Mitchell is covered by R. F. Futrell, *Ideas, Concepts, Doctrine: A History of Basic Thinking in the United States Air Force, 1907–1964* (Maxwell AFB, Ala.: Air War College, 1971), especially p. 26. See also Gerald Wheeler, "Mitchell, Moffett, and Air Power," *The Airpower Historian* 8 (April 1961): 79–87. There is a biography of Moffett: W. F. Trimble, *Admiral William A.*

Moffett, Architect of Naval Aviation (Washington, D.C.: Smithsonian Institution, 1994). Moffett as bureaucrat and political strategist is covered in T. Hone, "Navy Air Leadership: Rear Admiral William A. Moffett as Chief of the Bureau of Aeronautics," in *Air Leadership,* ed. Wayne Thompson (Washington, D.C.: Office of Air Force History, 1986), 83–117. The work of John Towers with the Morrow Board is described in Reynolds, *Admiral John H. Towers,* 184–95. The comment about *Langley* by the commander in chief, U.S. Fleet, is in his "Annual Report" of 30 June 1925, par. 50, p. 16. Record Group 80, Microfilm 971, Roll 5, National Archives.

11. Reeves assumed his post as Commander, Aircraft Squadrons, Battle Fleet, on 13 October 1925. The source is "Logbook, USS *Langley,* Jan. 1, 1925–Dec. 31, 1925," p. 568, in the National Archives. References to Wilson's memoir, *Slipstream,* are to chap. 13 and 14. More on Reeves is in Rear Admiral J. Hayes, USN (Ret.), "Admiral Joseph Mason Reeves, USN (Part One: to 1931)," *Naval War College Review* 23 (November 1970).

The times for clearing *Langley*'s deck and for aircraft landings are from a letter, "from Commander, Aircraft Squadrons, Battle Fleet, to Commander-in-Chief, Battle Fleet, subj: Force Battle Practice 1925, Report of," 3 April 1925 (90-FFW-CWM), in File UAN/1925, Naval War College Archives.

Capt. W. H. Standley, USN, Office of the Chief of Naval Operations, refers to the problem facing Pratt in a letter to him dated 21 November 1925, WHS-CD, Record Group 8 (UA), Naval War College Archives. Carrier weaknesses are from a memo written to Pratt by J. K. Taussig, head of the Department of Strategy and former assistant in the Tactics Department at Newport, dated 23 November 1925, also in Record Group 8 (UA). Data on battleships firing with air spot are from "Battle Fleet Annual Report," Commander-in-Chief, Battle Fleet, 1 July 1924 to 30 June 1925, p. 68, par. 175 and 176, Microfilm M971, Roll 5, National Archives.

Times on takeoffs and landings for *Langley* on 18 December 1925 are from her logbook, 1 January–31 December 1925, p. 733.

12. The comments of Commander-in-Chief, Battle Fleet, are in his "Annual Report . . . 4 Oct 1925 to 30 June 1926," p. 69, par. 243, Microfilm M971, Roll 5, National Archives. Photographs of planes landing on *Langley* are in L. M. Pearson, "Only the BuNo Has Changed," *Approach* 5 (September 1959), especially p. 4. The process of moving planes forward after they had landed is described in "Annual Report of Aircraft Squadrons, Battle Fleet, 4 Sept. 1926 to 30 June 1927," p. 5, par. (2), Microfilm M971, Roll 6, National Archives. There is also material in Reynolds, *Admiral John H. Towers,* 205, and in Rear Adm. George van Deurs, USN, "Navy Wings between Wars," Naval Historical Center Microfilm AR-233-76, 1975. The role of Aeronautics is from a letter signed by the chief of BuAer to the president of the Naval War College, "subj: Excerpt from Weekly News Letter, U.S. Battle Fleet, period 29 August–4 September 1926," dated 11 November 1926 (Aer-A-5-O'M, A7-1/FF2), in File UANOP/1926135, Naval War College Archives.

13. Tactical innovations are described in "Annual Report of Aircraft Squadrons, Battle Fleet, 4 Sept. 1926 to 30 June 1927," p. 7, par. (g)(3) [II. Combat], M971, Roll 6, National Archives. There is also a letter from "Commander, Aircraft Squadrons, Battle Fleet, to the Chief of Naval Operations, via the Commander-in-Chief, Battle Fleet and Commander-in-Chief, U.S. Fleet, subj: Forwarding Confidential Report 'Aircraft Tactics, Development of,'" A16-3(VV)FF2-3 [546], 01-PED, 15 February 1927, CNO Files, National Archives. The report itself ("Aircraft Tactics, Development of") was furnished to the authors by Capt. A. L. Raithel Jr., USN (Ret.). Engine development is described in Wilson, *Slipstream,* chap. 3, as well as in his report, "The Trend of Aircraft Engine Development," *Journal of the American Society of Naval Engineers* 38 (February 1926). The reaction of Adm. Hughes is from W. R. Braisted, "Charles Frederick Hughes," in *The Chiefs of Naval Operations,* ed. R. W. Love (Annapolis, Md.: Naval Institute Press, 1980), 49–68.

14. Carrier design is discussed in a memo (then Secret), "from: Capt. Stanford E. Moses, USN, to: President Naval War College, subj: 'Aircraft Carriers,'" 8 December 1926, File RG-8 UNC, Naval War College Archives. The quotation of the Commander-in-Chief, Battle Fleet, is from "Annual Report . . . , 4 Oct 1925 to 30 June 1926," p. 67, par. 236. Sherman's contributions are from a memo, "from: Lieutenant Forrest Sherman, U.S. Navy, to: Chief of Staff; subj: Aircraft Carriers—Characteristics," 1 December 1926, "B4," in File RG-8 UNC, Naval War College Archives. The comment about the open hangar deck is from the same memo, p. 3, par. 5, and the point about large carriers is from the memo's "Summary of Conclusions," p. 4. The link between the War College and *Langley* is from a letter, "from: President, Naval War College, to: Chief of the Bureau of Aeronautics, subj: 'Excerpt from Weekly News Letter, U.S. Battle Fleet, period 29 August–4 September 1926,'" 15 November 1926, File UANOP (1926135), Naval War College Archives. The importance of games to *Ranger*'s design is documented in Friedman, *U.S. Aircraft Carriers,* 57. Use of the paper and cardboard models is explained in a memo, "from: Lt. Forrest P. Sherman, to: President, Naval War College, subj: 'Aircraft Carriers—Design and Operation,'" 26 March 1927, in File RG-8, UNC, Naval War College Archives. Pratt's letter to OPNAV is a letter (then Secret), "from: President, Naval War College; to: Chief of Naval Operations; subj: Airplane Carriers," 11 April 1927, UNC (1927–83), File RG-8 UNC, Naval War College Archives. The quotation is from ibid., p. 1, par. 3. For *Langley*'s air group, see W. T. Larkins, *U.S. Navy Aircraft, 1921–1941* (New York: Crown Publishers Reprint, 1988), 48 and 56. See also "Annual Report of Aircraft Squadrons, Battle Fleet, 4 Sept, 1926 to 30 June, 1927," pp. 5–6, par. (g) (2). Van Deurs makes the point about Reeves's position in "Navy Wings between Wars." The work of Towers and Mitscher is documented in Reynolds, *Admiral John H. Towers,* 204. Reynolds, relying on Towers's letters, also describes the use of movies to analyze the cause of crashes.

15. The decision of Secretary of the Navy Curtis Wilbur is discussed in Melhorn, *Two-Block Fox,* 109–10. The argument for more carriers was made by Admiral Pratt

in a letter to the CNO, "subj: Airplane Carriers," 11 April 1927, UNC (1927–83), File RG-8 UNC, Naval War College Archives, p. 8. Pratt's observation regarding faulty lessons is from the same letter, p. 7. The Taylor Board was created by a memo from the secretary of the Navy to Rear Adm. M. M. Taylor, USN, Office of the Chief of Naval Operations, "subj: Board to consider the Naval Aeronautic Policy," T-7695, 4 April 1927, 2028-138, RG-8, Naval War College Archives. The Taylor Board's conclusions are from Clifford L. Lord, "The History of Naval Aviation," 1898–1939," Part IV, "Between the Wars," pp. 1178–80. The quote from the instructions to the Taylor Board is from the memo in the Naval War College Archives, "Board to consider the Naval Aeronautic Policy," 4 April 1927, Enclosure A.

16. Reeves's plans are in a letter, "from: Commander, Aircraft Squadrons, Battle Fleet, to: Commander-in-Chief, Battle Fleet, subj: Plans for operating aircraft carriers *Saratoga* and *Lexington,*" 25 October 1927 (A4-3/A3-2[2830]), File UNOpM, No. 1927-137, Naval War College Archives. Reeves's letter to Moffett about the visit of the Royal Navy vice admiral is in the Moffett papers, Naval Academy Library, Annapolis, Maryland. The problems of converting *Lexington* and her sister are described in Cdr. C. S. Gillette, USN, "History, Description, and Acceptance Trials of the U.S.S. *Lexington,*" *Journal of the American Society of Naval Engineers* 40 (August 1928). Work on *Langley*'s arresting gear is described in van Deurs, "Navy Wings between Wars." Problems with the arresting gear on the converted battle cruisers are taken from Lt. Cdr. S. R. Heller Jr., USN, "The Development of Attack Aircraft Carriers," *Journal of the American Society of Naval Engineers* 65 (1953): 522–23.

Fleet Problem IX is described in National Archives Publication M964. Aircraft complements are from "Report of the CINC, US Fleet," to the chief of naval operations, Part III, pp. 29–30. Wilson's quote is from *Slipstream,* 148. Wilson also prepared an account, much later, for the Naval Institute: "The Navy's First Carrier Task Force," U.S. Naval Institute *Proceedings* (February 1950): 159–69. Wilson's memory not being infallible, we consulted the primary documents. The citations for *Saratoga*'s strike are from National Archives Publication M964, "Report of the CINC, US Fleet," to the CNO, pp. 26, 23, 71, 103, and 67, respectively. For the symbolic effect of *Saratoga*'s maneuver, see ibid., "Blue Remarks, Critique of Fleet Problem IX," Aircraft Squadrons, Battle Fleet, pp. 37–41.

The descriptions of the formal critique are, first, "Memo, from: Commander-in-Chief, United States Fleet, to: Chief of Naval Operations, subj: United States Fleet Problem IX—Report of Commander-in-Chief, United States Fleet," (FP9 [139], 11-me[0], 18 March 1929), Part II, p. 1, on Roll 12, Fleet Problem IX, RG-80, National Archives. The second is Appendix XIII, "BLUE Situation and Instructions for Conducting U.S. Fleet Problem IX; memo, from: Commander-in-Chief, United States Fleet, to: Commander Scouting Fleet, Commander Control Force, Commander Train Squadron ONE, Commanding Officer, USS Lexington, subj: United States Fleet Problem IX," p. 115, on Roll 12, Fleet Problem IX, RG-80, National Archives.

Praise for the carrier force is in Appendix XII, "Critique of Fleet Problem IX," Remarks of Commander-in-Chief, Black Naval Force, p. 103, also on Roll 12. Cdr. Towers's remarks are from "Hearings before the General Board of the Navy, 1929," vol. 2, 1 October 1929, p. 249, RG-80, National Archives Microfilm 20. The presentation to the Naval War College was Capt. John Halligan, "Airplane Carrier Operations," 15 August 1930, File UANOp 1930-114, pp. 1–2, in the Naval War College Archives.

Chapter 3. Fleet Carriers—or Fleets of Carriers

1. Hughes, *Fleet Tactics,* chap. 4.

2. Rear Admiral Moffett's remarks are from "Design of Future Aircraft Carriers," Annex A, 7 October 1931, Serial No. 1533, in General Board File 420-5, National Archives.

3. Clark G. Reynolds, *The Fast Carriers: The Forging of an Air Navy* (New York: McGraw-Hill, 1968; Annapolis, Md.: Naval Institute Press, 1992), 36 (page citations are to the reprint edition).

4. Reynolds, *Fast Carriers,* 165–66. Adm. F. C. Sherman, *Combat Command, The American Aircraft Carriers in the Pacific War* (New York: E. P. Dutton, 1950).

5. Hughes, *Fleet Tactics,* 93. For Fleet Problem XX, see "Fleet Problem XX, Comments and Recommendations," from Commanding Officer, *Ranger,* to Commander-in-Chief, U.S. Fleet, CV4/A16-3/FPXX, 31 March 1939, National Archives.

6. *Report of Fleet Problem XV,* 1 June 1934, Commander-in-Chief, U.S. Fleet, "Exercise M," p. 20, Records of the Office of the Chief of Naval Operations, RG 38, National Archives.

7. Henry M. Dater, "Tactical Use of Air Power in World War II: The Navy Experience," *Military Affairs* 14 (Winter 1950): 193–94.

8. The quote from Moffett is from "Design of Future Aircraft Carriers," Annex A, 7 October 1931, Serial No. 1533, in General Board File 420-5, National Archives. The decision of Congress to authorize only one carrier for 1928 is in C. L. Lord, "The History of Naval Aviation, 1898–1939," Part IV, "Between the Wars," p. 1182.

9. The London Treaty negotiations are described in Raymond O'Connor, *Perilous Equilibrium, The United States and the London Naval Conference of 1930* (Lawrence, Kans.: University of Kansas Press, 1962).

10. For the problems of maneuvering carriers in battle, see Dater, "Tactical Use of Air Power in World War II." The quote about President Hoover is from Baer, *One Hundred Years of Sea Power,* 123.

11. Memo, "from: Commanding Officer, USS *Lexington,* to: Commander Aircraft, Battle Force, subj: Special Carrier Report," 26 April 1932 (CV2/A9/(Y4)), p. 1. Rear Admiral Moffett's memo is "Budget, 1934—Alterations to Bomb Handling Arrangements on the USS SARATOGA and the USS LEXINGTON," 16 August 1932. Both

memos are in the Confidential Correspondence File of the Secretary of the Navy, 1927–1939, Box 159, Folder "CV 1932," in Record Group 80, National Archives.

12. *Hearings before the General Board of the Navy, 1934,* "Facilities for Enlarged Aviation Program," 10 August 1934, p. 25.

13. The debate about carrier designs is described in detail in Friedman, *U.S. Aircraft Carriers.* In March 1939, then Capt. John S. McCain prepared a memo for the chief of naval operations arguing for armored deck carriers smaller than *Enterprise* and *Yorktown,* "subj: Suggested Design for New Carriers" (March 1, 1939), General Board Records, File 420-5, No. 1861. Rear Admiral King, then Commander Aircraft, Battle Force, rejected this idea. See "Suggested Design for New Carriers," memo from King to McCain, April 28, 1939, File 420-5, No. 1861.

14. The quote from Wilson is in *Slipstream,* 186. The quote from Baer is in *One Hundred Years of Sea Power,* 129. Other details are in Lord, "The History of Naval Aviation," Part IV, chap. 3 and 4.

15. Data on the progress in battleship design and engineering are from "Characteristics of Capital Ships," in Hearings before the General Board of the Navy, 1936 (30 October 1936), p. 134, in the National Archives. See also "Capital Ships," Hearings before the General Board of the Navy, 1935 (22 October 1935), pp. 204–5. On the costs of modernization, see T. Hone, "Spending Patterns of the United States Navy, 1921–1941," *Armed Forces and Society* 8 (Spring 1982): 443–62.

16. *Hearings before the General Board of the Navy, 1937,* "Aircraft Building Program—1939," 5 October 1937, p. 9.

17. The estimates from BuAer on numbers of aircraft procured are from "Treaty Navy Aircraft Procurement Program," 14 July 1934, Bureau of Aeronautics Records, RG-72, National Archives. Rear Admiral King's quotation is from "Hearings before the General Board of the Navy," vol. I, 1934, p. 108, Record Group 80, Microfilm No. 22, National Archives. The support of the General Board for airships is from "Hearings before the General Board of the Navy," 1 February 1937, Microfilm 23. The concept of an "effective air effort" is from Annex A to a memo from the General Board to the secretary of the Navy, "Design of Future Aircraft Carriers," General Board No. 420-5, Serial No. 1533, 7 October 1931.

18. *Hearings before the General Board of the Navy, 1937,* "Aircraft Building Program–1939," 4 October 1937, p. 24.

19. Data on the cost of aircraft are taken from "Memo, from: General Board, to: Secretary of the Navy, subj: Force Operating Plan Based on Treaty Navy," 8 September 1931, General Board Records, File 420, par. 5. On limitations of carrier aircraft, see Lord, "The History of Naval Aviation," Part IV, pp. 1214 and 1398–1404.

20. The pilot recruitment and retention problem is discussed in Lord, "The History of Naval Aviation," Part IV, pp. 1272, 1279, 1313, and 1331. For a firsthand account of the cadet program, see R. A. Winston, *Dive Bomber* (New York: Holiday House, 1939).

21. *Hearings before the General Board of the Navy, 1937,* "Aircraft Building Program–1939," 5 October 1937, p. 4.

22. Damage information from Fleet Problem XV is from "Report of Assistant Umpire (R. K. Turner, Commander), CARDIV 21, to Chief Umpire, *Saratoga,* 8 May 1934," in *Report of Fleet Problem XV,* 1 June 1934. Damage information from Fleet Problem XVIII is from "Fleet Confidential Notice 1 CN-37," in Roll 22, *Report of Fleet Problem XVIII,* June 1937, National Archives.

23. Data on aircraft performance are from Gordon Swanborough and Peter M. Bowers, *United States Navy Aircraft since 1911,* 2d ed. (Annapolis, Md.: Naval Institute Press, 1976). Ordnance loads are taken from the original BuAer data sheets in the files of the historian, Naval Air Systems Command. The quotation from Wilson is in *Slipstream,* 194. Wilson discusses the controllable-pitch propeller and the cowl flap on pp. 170 and 188, respectively. For the discussion of wing loadings and what they meant for military aircraft, see T. Hone and M. Mandeles, "Interwar Innovation in Three Navies: U.S. Navy, Royal Navy, Imperial Japanese Navy," *Naval War College Review* 40: 63–83. The quotation about blindfolded men with daggers is from Fleet Problem X, CINCUS Report, 7 May 1930, "Comment of Commander Aircraft Squadrons, Scouting Fleet," p. 66, RG-80, National Archives. Aircraft tactics are explained in "Aircraft Tactics—Development of," 3 February 1927, P-8 File 111-174, p. 85, RG-80, National Archives.

24. The testimony of the director of the War Plans Division is in "Aircraft Building Program—1939," 4 October 1937, Hearings before the General Board of the Navy, No. 271, p. 2, RG-80, Microfilm 23. The problem of having enough aircraft to train pilots is covered by Lord, "The History of Naval Aviation," Part IV, pp. 1316–36.

25. The Coontz recommendation is from "Annual Report of the Commander-in-Chief, U.S. Fleet–1 July, 1924 to 30 June, 1925," p. 26, par. 87, RG-80, Microfilm M971, Roll 5, National Archives. The exam is from "Bureau of Navigation Circular Letter No. 43-31, to: All Ships and Stations, subj: Examination of Line Officers for Promotion, to Include Principles of Aviation," Nav-143-ES, P17-2/00 (608), 19 May 1931, par. 1, File ZV (Administration, Navy Dept., Folder "Aviation—Hawaii Flight 1925, 1934"), Navy Operational Archives, Washington Navy Yard, Washington, D.C.

26. Memo, "from: Director, War Plans Division, to: The Chief of Naval Operations, subject: New Carrier Characteristics," 5 November 1938 ([SC]CV/S1-1). There is also, in the same box of records, a memo from War Plans to the CNO, "Conversion of merchant vessels to carriers," 15 September 1939 (SC), which advocates converting merchant ships to carriers and to "seaplane carriers" in response to "interest" expressed by President Roosevelt. See Folder "CV/A4 to CV8/S1-1," Box 253, Office of the Secretary of the Navy, Formerly Secret Correspondence, 1927–1939, RG 80, National Archives.

27. Rear Admiral Ghormley's position is taken from a memo he prepared for the General Board: "Memorandum for General Board Hearing 17 July 1939," dated 15

July 1939 and included in the records of General Board hearing, "Characteristics of New Aircraft Carriers," 17 July 1939, pp. 3–4. Captain Cooke testified before the General Board on 13 November 1939 at a hearing entitled, "Cruiser Design for Future Construction," p. 24. Rear Admiral Towers prepared a statement for the board for the hearing scheduled for 17 July 1939. His quotation is from p. 5. The intelligence division representative testified at the same hearing, p. 30. See "Hearings before the General Board of the Navy, 1939," vol. I.

28. "Remarks of Rear Adm. W. F. Halsey at Joint Army and Navy Critique, 30 January 1940," p. 6, Folder A16-3 #2, Box 128, Record Group 313, "US Fleet, Battle Force," National Archives.

29. The installation of the CXAM radar on *Yorktown* is documented in Robert Cressman, *That Gallant Ship* (Missoula, Mont.: Pictorial Histories, 1985), 29. The summer 1941 exercises are described in "Memo, from: Commander Aircraft, Battle Force, to: Commander-in-Chief, U.S. Pacific Fleet, subject: 'Exercises 151 and 153 held on 1 and 2 July 1941, respectively,'" (0532) 7 July 1941, from Folder 1, Box 1, Record Group 313, "Commander Aircraft: Tactics Branch, General Administrative File," National Archives. Later exercises are discussed in "Tactical Exercises, 29 July–1 August 1941—Report of," (0679) 25 August 1941, in Folder 3, Box 2, same record group, and in "Fleet Tactical Exercises, 27–30 August 1941, Reports," (0727) 7 September 1941, also in Folder 3, Box 2, same record group. The quotation about the radar plot organization is from the 25 August memo.

30. The "Annual Estimates" of the Chiefs of Naval Operations are in File L1-1, Office of the Secretary of the Navy, Confidential Correspondence, 1927–1939, Record Group 80, National Archives. The specific citations are from "Budget—1935. Annual Estimate of the Situation, including Shore Establishment Projects," p. 34, and "Fiscal Year 1937—Annual Estimate of the Situation," p. 74.

31. Duncan S. Ballantine, *U.S. Naval Logistics in the Second World War* (Princeton, N.J.: Princeton University Press, 1949). The quotations are from pp. 247 and 176–77.

32. Baer, *One Hundred Years of Sea Power,* 245.

33. Rear Admiral Pratt's comment about the purpose of the Naval War College course is taken from Kennedy, "The United States Naval War College," 132. The reforms of admirals Pratt and Laning are described in Kennedy and in J. B. Hattendorf, B. Mitchell Simpson III, and J. R. Wadleigh, *Sailors and Scholars, The Centennial History of the U.S. Naval War College* (Newport, R.I.: Naval War College Press, 1984), 141–46. Spector, *Professors of War,* also describes the Pratt and Laning reforms (p. 145). The quotations from the operations problem are taken from "Operations Problem IV—1933, Critique, General Comments," by Capt. S. C. Rowan, Dept. of Operations, Naval War College, May 1933 (No. 2819, 1-16-34, Enclosure M-1, Serial No. 2), Strategic Plans Division Records, Naval War College Operations Problems 1933–34, Box 19, pp. 6 and 7, Classified Operational Archives, Naval Historical Center, Washington Navy Yard.

34. The Spector quote is from *Professors of War,* 113. The problem of getting good officers into Naval War College classes in the 1930s is discussed by Kennedy, "The United States Naval War College, 1919–1941," at p. 292. Rear Admiral Upham's quotation is in Hattendorf, Simpson, and Wasleigh, *Sailors and Scholars,* 149.

35. The views of Wiley and Pratt are summarized in Gerald Wheeler, *Admiral William Veazie Pratt, U.S. Navy: A Sailor's Life* (Washington, D.C.: Naval History Division, Department of the Navy, 1974), 286–88.

36. Rear Adm. J. A. Furer, *Administration of the Navy Department in World War II* (Washington, D.C.: Naval History Division, 1959), 174.

37. Reeves's position is expressed in his "Annual Report of the Commander-in-Chief, United States Fleet, for the period 1 July, 1935, to 24 June, 1936," 24 June 1936 (CinC File No. A9-1/FF1/3282), p. 11, File "Fleet Organization and Command," 30 April 1937, Box 55, Subject File GB-420, Record Group 80, Records of the General Board of the Navy, National Archives. Standley's response is in his memo, "Fleet Organization and Command," to the General Board, 12 October 1936 (Op-12-MG, [SC]P17-1, Serial 352), p. 8, same file. Hepburn's memo is Fleet Organization and Command (CinC File No. A3-1, 4921), to the chairman of the General Board, 1 Oct. 1936, pp. 4 and 5, same file. Admiral Hart's paper to the secretary of the Navy, dated 30 April 1937, is "Fleet Organization and Command" (GB No. 420, Serial No. 1723) in File "420-1936–1937," also in Box 55, and the quotation is from p. 18. Rear Admiral King's concept is in Folder "VB to VV," Box 212, Record Group 80, Office of the Secretary of the Navy, Formerly Confidential Correspondence, 1927–39, National Archives.

38. Wilson's memories (sometimes fallible; he credits *Saratoga* with ten-inch guns when in fact she carried eight-inch) are from *Slipstream,* 2d ed. (1965), 128 and 136–37. The discussion between Admiral Reeves and the General Board is in "Facilities for Enlarged Aviation Program," *Hearings before the General Board,* 14 August 1934, pp. 132–35.

39. For the administration of the fleet, see Donald B. Duncan and Henry M. Dater, "Administrative History of U.S. Naval Aviation," *Air Affairs* 1(4): 533. The responsibility of BuAer was set out in General Order 68, 13 May 1935. See "Pre–World War II Operational Responsibilities of the Bureau of Aeronautics," by the BuAer Scientific Historian, Aer-123, 12 April 1957, p. 7, Naval Aviation Systems Command Historian's files.

40. Reynolds, *The Fast Carriers,* 48.

41. For organizational changes during the war, see *The Navy's Air War,* ed. A. R. Buchanan, OP-519B, DCNO(Air) (New York: Harper, 1946), 23. See also Reynolds, *Admiral John H. Towers,* chap. 14, and W. J. Armstrong, "The Establishment of the DCNO(Air)," unpublished paper prepared for the Commander, Naval Air Systems Command, n.d., 15. This paper is in the files of the Historian, Naval Air Systems Command.

42. Heinrichs, "The Role of the United States Navy," 197–223.

43. Letter from Adm. E. J. King to Chairman, General Board, subject: "Priorities in 2-Ocean Navy Building Program," 30 July 1941, Records of the Navy's General Board, File 420-2 (1941), par. 12, National Archives.

44. Rear Adm. E. C. Kalbfus, President, Naval War College, "A Study of the Relative Merits of a Balanced Navy and a Carrier Navy and the Conclusions Reached," September 1941, Folder "July–Dec. 1941," Box 56, Record Group 80, General Board, Subject File 420, National Archives.

45. "Aircraft Carrier Characteristics," 30 July 1938, in Folder "CV/S1-1 to CV/S24-2," Box 160, Office of the Secretary of the Navy, Confidential Correspondence File, 1927–39, RG 80, National Archives.

Chapter 4. The Fleet Air Arm: A Failed Revolution?

1. See H. Montgomery Hyde, *British Air Policy between the Wars, 1918–1939* (London: Wm. Heineman, 1976). See also *Documents Relating to the Naval Air Service,* ed. S. W. Roskill (London: Navy Records Society, 1969), vol. 1.

2. W. D. McIntyre, *The Rise and Fall of the Singapore Naval Base* (London: Macmillan, 1979), especially the chapter on "Guns v. Air," 69–85.

3. G. C. Peden, *British Rearmament and the Treasury, 1932–39* (Edinburgh: Scottish Academic Press, 1979), 118–21, 128–34.

4. John Ferris, "A British 'Unofficial' Aviation Mission and Japanese Naval Developments, 1919–1929," *Journal of Strategic Studies* 5: 416–39. Toshikazu Ohmae, "Japanese Naval Aviation," U.S. Naval Institute *Proceedings,* December 1972.

5. See "Progress in Tactics 1937," the first post-Ethiopian crisis edition, pp. 25–26, Public Records Office (PRO). The description of the remote-controlled semisubmersible is in Ship's Cover 486 ("Job No. 1") at the National Maritime Museum, Greenwich.

6. The 1930–39 series of "Progress in Tactics" is in the Naval Historical Branch, Ministry of Defence, London. But no interwar intelligence publications had been released to the PRO when this book was being written. None were cited in Arthur J. Marder's *Old Friends, New Enemies* (Oxford: Oxford University Press, 1981) except a prewar paper on Japanese psychology and consequent operational impediments.

7. "Progress in Tactics 1939," pp. 29–31. The first RDF sets were fitted in cruiser *Sheffield* and battleship *Rodney* in the fall of 1938.

8. For British efforts in Washington, see S. Roskill, *Naval Policy between the Wars,* vol. 1, *The Period of Anglo-American Antagonism, 1919–1929* (London: Collins, 1968), 323–24.

9. In the U.S. Navy, the cost of battleship *Washington,* commissioned in 1941, was approximately $43.2 million (in then-year dollars). The cost of carrier *Enterprise,*

commissioned in 1938, was approximately $23.8 million (in then-year dollars). Carrier *Hornet*, an improved *Enterprise* commissioned in 1941, cost about $27 million in then-year dollars. Navy Department, Bureau of Supplies and Accounts, *Naval Expenditures, 1941* (Washington, D.C.: Government Printing Office, 1941), 326–27.

10. David MacGregor, "Former Naval Cheapskate: Chancellor of the Exchequer Winston Churchill and the Royal Navy, 1924–1929," *Armed Forces and Society* 17 (Spring 1993): 319–34.

11. N. H. Gibbs, *History of the Second World War, Grand Strategy*, vol. 1 (London: HMSO, 1976), 368.

12. Wheeled aircraft *flew* off. Amphibians, carried by all the early carriers, were often catapulted, but they were clearly the exception because of the time it took to set up for catapult launchings. See memo, "from: Commander Aircraft Squadrons, Battle Fleet, to: Commander-in-Chief, Battle Fleet, subj: Exercise No. 1—Report on," 2 April 1927, p. 2, in File UNT-1927, Naval War College Archives.

13. Friedman, *British Carrier Aviation*, 160–63.

14. The rate-measuring (tachymetric) system ultimately adopted by the U.S. Navy was recommended in 1921 by the Royal Navy's Anti-Aircraft Gunnery Committee. The Admiralty rejected it as too complex. The High Angle Control System bought instead required the gunner to estimate target speed—a task nearly impossible for aircraft flying in 1939 and later. In 1937, the Director of Naval Ordnance strongly recommended a tachymetric system, but by then it was too late. Geoffrey Till, *Air Power and the Royal Navy, 1914–1945* (London: Jane's, 1979), quotes the First Sea Lord, Admiral Sir Ernle Chatfield, as saying in the wake of the Ethiopian crisis in 1936 that he expected to equip the fleet with so many antiaircraft guns that air attack would become unprofitable (pp. 142–43).

15. The Future Building Committee papers are in the Public Records Office (ADM 116/5150-5152). The papers of the related Naval Aircraft Design Committee are ADM 116/5977.

16. Till, *Air Power and the Royal Navy*, 57.

17. John Terraine, *A Time for Courage* (New York: Macmillan, 1985; published in England as *The Right of the Line*), 140–47. See also the papers by Terraine ("Theory and Practice of the Air War: The Royal Air Force") and Williamson Murray ("The Influence of Pre-War Anglo-American Doctrine on the Campaigns of the Second World War") in *The Conduct of the Air War in the Second World War: An International Comparison*, ed H. Boog (New York: Berg, distributed by St. Martin's Press, 1992).

18. The citation from Shores (*Ground Attack Aircraft of World War II*) about the RAF having few officers with experience in close air support is from p. 15. The light bombers are discussed in P. Lewis, *The British Bomber since 1914* (London: Putnam, 1967), 297–98. The February 1934 date is from the companion volume on Hawker aircraft (the other P.4/34 contender was the Hawker Henley). Lewis dates the specification 12 November 1934, but that is probably the date of final, rather than preliminary, issue.

19. See N. H. Gibbs, *History of the Second World War, Grand Strategy,* vol. 1 (London: HMSO), 362–69.

20. "Progress in Tactics 1931," pp. 110–11. "Progress in Tactics 1935," pp. 122–23.

21. See Till, *Air Power and the Royal Navy,* 122–25.

Chapter 5. The Fleet Air Arm before World War II

1. Till, *Air Power and the Royal Navy,* 137–39.

2. "Progress in Tactics 1930," and "Progress in Tactics 1931," p. 110. Both are located in the Naval Historical Branch, Ministry of Defense, London.

3. "Progress in Tactics 1935," p. 124.

4. *The Development of British Naval Aviation 1919–1945,* vol. I (1954: ADM 234/383) and vol. II (1956: ADM 234/384), in the Public Record Office, London. An additional volume reached the page proof stage but was never printed. A marked-up copy is in the Naval Historical Branch, Ministry of Defence, but we were unable to consult it. The first volume covers prewar policy but does not quite accord with other documents in the PRO. This work seems to be the only one to make the point about the loss of trained aircrew as the cause of failed Swordfish attacks during 1941, including the fortunately unsuccessful one made by mistake against cruiser *Sheffield* during the pursuit of *Bismarck.* During the war, the RAF fought hard to cut Royal Navy demands for replacement squadrons (e.g., of Seafires) aboard carriers.

5. For data on the aircraft, see R. C. Mikesh and S. Abe, *Japanese Aircraft, 1910–41* (London: Putnam, 1990), 171. For the story of Adm. Yamamoto's influence in developing the G3M Type 96, see R. Francillon, *Japanese Aircraft of the Pacific War* (London: Putnam, 1987), 350–57. The full British intelligence manual CB.1815 is in the Naval Historical Branch of the Ministry of Defence. The version in the PRO lists only British ships and aircraft. The role of the shore-based naval airplane is described in "Progress in Tactics 1938," p. 102.

6. "Progress in Tactics 1938," p. 98 (foreign section).

7. "Progress in Tactics 1932," p. 12.

8. See Friedman, *British Carrier Aviation,* especially pp. 19 and 155–72.

9. "Progress in Tactics 1932," p. 16.

10. See "Progress in Tactics 1934," p. 34, and "Progress in Tactics 1937," p. 59.

11. See "Progress in Tactics 1934," pp. 33–34. On gasoline stowage, see Friedman, *British Carrier Aviation,* 163.

12. Data comes from "Progress in Tactics 1930" (issued July 1931 by the Admiralty Tactical Division), in a discussion of carrier operations as typified by HMS *Courageous.* There appears to be no equivalent statement of planned changes in air complement in Admiralty papers in the Public Record Office.

13. None of the navies (U.S., British, and German) that developed magnetic torpedo exploders before World War II enjoyed much success with them during the

war, but they had good reason to pursue this line of development. The damage a torpedo does is a result of the incompressibility of water. When a torpedo detonates alongside a ship, the force of its explosion is vented into the hull. That damage can be predicted and absorbed. When a torpedo detonates beneath a ship's hull, however, the explosion creates an enormous bubble, which lifts the hull as it rises. Once the bubble has passed (sometimes through the bottom of the ship, into the hull), the ship's hull falls back. This sudden up and down movement buckles the hull, breaking it. The result is either sinking or severe damage.

14. Till, *Air Power and the Royal Navy,* 144.

15. Swordfish were massacred by German radar-directed fighters covering the passage of the battle cruisers *Scharnhorst* and *Gniesenau* up the English Channel in 1942. That was their last "classic" torpedo attack.

16. For a discussion of U.S. Navy dive-bombing, see "Progress in Tactics 1931," p. 111. For the 1933 trials, see "Progress in Tactics 1934," pp. 17–18. The figure on how many bombs it would take to score a hit on a cruiser is from "Progress in Tactics 1938," p. 14.

17. The official Fleet Air Arm history blames the Royal Navy's virtual abandonment of dive-bombing on the RAF's reluctance to develop a proper dive-bomber bombsight. This sounds incorrect. In the contemporary U.S. Navy, for example, dive-bomber bombsights were very simple.

18. CB.1815 ("World naval vessels and naval aircraft"), in the Naval Historical Branch of the Ministry of Defence. For the story of the B4Y and D1A, see Francillon, *Japanese Aircraft of the Pacific War,* 449.

19. Till, *Airpower and the Royal Navy,* 147. See "Progress in Tactics 1939," p. 14, for the attack on the carrier.

20. See the Ship's Cover for HMS *Eagle* (Cover 407B), National Maritime Museum, Greenwich. The "Cover" is a collection of documents affecting the design and modification of the ship.

21. Christopher Dandeker, "Bureaucracy, Planning and War: The Royal Navy, 1880–1918," *Armed Forces and Society* 11 (Fall 1984): 130–46.

22. See William J. Armstrong, "William A. Moffett and the Development of Naval Aviation," in *Aviation's Golden Age,* ed. W. M. Leary (Iowa City, Iowa: University of Iowa Press, 1989), 60–73. Also Wilson, *Slipstream,* 10.

23. See "Progress in Tactics 1931," p. 108, for the quotation.

24. *War Instructions, U.S. Navy, 1934* (Fleet Tactical Publication 143), Navy Department, Washington, D.C., 1942, chap. 9, pp. 37–45. See "The Similarity of Past and Present Standoff Threats," by T. Hone, U.S. Naval Institute *Proceedings,* September 1981, p. 114.

25. See Vice Adm. Sir Louis le Bailly, *From Fisher to the Falklands* (London: Marine Management (Holdings) Ltd. for the Institute of Marine Engineers, 1991).

Chapter 6. Two Navies on the Eve of War

1. "Fleet Problem XIV," CINCUS Report, 20 April 1933, p. 24, and "Report of Fleet Problem XV," 1 June 1934, CINC, U.S. Fleet, pp. 19–20.

2 "Fleet Problem XX, Comments and Recommendations," from Commanding Officer *USS Ranger* to CINCUS, 31 March 1939 (CV4/A16-3/FPXX), Roll 26, U.S. Navy Fleet Problems, National Archives.

3. There were, in fact, only two U.S. carriers that might have intervened at Pearl Harbor—*Enterprise* and *Lexington*—but Vice Admiral Nagumo did not know that. He thought that there might be four. He *did* know, based upon similar games and exercises conducted by both the Japanese and U.S. navies, that collectively carriers delivered their power as a pulse and that, as a result, one side, striking by surprise, might overwhelm the other, even if the latter had more aircraft and more carriers. A six-to-four ratio did not guarantee victory, especially if the other side struck first. See Hughes, *Fleet Tactics.*

4. *War Instructions, U.S. Navy, 1934* (Fleet Tactical Publication 143), Navy Department, Washington, 1942, chap. 9, pp. 37–45.

5. The long quotation is from N. H. Gibbs, *Grand Strategy,* vol. 1, *Rearmament Policy* (London: HMSO, 1976), 332–33. See also Hone, "Spending Patterns of the United States Navy," cited in n. 14, chap. 3, above, and T. Hone, "The Effectiveness of the 'Washington Treaty' Navy," *Naval War College Review* 32 (November–December 1979).

6. Jon T. Sumida, "'The Best Laid Plans': The Development of British Battle-Fleet Tactics, 1919–1942," *The International History Review* 14 (November 1992): 697.

7. Figures on U.S. Navy ship costs are from "Statement 33 (Property Investment —Ships)," "Bureau of Supplies and Accounts, report of," *Annual Reports of the Navy Department for the Fiscal Year 1926* (Washington, D.C.: Government Printing Office, 1927), p. 1114. See also T. Hone, "Battleships vs. Aircraft Carriers: The Patterns of U.S. Navy Operating Expenditures, 1932–1941," *Military Affairs* (October 1977), n. 21, p. 141. Data on British military expenditures are from Gibbs, *Grand Strategy,* vol. 1, p. 532, notes.

8. The 1935 quotation from *Brassey's* is included in Bryan Ranft, ed., *Ironclad to Trident, 100 Years of Defence Commentary, Brassey's 1886–1986* (London: Brassey's, 1986), 154. The quotations from the essay by Rear Admiral King are from the same source, pp. 167 and 168. The quotation from the report of the Bureau of Aeronautics is on p. 596, *Annual Reports of the Navy Department for the Fiscal Year 1926.*

9. See Gibbs, *Grand Strategy,* 367–68.

10. Hone and Mandeles, "Interwar Innovation," 77–78.

11. Gibbs, *Grand Strategy,* 368.

12. See ibid., 249.

13. Sumida, "'The Best Laid Plans,'" 696.

Chapter 7. Analysis

1. Thomas C. Hone, "Navy Air Leadership: RADM William A. Moffett as Chief of the Bureau of Aeronautics," in *Air Leadership*, ed. Wayne Thompson (Washington, D.C.: Government Printing Office, 1986), 83–118.

2. Letter, Sims to William S. Benson (later CNO), quoted in David F. Trask, "William Sowden Sims: The Victory Ashore," in *Admirals of the New Steel Navy*, ed. James C. Bradford (Annapolis, Md.: Naval Institute Press, 1990), 285.

3. J. B. Hattendorf, "Stephen B. Luce: Intellectual Leader of the New Navy," in Bradford, ed., *Admirals of the New Steel Navy*, 15.

4. *Transactions of the Society of Naval Architects and Marine Engineers* 29 (1921): 94; 52 (1944): 439–40.

5. The first British military aircraft to take off from a ship did so on 10 January 1912. By the fall of 1917, the Royal Navy's Grand Fleet had 33 aircraft accompanying it on what can only be called aircraft carriers. Friedman, *British Carrier Aviation*, 24, 52.

6. Friedman, *British Carrier Aviation*, 26.

7. Friedman, *British Carrier Aviation*, 25.

8. The famous sociologist Robert K. Merton noted the phenomenon of simultaneous discovery in his "Singletons and Multiples in Scientific Discovery: A Chapter in the Sociology of Science," *Proceedings* of the American Philosophical Society 105 (October 1961), 470–86.

9. Norman Friedman, "The Genesis of the Big Fleet Carrier, USS *Lexington*, CV2," *Warship Quarterly* (Conway Maritime Press) 2 (1978): 14–19.

10. Friedman, *British Carrier Aviation*, 32.

11. David MacGregor, "Former Naval Cheapskate: Chancellor of the Exchequer Winston Churchill and the Royal Navy, 1924–1929," *Armed Forces and Society* 17 (Spring 1993): 319–34.

12. Hone, "Spending Patterns of the U.S. Navy, 1921–1941," gives the numbers. Melhorn, in *Two-Block Fox*, describes the relationship between Moffett and members of Congress.

13. Sumida, *In Defense of Naval Supremacy*.

14. Pratt & Whitney Aircraft Division, United Aircraft Corporation, *The Pratt & Whitney Aircraft Story*, 1950.

15. Sir Ivor Jennings, *Cabinet Government*, 2nd ed. (Cambridge: Cambridge University Press, 1951), chap. 10. On the Norden bombsight, see David Zimmerman, *Top Secret Exchange, The Tizard Mission and the Scientific War* (Montreal: McGill-Queen's University Press, 1996), chap. 2.

16. Rear Adm. W. V. Pratt, "The Naval War College: An Outline of the Past and Description of the Present," 20 May 1927, in File UNT, Naval War College Archives.

17. Benjamin S. Kelsey, *The Dragon's Teeth?* (Washington, D.C.: Smithsonian Institution Press, 1982).

18. The maneuverings are detailed in Hone, "Navy Air Leadership."

19. Office of the Chief of Naval Operations, "Aircraft Tactics, Development of," 3 February 1927, File A-16-3(4), National Archives. In a cover letter (A16-3[VV]FF2-3), Commodore J. M. Reeves, USN, noted : "This report was made possible by the concentration of aircraft of the Battle Fleet . . . for a period of about three months during the summer and early fall of 1926." The file was given to us by Capt. A. L. Raithel Jr., USN (Ret.).

20. "Final Report of Board to Test Effectiveness of Aircraft Bombs on the U.S.S. Pittsburgh," 24 October 1931, A5-5 (Folder 2), Box 214, Office of the Secretary of the Navy, Secret Correspondence, 1927–1939, RG 80, National Archives.

21. C. L. Lord, "The History of Naval Aviation, 1898–1939," Part IV, "Between the Wars," p. 1211.

22. See "Appendix 2: Carrier Aircraft Data," in Friedman, *Carrier Air Power.*

23. "Aircraft Tactics—Development of," 3 February 1927, 105–106.

24. Letter, "from: Commander-in-Chief, U.S. Fleet, to: Chief of Naval Operations, subj: Radio Controlled Target Airplanes—Exercises with during current quarter, advance partial report, 12 Feb. 1939 (41-10/0245)," General Board Number 436, Serial 3908, National Archives.

25. Memo, from chief, Bureau of Aeronautics, to the secretary of the Navy via the CNO, "Naval Aeronautic Policy," 10 August 1922, Moffett papers, Naval Academy Library, Annapolis, Maryland.

26. See, for Pratt's position on preventing the creation of a separate flying corps within the Navy, his letter to H. A. Wiley, Commander-in-Chief, U.S. Fleet, 20 September 1928, in the Pratt Correspondence File, Naval War College Archives.

27. We are indebted to Dr. William J. Armstrong for this insight. But the wisdom of Rear Adm. Taylor's support for aviation as a technology was borne out by the many contributions BuAer personnel made, later, to aviation generally.

28. Letter, Moffett to Carl Vinson, 23 December 1931, Moffett papers, Naval Academy Library, Annapolis, Maryland.

29. Emory S. Land, later an admiral and then head of the Maritime Commission, cited in Melhorn, *Two-Block Fox,* 142.

30. *Life,* 28 October 1940, 23.

31. Erik Lund, "The Industrial History of Strategy: Reevaluating the Wartime Record of the British Aviation Industry in Comparative Perspective, 1919–1945," *The Journal of Military History* 62 (January 1998).

32. Hone, "Navy Air Leadership." Also, Armstrong, "William A. Moffett and the Development of Naval Aviation," in *Aviation's Golden Age,* ed. W. M. Leary (Iowa City: University of Iowa Press, 1989).

33. Vincent Davis, *The Admirals Lobby* (Chapel Hill, N.C.: University of North Carolina Press, 1967).

34. A case can be made that in fact the Navy's aviators did get their own "service

within a service," but nonetheless efforts were made to head off potential parochialism. Then surface officer Capt. Arleigh Burke (later CNO) was chief of staff to carrier task force commander Vice Adm. Marc Mitscher in World War II, for example, and aviator Capt. Forrest Sherman served as Admiral Nimitz's chief of staff in Hawaii during the war.

35. R. A. Winston, *Dive Bomber* (New York: Holiday House, 1939) provided a vivid and light-hearted description of the training program.

36. Melhorn, *Two-Block Fox,* 146, n. 21.

37. "Fleet Problem XV—Exercises L, M & N" (5–10 May 1934), CINCUS Report, 1 June 1934, Record Group 38, Records of the Office of the CNO, National Archives, 30.

38. "Fleet Problem XV—Exercises L, M & N," 31.

39. Hone, "Spending Patterns of the U.S. Navy, 1921–1941."

40. Joint Board No. 349 (Serial 629), memo, "to: Secretary of the Navy, subject: Army Bombardment and Reconnaissance Aviation—Limitation of Development of," 29 June 1938, in RG 80, Joint Army-Navy Board, Navy Secretariat, Box 14, Folder "Serial 582 to 637 Incl.," National Archives.

41. In 1941, the Navy and Marine Corps had 3,437 aircraft and 4,617 pilots. By 1945, the aircraft inventory had risen to over 40,000 and there were more than 60,000 pilots.

42. Erik Lund, "The Industrial History of Strategy."

43. Memo, 3 November 1938, Op-12A-MG (SC) A6-2 (14), "from: Director, War Plans Division, to: Director, Technical Division, 'Information in connection with naval aeronautical communications,'" Box 215, RG 80, Office of the Secretary of the Navy, Secret Correspondence, 1927–1939, National Archives.

44. Alex Roland, *Model Research: The National Advisory Committee for Aeronautics* I (Washington, D.C.: Government Printing Office, 1985).

45. The Air Corps Act of 1926 allowed the services to negotiate contracts for experimental prototypes and for "educational orders" (buys of aircraft that would "educate" contractors in the ways of producing aircraft for military use). But the intent of the act was undercut by specific legal interpretations of its meaning and by a congressional atmosphere of hostility toward anything but sealed-bid contracts. See Thomas C. Hone, "Fighting on Our Own Ground: The War of Production, 1920–1942," *Naval War College Review* 45 (Spring 1992): 93–107.

46. Irving B. Holley Jr., "Jet Lag in the Army Air Corps," in *Military Planning in the Twentieth Century,* ed. Harry R. Borowski (Washington, D.C.: Government Printing Office, 1986), 123–53.

47. Holley, "Jet Lag in the Army Air Corps," 125–26.

48. Ibid., 135–36. Aerodynamicist Theodore von Kármán attended the Fifth Volta Conference in Italy in 1935. On his return, he tried to persuade George Lewis, head of the NACA, to ask Congress for funds to build a large supersonic wind tunnel. Lewis did not. See Theodore von Kármán with Lee Edson, *The Wind and Beyond:*

Theodore von Karman, Pioneer in Aviation and Pathfinder in Space (Boston: Little, Brown & Co., 1967), 223–24.

49. Hone and Mandeles, "Interwar Innovation in Three Navies: USN, RN, IJN."

50. Stephen Roskill, *Naval Policy between the Wars,* II (Annapolis, Md.: Naval Institute Press, 1976), 406–07.

51. David C. Evans and Mark R. Peattie, *Kaigun* (Annapolis, Md.: Naval Institute Press, 1997), 341–42.

52. Stephen Rosen, *Winning the Next War: Innovation and the Modern Military* (Ithaca, N.Y.: Cornell University Press, 1991).

Chapter 8. Conclusion

1. John Wellham, *With Naval Wings* (Kent, UK: Spellmount, 1995).

2. Hone and Mandeles, "Managerial Style in the Interwar Navy: A Reappraisal."

3. A. D. Zimm, "The U.S.N.'s Flight Deck Cruiser," *Warship International* 16 (1979): 220–21.

4. Letter "from: Chief of Naval Operations, to: President, Naval War College, subj: Test between 8" gun ship and 6" gun ship carrying flying on deck," 18 December 1930, General Board Records, Serial No. 1515, National Archives.

5. Testimony of Capt. John H. Towers, Hearings of the General Board, 5 December 1930, p. 10, National Archives.

6. Comment by Admiral Bristol, Hearings of the General Board, 5 December 1930, p. 31.

7. The hearings consulted were held on 4 December, 5 December, 23 December, 16 July, and 17 July.

8. Testimony by Rear Adm. M. M. Taylor, Hearings of the General Board, 23 December 1930, p. 39.

9. A. D. Zimm, in his "The U.S.N.'s Flight Deck Cruiser," argues that what really killed the flight-deck cruiser concept was opposition from surface line officers and the death and retirement of the concept's three main supporters. These were Moffett, CNO Adm. W. V. Pratt, and Rear Adm. Harris Laning, president of the Naval War College under Pratt.

10. Sir Oswyn A. R. Murray, "The Administration of a Fighting Service," *Journal of Public Administration* 1 (July 1923).

11. Friedman, *U.S. Aircraft Carriers: An Illustrated Design History,* 116.

12. Jon Sumida, in his review of Andrew Gordon's *The Rules of the Game: Jutland and the British Naval Command,* in *The American Neptune* 57: 383.

13. Adm. Marc A. Mitscher, Foreword to *The Navy's Air War,* ed. by Lt. A. R. Buchanan, OP-519B, Deputy Chief of Naval Operations (Air), (New York: Harper, 1946), ix.

Bibliography

Books

Baer, George W. *One Hundred Years of Sea Power.* Stanford, Calif.: Stanford University Press, 1994.

Ballantine, Duncan S. *U.S. Naval Logistics in the Second World War.* Princeton, N.J.: Princeton University Press, 1949.

Berg, Dorothy, and Shumpei Okamoto, eds. *Pearl Harbor as History.* New York: Columbia University Press, 1973.

Biddle, Wayne. *Barons of the Sky.* New York: Simon and Schuster, 1991.

Boog, H., ed. *The Conduct of the Air War in the Second World War: An International Comparison.* New York: St. Martin's Press, 1992.

Borowski, Harry, ed. *Military Planning in the Twentieth Century.* Washington, D.C.: Government Printing Office, 1986.

Bradford, J. C., ed. *Admirals of the New Steel Navy.* Annapolis, Md.: Naval Institute Press, 1990.

Buchanan, A. R. *The Navy's Air War.* New York: Harper, 1946.

Buell, Thomas B. *The Quiet Warrior: A Biography of Admiral Raymond Spruance.* Boston: Little, Brown, 1974.

Cooling, B. F. *Gray Steel and Blue Water Navy: The Formative Years of America's Military-Industrial Complex, 1881–1917.* Hamden, Conn.: Archon Books, 1979.

Cressman, Robert. *That Gallant Ship: U.S.S. Yorktown.* Missoula, Mont.: Pictorial Histories, 1985.

Davis, Vincent. *The Admirals Lobby.* Chapel Hill: University of North Carolina Press, 1967.

Dyer, G. C., Vice Adm. *The Amphibians Came to Conquer: The Story of Admiral Richmond Kelly Turner,* vol. 1. Washington, D.C.: Government Printing Office, 1969.

Evans, David C., and Mark R. Peattie. *Kaigun.* Annapolis, Md.: Naval Institute Press, 1997.

Fleet Air Arm, Royal Navy. *The Development of British Naval Aviation, 1919–1945,* vols 1 and 2. London: Public Record Office, 1954 and 1956, respectively.

Francillon, R. *Japanese Aircraft of the Pacific War.* London: Putnam, 1987.

Friedman, Norman. *British Carrier Aviation.* London: Conway Maritime Press, 1988.

———. *Carrier Air Power.* New York: Rutledge, 1981.

———. *U.S. Aircraft Carriers, An Illustrated Design History.* Annapolis, Md.: Naval Institute Press, 1983.

———. *U.S. Battleships, An Illustrated Design History.* Annapolis, Md.: Naval Institute Press, 1985.

Furer, J. A., Rear Adm. *Administration of the Navy Department in World War II.* Washington, D.C.: Naval History Division, Navy Department, 1959.

Futrell, Robert F. *Ideas, Concepts, Doctrine: A History of Basic Thinking in the United States Air Force, 1907–1964.* Maxwell AFB, Ala.: Air War College, 1971.

Gibbs, N. H. *History of the Second World War, Grand Strategy,* vol. 1. London: HMSO, 1976.

Hattendorf, J. B., B. Mitchell Simpson III, and J. R. Wadleigh. *Sailors and Scholars, The Centennial History of the U.S. Naval War College.* Newport, R.I.: Naval War College Press, 1977.

Holland, Maurice, with T. M. Smith. *Architects of Aviation.* New York: Duell, Sloan & Pearce, 1951.

Holley, I. B., Jr. *Ideas and Weapons.* New Haven: Yale University Press, 1953.

Hughes, Wayne. *Fleet Tactics.* Annapolis, Md.: Naval Institute Press, 1986.

Hyde, H. Montgomery. *British Air Policy between the Wars, 1918–1939.* London: Wm. Heineman, 1976.

Jamieson, P. D. *Crossing the Deadly Ground: United States Army Tactics, 1865–1899.* Tuscaloosa: University of Alabama Press, 1994.

Jennings, Ivor. *Cabinet Government.* Cambridge: Cambridge University Press, 1951.

Jones, H. A. *The War in the Air,* vol. 6. Oxford: Oxford University Press, 1937.

Kaufman, R. G. *Arms Control during the Pre-Nuclear Era: The United States and Naval Limitation between the Two World Wars.* New York: Columbia University Press, 1990.

Kelsey, Benjamin S. *The Dragon's Teeth?* Washington, D.C.: Smithsonian Institution Press, 1982.

La Guardia, Fiorello. *The Making of an Insurgent.* Philadelphia: Lippincott, 1948.

Lamb, Charles. *To War in a Stringbag.* New York: Bantam Books, 1980.

Larkins, William T. *Battleship and Cruiser Aircraft of the United States Navy, 1910–1949.* Atglen, Pa.: Schiffer, 1996.

———. *U.S. Navy Aircraft, 1921–1941.* New York: Crown Publishers, 1988.

Leary, W. M., ed. *Aviation's Golden Age.* Iowa City: University of Iowa Press, 1989.

le Bailly, Louis, Vice Adm. Sir. *From Fisher to the Falklands.* London: Marine Management (Holdings) Ltd. for the Institute of Marine Engineers, 1991.

Lewis, P. *The British Bomber since 1914.* London: Putnam, 1967.

Love, R. W. *The Chiefs of Naval Operations.* Annapolis, Md.: Naval Institute Press, 1980.

MacDonald, Scot. *Evolution of the Aircraft Carrier.* Washington, D.C.: Office of the Chief of Naval Operations, Navy Department, 1964. This volume is a compilation of short articles from the following issues of *Naval Aviation News*: February 1962, March 1962, May 1962, June 1962, August 1962, September 1962, October 1962, November 1962, December 1962, January 1963, April 1963, May 1963, October 1963, and November 1963.

McIntyre, W. D. *The Rise and Fall of the Singapore Naval Base.* London: Macmillan, 1979.

Marder, Arthur J. *Old Friends, New Enemies.* Oxford: Oxford University Press, 1981.

Melhorn, Charles M. *Two-Block Fox, The Rise of the Aircraft Carrier, 1911–1929.* Annapolis, Md.: Naval Institute Press, 1974.

Mikesh, R. C., and S. Abe. *Japanese Aircraft, 1910–41.* London: Putnam, 1990.

Miller, Edward S. *War Plan ORANGE.* Annapolis, Md.: Naval Institute Press, 1991.

North, Douglass C. *Institutions, Institutional Change and Economic Performance.* New York: Cambridge University Press, 1993.

O'Connor, Raymond. *Perilous Equilibrium, The United States and the London Naval Conference of 1930.* Lawrence: University of Kansas Press, 1962.

Peden, G. C. *British Rearmament and the Treasury, 1932–39.* Edinburgh: Scottish Academic Press, 1979.

Perla, Peter. *The Art of Wargaming.* Annapolis, Md.: Naval Institute Press, 1990.

Potter, E. B. *Nimitz.* Annapolis, Md.: Naval Institute Press, 1976.

Pratt & Whitney Aircraft Division, United Aircraft Corporation. *The Pratt & Whitney Aircraft Story.* United Aircraft Corporation, 1950.

Ranft, Bryan, ed. *Ironclad to Trident, 100 Years of Defence Commentary, Brassey's 1886–1986.* London: Brassey's, 1986.

Reynolds, Clark. *Admiral John H. Towers, The Struggle for Naval Air Supremacy.* Annapolis, Md.: Naval Institute Press, 1991.

———. *The Fast Carriers.* Annapolis, Md.: Naval Institute Press, 1992.

Robinson, Douglas H., and Charles L. Keller. *"Up Ship": U.S. Navy Rigid Airships 1919–1935.* Annapolis, Md.: Naval Institute Press, 1982.

Roland, Alex. *Model Research: The National Advisory Committee for Aeronautics, 1915–1958,* vol. 1. Washington, D.C.: Government Printing Office, 1985.

Roskill, Stephen W., ed. *Documents Relating to the Naval Air Service,* vol. 1. London: Navy Records Society, 1969.

———. *Naval Policy between the Wars,* vol. 1. New York: Walker, 1968.

———. *Naval Policy between the Wars,* vol. 2. Annapolis, Md.: Naval Institute Press, 1976.

Smith, Richard K. *The Airships* Akron *and* Macon, *Flying Aircraft Carriers of the United States Navy.* Annapolis, Md.: Naval Institute Press, 1965.

Spector, Ronald. *Professors of War.* Newport: Naval War College Press, 1977.

Sprout, Harold, and Margaret Sprout. *Toward a New Order of Seapower.* Princeton, N.J.: Princeton University Press, 1940.

Stinchcombe, Arthur L. *Constructing Social Theories.* New York: Harcourt, Brace & World, 1968.

Sumida, Jon T. *In Defense of Naval Supremacy: Finance, Technology, and British Naval Policy, 1889–1914.* London: Routledge, 1993.

Swanborough, Gordon, and Peter M. Bowers. *United States Navy Aircraft since 1911,* 2d ed. Annapolis, Md.: Naval Institute Press, 1976.

Terraine, John. *A Time for Courage.* New York: Macmillan, 1985.

Till, Geoffrey. *Air Power and the Royal Navy, 1914–1945.* London: Jane's Publishing, 1979.

Trimble, W. F. *Admiral William A. Moffett, Architect of Naval Aviation.* Washington, D.C.: Smithsonian Institution, 1994.

———. *Wings for the Navy, A History of the Naval Aircraft Factory, 1917–1956.* Annapolis, Md.: Naval Institute Press, 1990.

Turnbull, A. D., and C. L. Lord. *History of United States Naval Aviation.* New Haven, Conn.: Yale University Press, 1949.

van Deurs, George, Rear Adm. *Anchors in the Sky: Spuds Ellyson, The First Naval Aviator.* San Rafael, Calif.: Presidio Press, 1978.

———. *Wings for the Fleet.* Annapolis, Md.: Naval Institute Press, 1966.

Van Fleet, Clark, and William J. Armstrong. *United States Naval Aviation, 1910–1980.* Washington, D.C.: Government Printing Office, 1981.

Van Wyen, Adrian, and the Editors of *Naval Aviation News. Naval Aviation in World War I.* Washington, D.C.: Chief of Naval Operations, 1969.

Vlahos, Michael. *The Blue Sword, The Naval War College and the American Mission, 1919–1941.* Newport, R.I.: Naval War College Press, 1980.

von Karman, Theodore, with Lee Edson. *The Wind and Beyond: Theodore von Karman, Pioneer in Aviation and Pathfinder in Space.* Boston: Little, Brown, 1967.

Wellham, John. *With Naval Wings.* Kent (UK): Spellmount, 1995.

Wheeler, Gerald. *Admiral William Veazie Pratt, U.S. Navy, A Sailor's Life.* Washington, D.C.: Naval History Division, Navy Department, 1974.

Wildenberg, Thomas. *Gray Steel and Black Oil: Fast Tankers and Replenishment at Sea in the U.S. Navy, 1912–1992.* Annapolis, Md.: Naval Institute Press, 1996.

Wilson, Eugene E. *Slipstream: The Autobiography of an Air Craftsman.* New York: McGraw-Hill, 1950.

Winston, R. A. *Dive Bomber.* New York: Holiday House, 1939.

Zimmerman, David. *Top Secret Exchange, The Tizard Mission and the Scientific War.* Montreal: McGill-Queen's University Press, 1996.

Zogbaum, R. F., Rear Adm. *From Sail to* Saratoga. Rome: Tipografia Italo-Orientale, n.d.

Articles

Anderson, Philip W. "More Is Different." *Science* 177 (4 August 1972).

Armstrong, William J. "William A. Moffett and the Development of Naval Aviation," in W. M. Leary, ed., *Aviation's Golden Age.* Iowa City: University of Iowa Press, 1989.

Braisted, William R. "Charles Frederick Hughes," in R. W. Love, ed., *The Chiefs of Naval Operations.* Annapolis, Md.: Naval Institute Press, 1980.

———. "Mark Lambert Bristol: Naval Diplomat Extraordinary of the Battleship Age," in J. C. Bradford, ed., *Admirals of the New Steel Navy.* Annapolis, Md.: Naval Institute Press, 1990.

Dandeker, Christopher. "Bureaucracy, Planning and War: The Royal Navy, 1880–1918." *Armed Forces and Society* 11 (Fall 1984).

Dater, Henry M. "Tactical Use of Air Power in World War II: The Navy Experience." *Military Affairs* 14 (Winter 1950).

Duncan, Donald B., and Henry M. Dater. "Administrative History of U.S. Naval Aviation." *Air Affairs* 1, No. 4.

Ferris, John. "A British 'Unofficial' Aviation Mission and Japanese Naval Developments, 1919–1929." *Journal of Strategic Studies* (September 1982).

Friedman, Norman. "The Genesis of the Big Fleet Carrier, USS *Lexington,* CV2." *Warship Quarterly* 2 (1978).

Fullam, William F., Rear Adm., USN. "Battleships and Air Power." *Sea Power* 7 (December 1919).

Gillette, C. S., Commander, USN. "History, Description, and Acceptance Trials of the U.S.S. *Lexington.*" *Journal of the American Society of Naval Engineers* 40 (August 1928).

Guilmartin, John F. "Changing the Guard." *Air University Review* 34 (March–April 1983).

Hattendorf, J. B. "Stephen B. Luce: Intellectual Leader of the New Navy," in James C. Bradford, ed., *Admirals of the New Steel Navy.* Annapolis, Md.: Naval Institute Press, 1990.

Hayes, J., Rear Adm., USN. "Admiral Joseph Mason Reeves, USN: Part One—to 1931." *Naval War College Review* 23 (November 1970).

Heinrichs, Waldo. "The Role of the United States Navy," in Dorothy Berg and Shumpei Okamoto, eds., *Pearl Harbor as History.* New York: Columbia University Press, 1973.

Heller, S. R., Jr., Lt. Cdr., USN. "The Development of Attack Aircraft Carriers." *Journal of the American Society of Naval Engineers* 45 (1953).

Holley, Irving B., Jr. "Jet Lag in the Army Air Corps," in Harry R. Borowski, ed., *Military Planning in the Twentieth Century.* Washington, D.C.: Government Printing Office, 1986.

Hone, T. "The Effectiveness of the Washington Treaty Navy." *Naval War College Review* (November–December 1979).

———. "Fighting on Our Own Ground: The War of Production, 1920–1942." *Naval War College Review* 45 (Spring 1992).

———. "Naval Reconstitution, Surge, and Mobilization: Once and Future." *Naval War College Review* 47 (Summer 1994).

———. "Navy Air Leadership: Rear Admiral W. A. Moffett as Chief of the Bureau of Aeronautics," in Wayne Thompson, ed., *Air Leadership.* Washington, D.C.: Government Printing Office, 1986).

———. "Spending Patterns of the U.S. Navy, 1921–1941." *Armed Forces and Society* (Spring 1982).

Hone, T., and M. Mandeles. "Interwar Innovation in Three Navies: USN, RN, IJN." *Naval War College Review* 40 (Spring 1987).

———. "Managerial Style in the Interwar Navy: A Reappraisal." *Naval War College Review* 32 (September–October 1980).

Lincoln, Ashbrook. "The United States Navy and the Rise of the Doctrine of Air Power." *Military Affairs* (Fall 1951).

Lund, Erik. "The Industrial History of Strategy: Reevaluating the Wartime Record of the British Aviation Industry in Comparative Perspective, 1919–1945." *The Journal of Military History* 62 (January 1998).

McBride, W. M. "Challenging a Strategic Paradigm: Aviation and the U.S. Navy Special Policy Board of 1924." *The Journal of Strategic Studies* 14 (1991).

MacGregor, David. "Formal Naval Cheapskate: Chancellor of the Exchequer Winston Churchill and the Royal Navy, 1924–1929." *Armed Forces and Society* 17 (Spring 1993).

Mandeles, Mark D. "Review Essay—*Crossing the Deadly Ground.*" *Journal of America's Military Past* 24 (Spring 1997).

Merton, Robert K. "Singletons and Multiples in Scientific Discovery: A Chapter in the Sociology of Science." *Proceedings of the American Philosophical Society* 105 (October 1961).

Murray, Sir Oswyn A. R. "The Administration of a Fighting Service." *Journal of Public Administration* 1 (July 1923).

Ohmae, Toshikazu. "Japanese Naval Aviation." U.S. Naval Institute *Proceedings* (December 1972).

Raithel, A. L., Capt., USN. "Sea Sleds." *Naval Aviation News,* September 1980.

———. "Trap 'Em." *The Hook* 10 (Fall 1982).

Sumida, Jon T. "'The Best Laid Plans': The Development of British Battle-Fleet Tactics, 1919–1942." *The International History Review* 14 (November 1992).

Transactions of the Society of Naval Architects and Marine Engineers 14 (1906), 18 (1910), 21 (1913), 29 (1921), 52 (1944).

Trask, David F. "William Sowden Sims: The Victory Ashore," in James C. Bradford, ed., *Admirals of the New Steel Navy.* Annapolis, Md.: Naval Institute Press, 1990.

Wheeler, Gerald. "Mitchell, Moffett, and Air Power." *The Airpower Historian* 8 (April 1961.

Wilson, E. E. "The Navy's First Carrier Task Force." U.S. Naval Institute *Proceedings* (February 1950).

———. "The Trend of Aircraft Engine Development." *Journal of the American Society of Naval Engineers* 38 (February 1926).

Woodhouse, Henry. "U.S. Naval Aeronautic Policies, 1904–1942." U.S. Naval Institute *Proceedings* 68 (February 1942).

Zimm, A. D. "The USN's Flight Deck Cruiser." *Warship International* 16 (1979).

Manuscripts and Theses

Armstrong, William J. "The Establishment of the DCNO (Air)." Unpublished paper prepared for Commander, Naval Air Systems Command, n.d. Historian's files, Naval Air Systems Command, Patuxent River, Maryland.

Campbell, Mark Allen. "The Influence of Air Power Upon the Evolution of Battle Doctrine in the U.S. Navy, 1922–1941." Master's thesis, University of Massachusetts–Boston, 1992.

Keith, Francis Lovell. "United States Navy Task Force Evolution: An Analysis of United States Fleet Problems, 1931–1934." Master's thesis, University of Maryland, 1974.

Kennedy, Gerald J. "The United States Naval War College, 1919–1941: An Institutional Response to Naval Preparedness." Ph.D. dissertation, University of Minnesota, 1975.

Lord, Clifford L. "The History of Naval Aviation, 1898–1939." Four volumes (1946). Manuscript, Office of the Historian, Naval Air Systems Command. Another copy is located in the Naval Historical Center library, Washington Navy Yard, Washington, D.C.

Turner, Stansfield. "The Growing Dominance of Naval Aviation," history honors thesis, Amherst College, April 1943.

Index

About the Authors

Thomas C. Hone is a member of the faculty of the Industrial College of the Armed Forces. He has also taught at the Naval War College, the Defense Systems Management College, and the George C. Marshall Center in Germany. He has worked at the Center for Naval Analyses and as the special assistant to the commander of the Naval Air Systems Command. He is the author of *Power and Change: The Administrative History of the Office of the Chief of Naval Operations, 1946–1986* and many articles analyzing naval history and administration.

Dr. Norman Friedman is an internationally known specialist in the fields of weapons design and development. He has written highly respected design histories of U.S. Navy carriers, battleships, cruisers, destroyers, submarines, and small attack craft. He has also published studies of naval radars, U.S. naval weapons, and carrier aviation in the Royal Navy. Other books by him include a study of the U.S. Navy's maritime strategy, an analysis of the 1990–91 campaign against Iraq, and his comprehensive series on world naval weapons systems. Dr. Friedman's articles have appeared in a number of journals, and he contributes a monthly column on world naval developments to the U.S. Naval Institute *Proceedings.* He is at work now on a history of the Cold War (*The Fifty-Year War: Conflict and Strategy in the Cold War,* forthcoming in November 1999 from the Naval Institute Press).

Dr. Mark D. Mandeles formed The J. De Bloch Group in 1993 to examine a wide range of national security and foreign policy issues for government agencies and private firms. Currently, he is writing an analysis of future military organization for the Office of Secretary of Defense/Net Assessment. He has served as chairman of the Air Warfare track of the American Military University. He has published articles and book chapters on command and control, naval weapons acquisition, professional military education, military doctrine, nuclear strategy, military innovation, the revolution in military affairs, and ballistic missile and nuclear weapons proliferation. Dr. Mandeles is author of *The Development of the B-52 and Jet Propulsion* and co-author of *Managing "Command and Control" in the Persian Gulf War.*

The Naval Institute Press is the book-publishing arm of the U.S. Naval Institute, a private, nonprofit, membership society for sea service professionals and others who share an interest in naval and maritime affairs. Established in 1873 at the U.S. Naval Academy in Annapolis, Maryland, where its offices remain today, the Naval Institute has members worldwide.

Members of the Naval Institute support the education programs of the society and receive the influential monthly magazine *Proceedings* and discounts on fine nautical prints and on ship and aircraft photos. They also have access to the transcripts of the Institute's Oral History Program and get discounted admission to any of the Institute-sponsored seminars offered around the country.

The Naval Institute also publishes *Naval History* magazine. This colorful bimonthly is filled with entertaining and thought-provoking articles, first-person reminiscences, and dramatic art and photography. Members receive a discount on *Naval History* subscriptions.

The Naval Institute's book-publishing program, begun in 1898 with basic guides to naval practices, has broadened its scope in recent years to include books of more general interest. Now the Naval Institute Press publishes about one hundred titles each year, ranging from how-to books on boating and navigation to battle histories, biographies, ship and aircraft guides, and novels. Institute members receive discounts of 20 to 50 percent on the Press's more than eight hundred books in print.

Full-time students are eligible for special half-price membership rates. Life memberships are also available.

For a free catalog describing Naval Institute Press books currently available, and for further information about subscribing to *Naval History* magazine or about joining the U.S. Naval Institute, please write to:

Membership Department
U.S. Naval Institute
291 Wood Road
Annapolis, MD 21402-5034
Telephone: (800) 233-8764
Fax: (410) 269-7940
Web address: www.usni.org